An Educator's Classroom Guide to America's Religious Beliefs and Practices

Benjamin J. Hubbard

John T. Hatfield

James A. Santucci

LIBRARIES
UNLIMITED

A Member of the Greenwood Publishing Group

Westport, Connecticut • London

Library of Congress Cataloging-in-Publication Data

Hubbard, Benjamin Jerome.
  An educator's classroom guide to America's religious beliefs and practices /
  Benjamin J. Hubbard, John T. Hatfield, and James A. Santucci.
    p. cm.
  Includes bibliographical references and index.
  ISBN-13: 978–1–59158–409–4 (alk. paper)
  ISBN-10: 1–59158–409–4 (alk. paper)
  1. United States—Religion—Handbooks, manuals, etc. 2. Religion in the public
  schools—United States—Handbooks, manuals, etc. I. Hatfield, John T.,
  1932– II. Santucci, James A. III. Hubbard,
  Benjamin Jerome. America's religions.
  IV. Title.
  BL2525.H82 2007
  200.71'073—dc22   2006037741

British Library Cataloguing in Publication Data is available.

Library of Congress Catalog Card Number: 2006037741
ISBN: 978–1–59158–409–4

First published in 2007

Libraries Unlimited, 88 Post Road West, Westport, CT 06881
A Member of the Greenwood Publishing Group, Inc.
www.lu.com

Printed in the United States of America

∞™

The paper used in this book complies with the
Permanent Paper Standard issued by the National
Information Standards Organization (Z39.48–1984).

10 9 8 7 6 5 4 3 2 1

Contents

Foreword

Today's classrooms reflect the increasing diversity in the United States. As we strive to meet our students' academic needs, we have neglected to gain a thorough understanding of students' cultural and religious practices and beliefs. Naturally, the term *religion* sends up red flags when used in association with public education, and rightfully so. The Constitution mandates a separation between church and state. We often hear about the ongoing legal battles and controversy involving the church–state issue. Still, we cannot neglect the fact that individual public school sites have student populations that may represent as many as fifty different languages, and this clearly reflects a global population.

Our job as educators is to teach this student population the essential skills needed to become literate readers, literate writers, and independent thinkers. We are responsible for molding our country's next adult generation. Problems arise when our actions as educators unknowingly offend or confuse students by creating conflicts with their cultural or religious beliefs. When this occurs, we cause unnecessary problems within our educational system. Many educators have heard the anecdote about the teacher who called a student to his desk with a hand signal, not realizing that this hand signal was a form of disrespect in the student's culture. I myself have heard this story used many times—as incitement for developing a greater awareness and respect of cultural diversity—yet I believe that few teachers are aware of the specific hand gesture or the culture that it offends.

Several years ago, I became aware of a situation that occurred in my former school district. A male member of a theater group performing at an elementary school assembly went into the audience and sat next to and placed his arm around a female student. This student had recently arrived from Somalia and was dressed in a full head veil. The actor may have thought that he was doing a good deed by involving this particular student in an auditorium of four hundred students. Perhaps he thought that his actions, directed at a student who looked different, would help an "outsider" feel more at ease. However, the actor had not realized that this student's attire was, foremost, an indicator of her cultural and religious differences. This young girl was Muslim, and she became so upset (because a male had placed his arm around her) that her mother had to come and remove her from school for the remainder of the day. I am sure the actor meant no harm by choosing this student, but the fact remains that this incident could have been avoided. The purpose of *An Educator's Classroom Guide to America's Religious Beliefs and Practices* is to help develop "trained eyes" so that such incidents are less likely to occur.

In the classroom, I have heard different groups of people referred to as "inconvenient" while a student from one of these groups was present. These inconveniences usually come in the form of special needs based on someone's religious or cultural background. This book explains the importance of individual customs and beliefs and give teachers concrete information that will help them with classroom management. Teachers are in a powerful position. Students look to teachers as models. I frequently see young students trying to dress like their teacher or use a phrase that the teacher often uses. If a young student looks to you so reverently that he or she wants to dress—and talk—like you, it is likely that you could make lasting impressions on the student regarding religious issues. This is why cultural and religious diversity in the classroom must be understood, respected, and handled with great care.

I grew up in a rather unusual situation and remember the effects it had on me. I attended a public elementary school in Canada where the class began each day by reciting the Lord's Prayer and reading from the New Testament. The Bible was passed around the classroom daily, so that students could read the day's passage aloud. It did not matter whether reading from the Bible was part of your religious background—this was simply something the class did. There were, of course, students who did not believe in what they were being asked to do, and parents who agreed with them. Consequently (although unnecessarily), there was tension in the classroom.

Students should feel that school is a safe environment where powerful learning is to take place. School is a place of education, not indoctrination. By familiarizing ourselves with people's customs, we as educators can fulfill our role while maintaining the proper level of respect for all cultures and religions in the classroom.

Think of this book as a dictionary of religion and culture. Within its pages are clearly stated definitions of the many different cultures, religions, and branches of religions you may encounter in your classroom. Use this book to familiarize yourself with religious beliefs and practices. This will help you avoid conflict with your students and their families. This book also helps explain the "fine legal line" between *teaching* about and *celebrating* religion in the classroom, an issue that is the focus of many court battles.

As a former public school teacher, assistant principal, principal, and current school administrator, I fully appreciate the time constraints that teachers face. Curricula, teachers, students, and administrators change; somehow, through all this change, we must continue to deliver a quality program. You have a new book in front of you, but to devote time to it means taking time from another area. I understand that frustration. What I can tell you is that the information you acquire from this book should help save you time in the future. Your time savings will come in the form of a well-tuned classroom where students are respected and experience a safe learning environment. This in turn can keep teachers from entering into unprofessional and embarrassing situations that often lead to time-consuming conferences with parents and administrators.

Finally, as an added benefit, I offer to you the following service: If you encounter a question about the religious practices of students that is not covered in this book, feel free to e-mail or write to Dr. Benjamin Hubbard (see contact information that follows). Either he or one of his coauthors will be happy to respond to your query. You will receive a response to your question, and it may be used in a future edition of this book.

Contact:
Dr. Benjamin Hubbard
Department of Comparative Religion
California State University, Fullerton
Fullerton, CA 92834-6868; (714) 278-3452; bhubbard@fullerton.edu

Dr. David A. Hubbard, School Administrator
Westminster School District, Westminster, California; dahubbard1@aol.com

Preface

Should religion be discussed in public schools? It could well be argued that the United States is the most multicultural and multireligious society that has ever existed. From around the world, people have been coming here in ever-increasing variety, bringing with them religious traditions both familiar and exotic. This mix of religions results in inevitable tensions that arise when people with different beliefs live together. But it also provides fertile opportunities that may ensue when people learn to reach out across their differences, thus making twenty-first-century America an exciting and dramatic stage on which to encounter religion.

At the same time, this proliferation of religions has brought about considerable confusion. In response, some people have turned to the secular world and dismissed religion as hopelessly outdated. Others have sought to simplify their confusion by adhering to one religion and shutting out the rest. Still others have tried to find common threads that would tie together the diversity into one synthetic religion. Amid this sometimes bewildering variety of opinion, the public schools have been caught in a dilemma. On one hand, teachers want students to learn about the many cultures that constitute the United States and the role religion has played in our history. On the other, however, teachers feel constrained by legislation and court rulings that seem to prohibit teaching about religion and by fears that parents might object to discussing religions different from the parents' faith. What are teachers to do?

Although it might be tempting simply to avoid teaching about religion, many teachers have said that if only they had the resources to help them develop lessons, they would be more comfortable with religion. Also, if only they had a readily available guide to the practices and beliefs of the students in their classrooms, if only they knew just a bit more about how to handle expressions of religion in public schools, they would be willing to take the challenge.

This book provides just such a resource, along with helpful bibliographies and Web sites. However, the book is not just for teachers, even though they are the primary audience. News reporters, for example, know that they cannot represent the news fully without including the religious dimension. The reading public can hardly be expected to understand current events without some knowledge of religious traditions. Islam, in particular, is quite unfamiliar to many people. Yet knowledge of the world's second largest faith community is indispensable to an understanding of our world. People who work in international business and overseas relief organizations, government service, tourism, scientific and educational fields, and international exchange programs—as well as social workers, therapists, health care professionals, and attorneys—all encounter unfamiliar religious beliefs and practices regularly. These people and others may find in this volume useful information to help them understand the religious backgrounds of people they encounter in their everyday work.

Religions Discussed

Including each and every religion one might encounter in the United States would make this book too large and unwieldy. We have used three criteria in deciding which traditions to include. First, the religion must be a living tradition in the United States. Second, it must command national or at least regional attention and interest. Third, it must be among those religions encountered in the public school system. The only exception to the third criteria might be the Chinese traditions Confucianism and Daoism. However, both—especially Confucianism—have shaped the cultures of Asian Americans from the Republic of China, Taiwan, Korea, and Japan, whether they fully realize this or not. Hence, the inclusion of these two worldviews.

Discussion Format

Each chapter is subdivided as follows: Origins, Beliefs, Sacred Books/Scriptures, Practices, Main Subgroups, Common Misunderstandings and Stereotypes, Classroom Concerns, Population Data, Further Reading, and Web Sites. Thus, the reader will be able to find information quickly and compare facts about different religions (e.g., population data on Muslims and Buddhists). The sections on origins and beliefs are as brief as possible, whereas those on common misunderstandings and stereotypes and classroom concerns have been given special attention.

Authors' Point of View

We have written this book from the point of view of sympathetic observers who are trying to understand religious traditions from the inside. However odd, strange, or different a religion may appear to those who are outsiders, it is not our role to judge whether it is true or false. Rather, we have tried to let each religion tell its own story.

For us, this is an ongoing effort to provide the most accurate and up-to-date information possible about the world's religions as encountered in the United States. Inevitably, we may distort or misrepresent. No offense is intended, and we are open to suggestions for improvement. Please send your comments to us via Dr. Hubbard (see address at the end of the Foreword) or to the publisher.

At the end of each chapter, the initials of the contributor are provided: **JH** (John Hatfield), **BH** (Benjamin Hubbard), **JS** (James Santucci).

Dating System

Instead of B.C. (Before Christ) and A.D. (*Anno Domini*, Latin for "In the year of the Lord"), we have adopted the more neutral and inclusive B.C.E. (Before the Common Era; i.e., before the era *common* to Jewish and Christian peoples); and C.E. (Common Era). The dates remain the same, only the designations (B.C. = B.C.E.; A.D. = C.E.) are different. Of course, we could have chosen the Muslim or some other dating system, but B.C.E./C.E. are widely used by most religion scholars.

Pronunciation of Foreign Words

We have developed a commonsense pronunciation system whereby unfamiliar terms are phonetically spelled in brackets following the word, with capital letters designating stress. For example, the word *Christmas* would be followed by this pronunciation: [KRISS-muss]. We hope this will help the reader to feel more at ease when trying to pronounce unfamiliar words, and we are certain that students, particularly those from minority religious backgrounds, will appreciate your effort.

Acknowledgments

We first need to acknowledge school administrator and former teacher David Hubbard, son of Benjamin Hubbard, who suggested to his father in the mid-1990s that a book of this nature would greatly benefit public school teachers. Each year David's classes—and those of thousands of teachers across the nation—were becoming more multicultural and, consequently, more multireligious. Yet there was no resource available to guide teachers through the customs and practices associated with particular religious backgrounds and to keep them from unintentionally offending students. Thus was born the idea of writing a book to fill this need and the publication in 1997 of *America's Religions (An Educator's Guide to Beliefs and Practices)*. Not only did David Hubbard come up with the idea for the book, he read the entire manuscript from the perspective of a public school teacher, removing jargon that only a religion scholar would understand and editing the manuscript for greater clarity. He also wrote the Foreword to the book. We are very much in his debt.

The current book represents a revision of the 1997 volume, including four new chapters, with a focus on making the new book available as a resource tool in K–12 school libraries, and in the hands of individual teachers and other professionals (journalists, social workers, physicians, attorneys, etc.) who need accurate information about the religious backgrounds of their students or clients. We are grateful to the editors at Libraries Unlimited, particularly Sharon Coatney, for agreeing that a revision of the 1997 book would be a valuable tool for teachers and other twenty-first-century professionals.

Benjamin Hubbard wishes to express sincere thanks to his two collaborators, John Hatfield and James Santucci, who again took his dream to heart and produced chapters full of accurate information and keen insight for this second edition.

We would like to thank the following experts for their help in reading and suggesting improvements to various chapters in the book: Dr. Julie Stokes (African American Christianity), Dr. Fiona Missaghian-Moghaddam (the Baha'i Faith), Dr. Ananda Guruge (Buddhism), Mary Roddie and Robert Gilbert (Christian Science), Dr. Zakyi Ibrahim (Islam), Rev. Bruce Montgomery (Jehovah's Witnesses), Rabbi Allen Krause (Judaism), Dr. Ronald Peterson (Mormonism), William N. Hatfield (Native American Religions: Luiseno/Wailaki Nation), Dr. Charles Frazee (Orthodox Christianity), Dr. Richard Johnson (Protestant Christianity), Dr. Paul Levesque (Roman Catholic Christianity), Dr. Gerald Larue (Secular Humanism), Dr. Dalton Baldwin (Seventh-Day Adventists), and Dr. James Nelson (Unitarian Universalism).

We also wish to express our gratitude to Dr. Robert W. Graeff, Assistant Superintendent for Educational Services of the Ramona (California) Unified School District, for allowing us to reproduce in Appendix A the policy statement "Recognition of Religious Beliefs and Customs."

Benjamin Hubbard would like to thank Judy Hubbard for allowing him the time during the summer of 2006 to complete revisions to the book while a number of home improvements were put on hold.

Finally, our thanks to Sharon Coatney, Sue Stewart, Emma Bailey and Elizabeth Budd of Libraries Unlimited who guided the book so skillfully through the editorial process.

Introduction

What follows is an overview of the key issues a classroom teacher is liable to encounter when teaching about religion or when dealing with questions or situations related to religion, and specific suggestions for dealing with them. The issues are arranged according to the eight topics discussed for each religion.

Origins

The United States has always been a religiously plural nation. In the past half century, the number of religions practiced in the United States has increased more than ever before. There are several reasons for this proliferation: (1) Generally, Americans regard religion as a matter of personal conscience and choice and believe that people should be free to select which religion to practice or to elect not to practice any religion. (2) Because the First Amendment—ratified in 1791—separated church from state, there is no central religious authority for the country. (3) Immigrants have brought their religions from all parts of the world. In particular, the 1965 reform of the McCarran-Walter Immigration Act opened the door to immigrants from countries such as India and Pakistan with predominantly non-Christian populations. (4) No one church or religion is dominant over another.

The establishment and implementation of the principles of the First Amendment have involved controversy and struggle that continues today. This momentous effort is part of the history of the United States, a unique experiment in freedom. If we overlook the connection between this country's history and its religious traditions, we cannot possibly understand what it means to be American.

Beliefs

The First Amendment to the Constitution begins: "Congress shall make no law respecting an establishment of religion, or prohibiting the free exercise thereof." Charles Haynes of the Freedom Forum First Amendment Center at Vanderbilt University has led the way in understanding how to use the first principles articulated in the Constitution to guide educational policies and practices about religion. In *Finding Common Ground,* he writes that the fundamental question in the modern United States is: "How to live with our deepest differences?"[1] The First Amendment's religion section has two clauses that protect the exercise of freedom of conscience for people of all faiths or none. The Establishment Clause protects citizens from religious persecution because no one religion is sponsored ("established") by the government, and the Free Exercise Clause guarantees the right of citizens to "reach, hold, exercise or change beliefs freely."[2]

In the United States, then, you can practice whatever religion you choose or not practice any. The two clauses together provide the principles by which we can learn to live with our sharpest differences and celebrate our religious diversity. Our common ground is a shared understanding of the "place of religion in public life and of the guiding principles by which people with deep religious differences can contend robustly but civilly with each other."[3] Because our religious liberty is a right extended to everyone, we need to be particularly vigilant in protecting that right for others so that we may enjoy it ourselves.

In the "Beliefs" section of each chapter, we present a concise summary of what is most central to the worldview of people in the various faith communities.

Sacred Books/Scriptures

Most living religious traditions are based on written records—books, scrolls, tapestries, tablets, clay vessels, and the like. Given the prominence of written records in most of the better-known religions discussed in this book, we decided to make this one of the elements in our summaries of the various religions. It is important to understand, however, that traditions without scriptures (e.g., Native American) are also worthy of study.

Practices

A comment by Supreme Court Justice Tom Clark in a case that outlawed Bible readings in public schools, provides a powerful justification for teaching about religion in public schools:

> In addition, it might well be said that one's education is not complete without a study of comparative religion or the history of religion and its relationship to the advancement of civilization. It certainly may be said that the Bible is worthy of study for its literary and historic qualities. Nothing we have said here indicates that such a study of the Bible or of religion, when presented objectively as part of a secular program of education, may not be effected consistently with the First Amendment.[4]

Although the First Amendment provides the guiding principles for religion in public schools, the Supreme Court, in two significant decisions, has interpreted how these principles may be applied. With regard to the Establishment Clause, the Lemon Test (*Lemon v. Kurtzman*, 1971) stipulates that a negative answer to any of the following three questions makes a law relating to religion unconstitutional: "(1) Does the law, or other government action, have a bona fide secular or civic purpose? (2) Does the primary effect neither advance nor inhibit religion? In other words, is it neutral? (3) Does the law avoid excessive governmental entanglement with religion?"[5] If all three questions can be answered in the affirmative, the law is constitutional. Because public schools represent the government, their policies and legal positions must pass the Lemon Test.

With regard to the Free Exercise Clause, the Sherbert Test (*Sherbert v. Verner*, 1963) stipulates that citizens, in attempting to practice their religion, can claim protection if their actions "(1) are motivated by a sincere religious belief, and (2) have been substantially burdened by the government."[6] It also says that government can prevail, nevertheless, if it can show that "(1) it is acting in furtherance of a 'compelling state interest,' and (2) it has pursued that interest in the manner least restrictive, or least burdensome, to religion."[7] Under this test, sincerely religious students may pray silently in class without fear of being "burdened," or restricted, by the government (school), but they cannot pray in a way that will interfere with the government's "interest" of conducting an orderly class or in ways that would coerce or harass others.

These guidelines will also help teachers decide how to treat religious holidays in the classroom; where and how to teach Creationism or Intelligent Design;[8] how to deal with challenges brought by parents; and how to treat particular religious practices, such as not saluting the flag.

The First Amendment provides that religions shall be neither advocated nor opposed, that fairness and neutrality should prevail. Fairness means that religions should be taught without injecting personal beliefs. This can be done by attribution ("most Hindus believe . . ."). Fairness involves a critical and careful approach that includes the positive and negative aspects of a religion. A stance of fairness will acknowledge the adverse effects religions have had on history as well as their uplifting and beneficial contributions. Fairness says that we should teach not only about religion but also about the absence of religion (often called Humanism, a worldview included in this book). Fairness means not making judgments about the comparative worth of religions. Each religion should be respected in its own right.

Finally, fairness dictates that we avoid "explaining away" religion. For example, we should not teach the view that all religions are the same, that they are merely outmoded ways of thinking, that they are all relative to one another, or that one is better than another. These views make assumptions about religion that are not factually demonstrable. Neither is it enough simply to tolerate other religions, because toleration too often is a patronizing stance in which those in power "put up with" others. Fairness means, rather, a positive respect for religious difference, as well as a desire to understand the way each religion understands truth, goodness, justice, and so forth. It means an appreciation of how religions affect the lives of their followers. The goal should always be to understand how the religion understands itself.

Main Subgroups

The variety of religions in the United States is greater than at any time or place in history. This, together with the unique experiment of making religion a constitutionally guaranteed choice, has given religion in the United States a very special flavor. We have supplied chapters on religions that are practiced today in at least some parts of the United States. You are liable to encounter many of these religions in your classroom:

The Baha'i Faith

Buddhism

Chinese Religions (Confucianism and Daoism)

Christianity (Orthodox, Roman Catholicism, Protestantism, and African American Christianity; Christian Science; Mormonism/Church of Jesus Christ of Latter-Day Saints; Jehovah's Witnesses; Seventh-Day Adventists)

Hinduism

Islam

Jainism

Judaism

Native American Religions

Rastafarianism

Scientology

Sikhism

Unitarian Universalism

Wicca

Zoroastrianism

We have also provided chapters on the following:

Fundamentalism

Secular Humanism/Atheism

New Age Religion

We have not included Shinto (the nature-oriented religion of Japan) but have provided chapters on Confucianism and Daoism. These two indigenous Chinese traditions, especially Confucianism, continue to influence immigrants from China, Taiwan, Korea, and Japan on a cultural if not a religious level—even those Asians who are Christian or secular.

Common Misunderstandings and Stereotypes

Some teachers may be reluctant to teach about religions for fear of making mistakes or offending someone. However, when teachers are making an honest and sympathetic effort to portray a religion, students and their parents seldom take offense and will often provide clarification.

Occasionally, teachers are challenged by parents who either believe religion should not be taught at all or want their faith taught rather than the religion currently being presented in class. When teachers take time to explain exactly what they are doing—teaching *about* religion as it occurs in the curriculum or in the calendar (e.g., at Christmas, the Buddha's birthday, etc.), without advocating any one religious point of view, and being neutral and fair toward all religions—parents usually are willing to forgo their disagreements in favor of education.

Some teachers may feel that their own religious convictions prevent them from teaching about other religions. They need to understand their responsibilities as public servants subject to the provisions of the Constitution. Personal convictions, whether for or against religion, should not be allowed to dominate. Nevertheless, this does not mean teachers cannot reveal their convictions to the class. What this does mean is that teachers should state their convictions only as *personal* beliefs, making it clear that the task of the teacher is to present fairly the various religions of the world. One important caution: Because students in the elementary grades are very impressionable, there is the danger that they may assume your beliefs should be true for them as well.

A note about religious studies classes at the high school level. It is important that anyone teaching world religions, the Bible as literature, or similar courses in grades nine through twelve have some training in these areas at the college level, preferably a major or minor in religious studies/comparative religion. These are complex subject areas— just like mathematics, biology, or world history—and they deserve to be taught by a knowledgeable person.

Classroom Concerns

Most teachers agree that students learn more when they are actively involved. Because there is a fine line between explaining a particular symbol or ritual and actually using it religiously, greater care than usual should be taken when dealing with religious activities. The secular and historical nature of the study should be carefully established so that students of any faith (or none) will not be put in a position of betraying their own faith. In establishing the factual and historical setting, students may read and study sacred literature as dramatic events, such as the Exodus of the Jews from Egypt. Then, dramatic presentations can represent the religious life of people, rather than imitate religious ritual. An appropriate time for such activities is in connection with the calendar of religious holidays that many school districts establish for study. Of course, students should understand that they may be excused from such activity if it compromises their own beliefs or values.

We suggest that teachers avoid asking students about their personal religious beliefs. However, on their own initiative, students may make reports, write papers, create artwork, and do homework about their faith. When relevant, they may express their religious beliefs in the course of classroom discussions. It is also permissible to invite knowledgeable adults to discuss religious topics in class, so long as they do it in a noncoercive, nonproselytizing manner. The teacher may make a general invitation to the class, asking for names of adults, including parents and community members, who might be available to speak about their religions. Suggested guidelines for topics include the following questions: Is it permitted by the Constitution? Is it educationally sound and culturally sensitive? Is it appropriate to the class level? Does it recognize that there is more than one view on any issue? Does it avoid generalizing and making "universal" (stereotypical) statements?

Art and music are effective sources of instruction in religious traditions. Artifacts and symbols may be displayed and used in instruction, with the understanding that they are not being used in a religious manner. Music may be studied to learn about religious attitudes and feelings. Architecture, painting, calligraphy, sculpture, and ceramics are vivid media for teaching about religions. In addition, students may draw, paint, sculpt, compose, or construct artifacts, music, and symbols as a way of learning about religions. As with plays, students should understand that they may be excused from these activities if their beliefs or values will be compromised. Finally, food associated with religious holidays (e.g., potato pancakes, or *latkes*, in connection with the Jewish festival of Hanukkah) might be brought to school, or even cooked at school if facilities are available.

Fundamentalists or highly conservative members of whatever faith should not be portrayed as fanatics or "Bible thumpers." Stereotypes abound on both sides, with liberals being portrayed as relativists or "do-gooders." We need to understand all points of view, without expecting that anyone will change. Deeply held religious convictions give meaning and purpose to people's lives. For this reason, people often have a desire to tell others what they have experienced. In this regard, it is possible that a well-meaning student or parent from one of these traditions may try to proselytize in class or invite religious spokespersons to do so. It would then be necessary to mention discreetly that the First Amendment prohibits such activity.

Different religions often have different moral views, especially on such issues as sexual orientation, abortion, drugs, warfare, and the environment. The First Amendment protects the right of all Americans to express their views. Within reason, this is true in the classroom as well. Sometimes, when students have had instruction at home or at their places of worship, they may become disinterested in the classroom lesson or raise questions about it. Usually, it is enough to mention that there are different ways of thinking about questions of morality, and we need to look at all sides. A variety of views should be encouraged as a way of learning how people with deeply held, but different, religious and moral convictions can live together.

To achieve the best situation for teaching about religion, all those who have an interest, positive or negative, should be included—parents, teachers, administrators, and especially school board members. When all points of view are heard and when clear and positive policies are established, there will be fewer conflicts, and conflicts that do arise will be treated in a civil manner. In Appendix A, we have provided a model policy on religion in the public school: "**Ramona [California] Unified School District Policy Instruction: Recognition of Religious Beliefs and Customs.**"

Religious expression in school is not prohibited under present law, although it may be controlled as a matter of fairness. Students may pray, read sacred scriptures, discuss and write about religious topics, meet in groups for religious activities, wear religious garments, distribute religious literature, be released for off-campus religious activities during the school day, and be excused from lessons and activities that are contrary to the teachings of their religion. The only restrictions are the following: (1) these activities cannot interfere with the normal processes of instruction, and (2) they cannot be conducted in a way that would coerce or harass others. What is prohibited by law is state sponsorship or initiation of religious (or antireligious) activities. For example, the school cannot sponsor or initiate celebrations of religious holidays, although teachers may teach about these, and the school can recognize the more secular aspects of religious holidays. These secular aspects might include the dreidel game associated with Hanukkah, the Christmas tree, Easter eggs, Tibetan mandalas, Indian (South Asian) dances, the Japanese zodiacal signs, money exchanges in connection with Chinese New Year, roasting corn in Native American style, Hatha yoga (breathing and posture techniques), and so on. Perhaps the most difficult challenge for the typical teacher is how to recognize Christmas and Easter in a manner that is informative yet not a veiled worship service.

Population Data

In 1990–91, Barry Kosmin and Seymour Lachman[9] conducted a survey of 113,000 randomly selected adults from across the nation, the largest survey of its type in the twentieth century. They found that 86.2 percent of this country's adult population was Christian, 8.2 percent had no religion, 3.3 percent belonged to other faiths, and 2.3 percent refused to answer. Then in 2001, Kosmin and Ariela Keysar replicated the survey with 50,000 respondents. The number of those describing themselves as Christian had dropped from 86 to 77 percent, and those who specified no religious affiliation rose from 8 to more than 14 percent. The percentage of adherents of non-Christian faiths increased modestly: from 3.2 to 3.7 percent of the total adult population, although their actual numbers rose from 5.8 to about 7.6 million.[10] Throughout the book, we use the Kosmin and Keysar data for each of the religions surveyed.

—J.H. and B.H.

Further Reading

Fraser, James W. *Between Church and State (Religion and Public Education in a Multicultural America)*. New York: St. Martin's Griffin, 1999.

Greenawalt, Kent. *Does Religion Belong in Pubic Schools?* Princeton, NJ: Princeton University Press, 2005.

Haynes, Charles C. *Religion in American History: What to Teach and How*. Alexandria, VA: Association for Supervision and Curriculum Development, 1990.

Haynes, Charles C., and Warren A. Nord. *Taking Religion Seriously across the Curriculum*. Nashville, TN: First Amendment Center, 1998.

Nord, Warren. *Religion and American Education: Rethinking a National Dilemma*. Chapel Hill: University of North Carolina Press, 1995.

Web Site

www.firstamendmentcenter.org

Notes

1. Charles Haynes, ed., *Finding Common Ground: A First Amendment Guide to Religion and Public Education.* Nashville, TN: First Amendment Center, 1994, sec. 1.2. See also Haynes et al., *The First Amendment in Schools.* Nashville: First Amendment Center, 2003.

2. Haynes, *Finding Common Ground,* sec. 2.3.

3. *Ibid.*

4. Supreme Court Associate Justice Tom Clark, *Abington v. Schempp,* 1963.

5. Haynes, *Finding Common Ground,* sec. 4.5.

6. *Ibid.*

7. *Ibid.,* 4.6.

8. Creationism or Creation Science attempts to establish scientifically that the world was created by God out of nothing in six days about 10,000 years ago. (See the chapter "Fundamentalism.") Intelligent Design (ID) is a more recent hypothesis that has replaced Creationism for many conservative or Evangelical Christians. It holds that human beings and the entire physical universe are simply too complex to have arisen on their own or by chance, as proponents of evolution contend. However, recent attempts by school boards to mandate equal time for the teaching of ID alongside evolution in science classes have been invalidated by the courts. See *Kitzmiller v. Dover Area School District et al.* (WL 578974 MD Pa. 2005) in which a federal judge ruled that ID is not science and must not be taught in public school science courses. (See also *Edwards v. Aguillard, 482* U.S. 578 [1987], which outlawed a Louisiana law that had required equal treatment for both evolution and Creationism in public school science classes.) However, consideration of ID or Creationism in a world religions, Bible as literature, or civics class would certainly be permissible. See Charles Hayes and Warren Nord, *Taking Religion Seriously across the Curriculum* (Nashville: First Amendment Center, 1998), pp. 155–61.

9. *One Nation under God: Religion in Contemporary American Society.* New York: Harmony Books, 1993, pp. 1–17.

10. Kosmin and Keysar. *Religion in a Free Market Religious and Non-Religious Americans: Who, What, Why, Where).* Ithaca, NY: Paramount Books, 2006, pp. 20–30.

The nine-pointed star of the Baha'i Faith represents the numerical value of the Arabic word baha, *meaning "Glory." In Arabic, as in Hebrew, every letter of the alphabet is assigned a numeric value (e.g., a = 1, b = 2, etc.).*

The Baha'i Faith

Origins

The Baha'i (buh-HAI) Faith officially began in 1863 in Baghdad, Iraq, under Mirza Husayn Ali Nuri, known as Baha'u'llah (buh-HA-u-lah) (Persian for "Glory of God"), who claimed to be a "Manifestation of God," another revealer of divine truth following in the tradition of Moses, Jesus, and Muhammad. He had been part of a movement within Shi'a Islam, Babism, begun by the Bab (Arabic for "gateway"), Siyyid Ali Muhammad, who claimed to be the Twelfth Imam (in Shi'a Islam, imams are spiritual successors of Muhammad who interpret religious truth for their age). He had disappeared centuries earlier and was to return as the Mahdi (MEH-dee), a messianic figure who would purify Islam. The Bab was executed in 1850, but not before proclaiming that another would follow him and be the prophet of a new, universal religion. Two years later, while imprisoned in the so-called Black Pit of Tehran, Baha'u'llah received his call to be God's messenger for the modern age.

After Baha'u'llah's death, the worldwide Baha'i community was first lead by his son Abbas Effendi, titled Abdu'l-Baha ("Servant of the Glory"), then by his great-grandson Shoghi Effendi. Since 1963, the Universal House of Justice has been the head of the international Baha'i community. This institution is elected every five years and is headquartered in Haifa, Israel.

Beliefs

The Baha'i Faith is monotheistic in the tradition of Judaism, Christianity, and Islam. Baha'is hold that all religions are essentially true because they come from the same divine source. It thus promotes mutual respect and reconciliation between the world's religions, as well as world peace. Baha'u'llah is regarded as the most recent messenger from God. There is, consequently, a strong effort to promote Baha'u'llah's mission, inspired by the work of his son who made missionary journeys to Egypt, Europe, and North America until his death in 1921.

Baha'is believe in continuous revelation of divine truth; each age requires a new message because of the progressing development of humanity. In fact, revelation will never be complete because divine truth is limitless. Even the Baha'i Faith itself will eventually be superseded—although not for a thousand years.

Baha'is hold that science and religion must cooperate because they are two sides of the same truth. Any religion that states something contrary to science is distorting the truth, which leads to superstition. Blind faith in science, on the other hand, leads easily to materialism.

One of the most important teachings of the Baha'i Faith is the oneness of humanity. The Baha'i Faith also stresses equality between men and women. Abdu'l-Baha wrote as follows on this subject:

> To accept and observe a distinction which God has not intended in creation is ignorance and superstition. The fact which is to be considered, however, is that woman, having formerly been deprived, must now be allowed equal opportunities with man for education and training. There must be no difference in their education. Until the reality of equality between man and woman is fully established and attained, the highest social development of mankind is not possible.[1]

Sacred Books/Scriptures

From 1852 to 1892, Baha'u'llah was either imprisoned or living in exile. During this time, he was continuously engaged in writing books and letters, making up Baha'i scripture. The Baha'i book of laws is the *Kitab-i-Aqdas* (Arabic for "The Most Holy Book"), which he completed in 1884. All in all, he wrote more than one hundred volumes that explain the faith's teachings.

Practices

Although the Baha'i Faith has hardly any public or private rites, it requires its followers to pray daily, to fast (much as Muslims do during Ramadan; see the chapter "Islam") for nineteen days during the final of the nineteen months in the Baha'i calendar, and to abstain from alcoholic beverages and drugs. There are no clergy to conduct worship services, which are usually held in a member's home in smaller communities and include prayer and readings from the *Kitab-i-Aqdas* and other scriptures. In place of local houses of worship, Baha'i followers have erected on each continent magnificent places of worship open to people of all faiths. The North American center is in Wilmette, Illinois.

Baha'is observe nine Holy Days on which work is to be suspended. These include:

Naw Ruz—The Baha'i and Iranian new year, celebrated March 20 or 21.

Ridvan—A celebration of the religion's founding, when Baha'u'llah revealed himself to his followers. Work is suspended on the first, ninth, and twelfth days of the celebration, April 21–May 2.

Martyrdom of the Bab—A commemoration of the day Baha'u'llah's forerunner was put to death by a firing squad, celebrated July 9.

Birth of the Bab—October 20.

Birth of Baha'u'llah—November 12.

Main Subgroups

It does not appear that there are any significant divisions within the Baha'i Faith.

Common Misunderstandings and Stereotypes

"Baha'i is a type of Islam."

Although the Baha'i Faith developed out of the Shi'a branch of Islam (compare Christianity's evolution from Judaism), it is an independent religion.

Classroom Concerns

The Baha'i Faith is generally not well known in the United States. However, Baha'i children should be accorded respect and recognition (including the mention of the holidays noted earlier in "Practices") in light of the noble principles—such as tolerance, peacemaking, and women's rights—that the religion promotes. Baha'is have been severely persecuted in Iran since the shah's overthrow in 1978 and the establishment of an Islamic theocracy there.

Population Data

There are about 7 million Baha'is in the world,[2] including 84,000 adults in the United States.[3]

—B.H.

Further Reading

Bowers, Kenneth E. *God Speaks Again: An Introduction to the Baha'i Faith*. Baha'i Publishing, 2004.

Web Site

http://www.bahai.org

Notes

1. *The Promulgation of Universal Peace: Talks Delivered by 'Abdu'l-Baha during His Visit to the United States and Canada in 1912*. 2nd ed. Willmette, IL: Baha'i Publishing Trust, 1982, p. 76.

2. Available at http://www.adherents.com. Retrieved June 27, 2006.

3. Kosmin and Keysar, *Religion in a Free Market*, p. 27.

The symbol of Buddhism is the wheel of dharma (Truth, or the teaching or doctrine encompassing Truth), first introduced after the Buddha's Awakening in the first Sermon, titled "The Turning of the Wheel of Dharma."

Buddhism

Origins

Buddhism arises out of the experience and teaching of a historical figure who lived 2,500 years ago. His family name was Gautama, but a number of titles and epithets describing his spiritual nature and accomplishments were claimed either by Gautama or by his followers: the *Buddha* (the Awakened One), Siddhartha (He Who Has Achieved His Goal), Shakyamuni (the Sage of the Shakyas), and Tathagata (Thus Come, or Thus Gone). Most scholars place his birth at about 563 B.C.E. and death at about 483. Born to a king or chieftain of the Shakya tribe near what is today the Indian-Nepali border (in the Lumbini grove outside the ancient city of Kapilavastu), Gautama, when he was still a young man of twenty-nine, renounced his birthright, wife, and child and chose to become a wandering ascetic in search of the ultimate Truth about existence and an escape from suffering. He sought the answer for six years before experiencing, at age thirty-five, release from suffering.

Following this "awakening," or *Nirvana* [Nir-VAH-nah], the Buddha chose to lead the life of a teacher "for the good, benefit, and happiness of gods and men."[1] After serving as a teacher for forty-five years, he died, or as the Buddhists call it, achieved the ultimate *Nirvana: Parinirvana,* or emancipation. To many Buddhists, the Buddha is considered to be a historical figure who accomplished the extraordinary feat of discovering and realizing the highest Truth and sharing this insight with those who sought his counsel. His most important function, therefore, was that of a teacher. This is the view of the Theravada [terra-VA-dah] school (see "Main Subgroups" below). There has always been a tendency, however, to elevate the Buddha to superhuman status. This tendency was resisted in the Theravada tradition but accepted in the later, more liberal, Mahayana [MA-hah-YAH-nah] tradition (see "Main Subgroups" below).

Beliefs

The teachings of the Buddha center around insight into the nature of suffering and how to end it. The earliest texts containing these teachings were written three centuries after he died. There is, nonetheless, a fair amount of certainty that the teachings of the Four Noble Truths and Noble Eightfold Path were, in some form or another, original teachings of the Buddha.

The Four Noble Truths state that (1) all of humanity is in a state of suffering or disharmony, expressed specifically as physical, mental, and existential (i.e., birth, aging, and death) suffering; (2) this situation has its origin in a thirst, or excessive and uncontrollable desire, for sensual experience and pleasure, continued existence, and even nonexistence or annihilation; (3) this suffering can be stopped by following a path or method designed to achieve this result; and (4) the method the Buddha urged his disciples to follow to achieve the end of suffering, or *Nirvana*, is the Noble Eightfold Path.

The eight steps of the Noble Eightfold Path are subdivided into three areas of cultivation: of insight, or wisdom; of morality; and of the mind through meditation. Thus the first two steps—*right views* and *right intention*—reflect the cultivation of wisdom; the next three—*right speech*, *right action*, and *right career*—reflect the cultivation of morality; and the last three—*right effort*, *right mindfulness*, and *right concentration*—reflect the cultivation of mind. Employing a medical model, the Buddha is viewed as a doctor who diagnoses the problem that afflicts all humanity and sets forth a cure.

Although the Buddha incorporated the doctrines of *karma,* rebirth, and the existence of various divine and demonic beings from Brahmanism, the dominant or mainstream religion of northern India, he rejected other elements of this religion. The Buddha rejected the most important religious activity of the time, ritual action—specifically, those rituals described in the Vedas, the sacred texts of Hinduism/Brahmanism. In addition to the Vedic ritual practices, the so-called low arts—such as astrology and palmistry—were also rejected. The basis of society itself was challenged. During the time of the Buddha, four classes were recognized: the brahmins, who regarded themselves as the most prestigious and important class because of their knowledge of the rituals, which in turn controlled the cosmos; administrators and warriors; the farmer/commercial class; and the serfs, or peasants, who served the other classes. This system, based on birth, was unacceptable to the Buddha, who argued that merit, not birth, defined a person's worth.

What was truly revolutionary, however, was the Buddha's rejection of these bedrocks of Hindu philosophy: (1) the Self as the permanent, unchanging life force that was the font of ultimate knowledge for the individual; and (2) the Brahman (Godhead) as the permanent, unchanging, transcendent, unknowable Supreme Force, which both lay beyond the cosmos and was the source of the cosmos. If one rejects these notions, nothing can be permanent and eternal: soul, self, God(s), heaven, hell, or anything within the cosmos.

It is this acceptance of the impermanence of everything—not only of those objects that exist outside of us but also of those elements that comprise the individual—that defines the purpose of Buddhist teaching: to overcome the tenacious grasping after the material and mental realms that we mistake as the source of the permanent and unchanging.

This impermanence of everything is the source of an unbalanced and unstable existence and experience that constantly impels us to desire things that we do not possess or, once a thing is in our possession, constantly to fear losing it. Indeed, nothing can be possessed because there is no thing that exists unto itself, for there is no substance or essence, no permanent model or ideal that underlies the material and mental realms. The natural consequence to the teachings of impermanence and nonself is that there is no personhood, only a bundle of physical and mental phenomena.

The tenets of Buddhism include the following: (1) We exist in a condition of dysfunctionality, constantly grasping after whatever we think will make us permanently happy, not mindful that there is nothing that can give us perfect and constant contentment simply because there is nothing that is permanent in this world. (2) The Noble Eightfold Path represents a regimen that avoids an addiction to self-torment—standard practice among the ascetics (practitioners of extreme penitence) of the Buddha's time—as much as it avoids the opposite extreme, an addiction to sensual pleasures. (3) Meditation is the primary practice that overcomes the ills of the human condition. It consists of calming the mind (compare the practice of yoga in Hinduism) and practicing "insight" meditation, in which the mind actively observes all bodily and mental processes. Out of such practices, insight-knowledge, that is, knowledge of the nature of things as they truly are, is gradually developed until there is an ultimate breakthrough: *Nirvana*, the transcendence of greed, hatred, and delusion.

The importance of pursuing such demanding and time-consuming practices helps to explain why early Buddhism and the Buddhism of South and Southeast Asia, Theravada Buddhism, is presented more as a monastic religion rather than as a religion of the masses. As a result, the Sangha [SUNG-gha]—the monastic community of monks and, previously, nuns—is given more importance than the ordinary lay community in achieving the goal set forth by the Buddha.

Sacred Books/Scriptures

The sacred compositions of Buddhism are vast in number and composed in many languages. The oldest collection surviving to this day is the Pali Canon (Pali is a literary language related to the language spoken by the Buddha), originating in what was to become the Theravada tradition. The earliest compositions in the Canon were based on the discourses and addresses of the Buddha, although they were not necessarily his exact words. These compositions were called *sutras* (discourses, dialogues, or teachings presented in prose), usually of the Buddha but sometimes also of his disciples. A later section was added to the Canon that presented an analysis of the teachings in the earlier compositions. Around the first century B.C.E., the canon was committed to writing on the island of Sri Lanka.

The Pali Canon comprises three *pitakas* (baskets): the Vinaya Pitaka, containing the rules for the monks and nuns of the monastic community; the Sutta Pitaka, consisting of the teaching of the Buddha; and the Abhidhamma Pitaka, discussing, through various analytical methods, the teaching (*dhamma*, Sanskrit *dharma*) on the factors of experience (*dhummas*).

Authoritative and influential texts also originated within the Mahayana and Vajrayana [vuhj-ruh-YAH-nah] (see "Main Subgroups" below) Buddhist traditions. Many of the texts were known as *sutras*, like the Pali texts mentioned above, because they were considered the Buddha's own words. In the Mahayana tradition, *sutras* made their appearance as early as the first century B.C.E., and they continued to be written until the eighth century C.E. Most prominent are the Wisdom Sutras, of which there are longer and shorter versions (including the Diamond and Heart Sutras), the Lotus Sutra, and the Pure Land Sutras, to name just a few. Vajrayana, or the "Apocalyptic Vehicle," originated with the introduction of new texts known as *tantras* (systems), esoteric (hidden and mysterious) ritual texts dating from the sixth century C.E. onward.

Practices

Buddhism began as a practice designed to overcome any opinion or emotional state that bound one to this world of suffering. Meditation (see "Beliefs" above), in which the mind is in a calm, observant state, is the principal practice of the majority of Buddhists.

Not every Buddhist school practices meditation, however. There is a devotional side to Buddhism: the Pure Land School, for example, emphasizes the recitation of a formula (*nien-fo* [Chinese] or *Nembutsu* [Japanese]): *"Namo Amituo Fo"* (Homage of Amida Buddha) that will make it possible for one to be reborn in the Western Paradise (an abode that has no connection to the world of suffering, karma or rebirth, making it possible to achieve Nirvana); the Nichiren School emphasizes that its members recite the *daimoku* (sacred phrase) *"Namu myo-ho-ren-ge kyo"* (Homage to the Lotus Sutra) as encompassing the perfect expression of the Buddhist teaching. For the Vajrayana, of which Tibetan Buddhism is an example, its monks and nuns practice elaborate rituals with the use of *mantras* (sacred syllables or phrases) and *mudras* (hand gestures) to effect a mystical state in the mind. The practices of laypeople within the entire Buddhist community mainly involve acts of merit designed to bring about a better existence in a future life, which in turn will eventually lead to final liberation. These acts include offering food and robes to monks, constructing *stupas* or *pagodas* (shrines to the Buddha, sometimes containing his relics), gilding statues of the Buddha with gold leaf, and visiting temples.

Vegetarianism is often associated with Buddhism, but it is not universal. It is a practice of monastics in China but not in Japan.

A Buddhist recitation called "Three Jewels" is common to all Buddhists and is also employed by one who converts to Buddhism: "I take refuge in the Buddha, I take refuge in the Sangha [monastic community], I take refuge in the Dharma [teaching]."

Major Buddhist festivals and holidays include **Wesak** (**Vesak** or **Visakha Puja**), the celebration of the Buddha's birth, enlightenment, and Parinirvana, usually celebrated on the full moon day in April or May depending on which Buddhist country; the **Asalha Puja** (Dhamma Day), held usually on the full moon day in July, the day which commemorates the Buddha's first sermon to his original disciples; **Ulambana** (**Yu-lan pen** or **Obon**) a three- to fifteen-day period in July or August during which the living offer food to the ancestors or the hungry ghosts to reduce their suffering; **Guan Yin's** (**Avalokiteshvara's**) birthday is celebrated in Mahayana countries such as Tibet and

China during the month of February or March; the Thai **Loy Krathong** (Festival of the Floating Bowls), a popular Thai festival held on the full moon night of November, when banana leaf cups with incense sticks, a candle, and a coin are floated on the waterways; and the **Songkran** Festival, or Thai New Year held for three days in April, when water is sprinkled on the elders and images of the Buddha as a sign of respect and on anyone else who gets in the way. As is expected, the New Year is an important event because it is a good time to perform acts of merit.

Other ceremonies and practices occur as well. For the Theravada Sangha, the **Uposatha** (or **Poya**) is one of the more important practices for monastics and lay alike. Monastics (*bhikkhus*), on the new and full moon days of the month, confess their transgressions and recite the 227 monastic rules of the Sangha. Laypeople observe the eight precepts (see note 8 to this chapter) as a means of strengthening their commitment to the Dharma. The **Anapanasati** Day, which commemorates the time when the Buddha extended the Rain Retreat by a month beyond the usual three-month period, celebrates the Buddha's discourse on the mindfulness of breathing (Majjhima Nikaya, sutra 118), given on the full moon day of the fourth month. The **Kathina** Ceremony, popular in Thailand and held one month after the Rain Retreat (October or November), is the time of offering new robes and other requisites to the monks.

Main Subgroups

Preliminary Remarks

Buddhism today is generally identified according to three traditions or *yana* (vehicles): Theravada,[2] Mahayana, and Vajrayana. To capture the primary emphasis of each of the three traditions, (1) Theravada (the Teaching of the Elders) is referred to as "Individual Vehicle,"[3] (2) Mahayana (Great[er] Vehicle) is called "Universal Vehicle," and (3) Vajrayana (Vehicle of the Thunderbolt) is referred to as "Apocalyptic Vehicle."[4] The term *yana,* also translated as "career" or "path" (Sanskrit, *marga*), is considered equivalent to Buddhist doctrine. Because the First Sermon of the Buddha was called the "Turning of the Wheel of Dharma," those Buddhists who recognized the Three Vehicles identified them respectively as the First, Second, and Third Turning of the Wheel of Dharma. The First Turning focuses on the Four Noble Truths and Eightfold Noble Path described in the First Sermon of the Buddha; the Second focuses on the Doctrine of Emptiness (the teaching that no thing possesses independence, substantiality, or inherent nature); and the Third focuses on the Buddha-Nature (the teaching that all beings possess the potential of becoming a Buddha).

Although Buddhism is identified by non-Buddhists according to vehicle or tradition, few Buddhists except the Theravadins identify themselves in this manner, for reasons explained later. Rather, it is the lineage or teacher, often called a school or subschool—a typically South Asian approach that carries over into the Far East and elsewhere—that is the badge of identity. For instance, Mahayana Buddhists identify themselves through one of the many schools established in China, Japan, or elsewhere, such as the **Pure Land School** (stressing the attainment of the Western Paradise through recitation of the name of the Amida Buddha, *"Namo Amituo Fo"* of the Japanese teacher Honen (1133–1212) or of Shinran (1173–1262); the **Chan or Zen school** (with its emphasis on meditation techniques) of the Japanese teacher Dogen (1200–1253), known as Soto Zen, or the Rinzai Zen school of the Japanese teacher Eisai (1141–1215); or the **Nichiren school** (inspired by the medieval Buddhist priest Nichiren (1222–1282) who taught that the best practice was the *daimoku* ("title") or *mantra "Namu myo-ho-ren-ge kyo."*[5]

Theravada

Based on the above remarks, Theravada may be viewed as both a *yana* (tradition) and a school. As the sole representative of the Individual Vehicle,[6] Theravada is the predominant form of Buddhism in South Asia (Sri Lanka) and Southeast Asia (Myanmar [Burma], Thailand, Cambodia, and Laos). From a modern-day perspective, it is through the South and Southeast Asian immigrants that Theravada is represented in the United States and other Western countries. Buddhism began to fragment fairly early in its history. Around 349 B.C.E., the first major schism took place resulting in two divisions: the **Sthavira-vada** (the Tradition or Doctrine of the Elders) and **Mahasanghikas** (Those Who Belong to the Great Assembly), with the latter separating from the former, according to the historical accounts. It is generally assumed within Buddhism that the orthodox teaching and monastic discipline developed along Sthavira lines. Yet even though the Sanskrit compound *Sthavira-vada* is equivalent to the Pali *Thera-vada,* we cannot automatically assume that Theravada Buddhism today is identical to original Buddhism. We may safely assume, however, that it represents an early strand of Buddhism. Around the time of the Indian Buddhist Emperor Ashoka (268–232 B.C.E.), the Theravada Buddhists identified themselves as **Vibhajyavadins** (Those Who Distinguish, referring to a method of analysis of distinguishing between those factors of existence or *dharmas* that "exist" and those factors that do not). It is likely that from this time or earlier, the Theravadins viewed themselves as a separate school from others that were appearing at this time.

When Ashoka instigated Buddhist missionary activity to foreign lands, it was Theravada that was established in Sri Lanka with the coming of Ashoka's son, Mahinda, in 243 B.C.E. With the arrival of Theravada in Sri Lanka, the tradition-school assumes a firm foundation in history, with its Pali Canon first set down in writing in the first century B.C.E. in an organized fashion.

The practice of Theravada focuses on the monastic life. The term *sangha* (community) generally refers to the monastic order (*bhikkhu-sangha*). Some monks are "forest-dwelling" monks who live in secluded locales and engage in meditation and ascetic practices (*dhutanga*) such as refusing to eat at the house of a layperson or refusing to dwell in a village or town.[7] They will also preach the Dharma or Buddhist teaching. They follow the traditional rules of the community of monks (*vinaya*) more strictly than the "village monks" who participate in the ceremonial needs of the laity, such as participating in funerals and other rituals.

Although a community of nuns (*bhikkhuni-sangha*) existed from the time of the Buddha, it died out in the eleventh century in Sri Lanka with the fall of Anuradhapura, its capital, to the Colas of South India, and from India as a whole with the Turkish Muslims invading northern India. The *bhikkhunis* that survived in Myanmar (Burma) died out when the Mongol emperor in China sacked Pagan, Myanmar's capital, in 1298. Recently, communities of women (known as *mae ji* or laywomen, who sometimes shave their heads and wear white robes) taking the first five or eight precepts (of the traditional ten of the monks)[8] have been established and are generally attached to temples. One of the principal proponents for the reintroduction of the Order is Venerable Dhammananda, a Buddhist. The possibility of the revival of the *bhikkhuni sangha* has been discussed extensively in Thailand both within the *bhikkhu sangha* and the Thai government. So far there is no official Bhikkhuni Order that is fully recognized. In Sri Lanka, a Bhikkhuni Order does exist because of the support of Venerable Sumangalo Maha Thera at Syamvamsa chapter in Dambulla. Some four hundred *bhikkhunis* belong to this chapter.

Laypersons conduct themselves differently from monastics. For one thing, it is generally assumed that *Nirvana* is out of reach for laypersons in this or the next life, so most of their religious activities are designed to gain merit (good karma) to achieve a better, more spiritual present and future life. *Nirvana* will be achieved in a more distant lifetime. Acts of merit for the lay community include listening to the Dharma and making donations to the monks and temple. A more intense practice might include taking the precepts (five or eight).

Mahayana

Around the first century B.C.E., a new literature began to appear that introduced different perspectives and insights into the Buddha's teachings: Mahayana, "Great(er) Vehicle" or "Career," as opposed to the earlier, monastically and scholastically oriented schools referred to earlier. Among the differences in attitude between Theravada, the sole surviving school of the Individual Vehicle, and Mahayana, as perceived by the Mahayana teachers, are the following:

1. A new path was introduced, that of the Bodhisattva (a being who strove for awakening or Buddhahood). Instead of pursuing *Nirvana,* which resulted in the total removal of the enlightened being from the world of suffering, Bodhisattvas vowed to continue to devote themselves to ensuring the salvation of all living beings in the world of suffering. As a result, the ideal individual of Theravada Buddhism, the Arhant [AR-hunt] (one who has achieved *Nirvana*) was rejected and replaced by the ideal individual in Mahayana, the Bodhisattva. Certain implications arise from this shift in teaching:

    a. The emphasis is on saving others, not just oneself.

    b. Saving others requires methods and conduct that are certain to cause the unenlightened to see the light. This is known as "Skillful Means."

    c. All beings have the potential to become Buddhas. This reflected the basic Buddhist teaching that the Buddha was a Bodhisattva prior to his enlightenment at age thirty-five. In the Theravada tradition, however, only one Buddha is recognized in this present world age—Gautama—and only one present Bodhisattva currently exists, Maitreya. He is expected to emerge many thousands or even millions of years from now as a Buddha. Contrary to this view is the Mahayanist view that Buddhahood is open to all because all beings possess Buddha Nature.

    d.   More emphasis is placed on the practice of compassion (i.e., wisdom put to practice).

2.   New, divine-like Buddhas and Bodhisattvas were introduced into the literature. Among the Bodhisattvas who are especially important are the Bodhisattvas of Compassion (*Guanyin*); the Bodhisattva of Wisdom (*Wenshu* or *Manjushri*); the Bodhisattva who saves the dead from hell and who (as *Jizo* in Japan) watches over the welfare of children, pregnant women, and travelers (*Dicang* or *Kshitigarbha*); the Bodhisattva who represents universal kindness (*Puxian* or *Samantabhadra*); and the future Buddha (*Miluofo, Maitreya*) who is often identified as the Laughing Buddha (see "Common Misunderstandings and Stereotypes"). Although in the literature, Maitreya is identified as a Bodhisattva or Future Buddha, the Chinese name incorporates the character *fo,* or Buddha. This partially explains his identification as a Buddha.

Among the Buddhas of note are the Buddha of the Western Paradise or Pure Land (*Amitabha*, Japan: *Amida*); the Medicine Buddha (*Yaoshi Liuliguangwang Rulai, Bhaishajyaguru),* who is popular in China as the curer of all diseases; the Sunlike Buddha (Japan: *Dai-nichi, Vairocana)*; the Buddha of the South (*Ratnasambhava,* Japan: *Hosho*); the Buddha of the East (*Akshobhya*); and of the North *(Amoghasiddha)*.

Vajrayana

In Tibet and Nepal around 500 C.E., the third type of Buddhism appeared with the introduction of new sacred books known as *tantras*. This tradition, called today Vajrayana, the "Diamond" or "Apocalyptic" Vehicle, which spread to Mongolia, parts of China, Bhutan, Sikkim, Ladakh, and parts of Russia among the Buriat Mongols and Kalmucks, emphasized ritual and magical means of achieving Buddhahood. The tradition was philosophically based on the Mahayana teachings but placed emphasis on technical, magical, and ritual means that were radically different from earlier practices to accelerate enlightenment. More specifically, *mantras* (sacred language), *mudras* (hand gestures), *mandalas* (symbolic models of the cosmos), special deities, and instruments such as the bell, ritual dagger, hand drum, and scepter are employed to this end.

Common Misunderstandings and Stereotypes

It is important to keep in mind that sweeping statements about Buddhist behavior and belief cannot be made. For instance, not all Buddhists meditate (some schools do not advocate it); not all Buddhists are vegetarians (this is especially true of Japanese Buddhists); not all Buddhist monks and nuns are celibate; and not all Buddhists hold to the teaching of nonviolence.

Furthermore, there is no general ethical system or rigid ethical code for Buddhists except perhaps for the Five Precepts (not to kill, steal, or lie; not to abuse speech or sex). Opinions about the rightness or wrongness of a specific action will often depend on one's national background or specific circumstances. Opinions differ on such important issues as warfare, abortion, and homosexuality. In general, however, the rule of thumb for Buddhists is that if an action is harmful to oneself or to others, it must be avoided. The problem that often arises in real-life situations, though, is that what is harmful to one may be helpful to another. The decision as to whether such an action is to be avoided or permitted will be open to debate among Buddhists.

> *"Buddhists worship statues of Shakyamuni (Buddhism's founder) and other Buddhas."*

Statues of Buddhas and Bodhisattvas do not constitute a form of worship in the Western sense. Although descriptions and Buddhist literature might give the impressions that these beings are divinities, they are not in the strict sense. They are not necessarily worshipped as gods, although it is quite possible for less sophisticated Buddhists to view the Buddhas and Bodhisattvas as gods or emanations of God.

> *"The Buddha is a fat, jolly figure who doesn't seem very religious."*

What is known as the Laughing Buddha—a fat, disheveled, figure standing with raised hands or sitting with a laughing visage found in gift shops and restaurants—is actually Maitreya (the future Buddha), or more accurately, the Chinese monk Budai (Hotei in Japan), who was posthumously connected to Maitreya in the eleventh century. Budai (Hemp Bag, Glutton) was known for his hemp bag containing all sorts of oddities that was the continual object of curiosity, especially of children. In Chan, or Zen, Buddhism, he represents a class of individuals who pose as religious eccentrics.

Classroom Concerns

Because of the general ignorance about Buddhist teaching and practice in the United States, some students might view it as a cult. It is important to explain its key ideas and its moral code as worthy of careful study and discussion.

It is also important to be aware that the different calendars employed by Buddhists of different traditions and nationalities—especially regarding the Buddha's birthday and New Year's celebrations—can be confusing. If you have Buddhist students in class, consult them or their parents about when they celebrate these events. (See Appendix B for a calendar.)

Population Data

It is very difficult to determine an accurate number of Buddhists worldwide. Numbers range from 250 million to 500 million, but a realistic estimate is 376 million.[9] Buddhist countries include Thailand (95% Buddhist), Cambodia (90%), Myanmar (Burma)

(88%), Sri Lanka (70%), Laos (60%), Vietnam (55%), Japan (50%), and Taiwan (43%). Kosmin and Keysar[10] (*Religion in a Free Market,* p. 27) report the adult population of U.S. Buddhists at 1,082,000.

—*J.S.*

Further Reading

Corless, Roger I. *The Vision of Buddhism.* New York: Paragon House, 1989.

Harvey, Peter. *An Introduction to Buddhism: Teachings, History, and Practices.* Cambridge and New York: Cambridge University Press, 1990.

Keown, Damien. *Buddhism: A Very Short Introduction.* Oxford: Oxford University Press, 1996.

Keown, Damien. *Buddhist Ethics: A Very Short Introduction.* Oxford: Oxford University Press, 2005.

Strong, John S. *The Buddha: A Short Biography.* Oxford: One World, 2001.

Strong, John S. *The Experience of Buddhism: Sources and Interpretations.* Belmont, CA: Wadsworth/Thomson Learning, 2002.

Snelling, John. *The Elements of Buddhism.* Longmead, Shaftesbury, Dorset, UK: Element Books, 1990.

Web Sites

Buddha Dharma Education Association Inc.: http://www.buddhanet.net

Ontario Consultants on Religious Tolerance: http://www.religioustolerance.org/buddhism.htm

Buddhist Studies WWW Virtual Library: http://www.ciolek.com/WWWVL-Buddhism.html

http://www.adherents.com/

Notes

1. Quoted from A. K. Warder, reviser of 2d ed., *The Anguttara-Nikaya,* vol. 1. Rev. Richard Morris, ed. London: Luzac for the Pali Text Society, 1961.

2. The term *Hinayana* (Lesser Vehicle) is considered a derogatory term by those within this tradition. Therefore, Theravada is used here.

3. The expression is taken from Marylin M. Rhie and Robert A. F. Thurman, *Wisdom and Compassion: The Sacred Act of Tibet.* New York: Harry N. Abrams, 1991, p. 15.

4. *Ibid.*

5. An offshoot of the Nichiren Buddhist tradition is Soka Gakkai, an organization founded in 1930 by Makiguchi Tsunesaburo (1871–1944) and now known as the Soka Gakkai International. Originally an independent organization that became affiliated with the Nichiren

Shoshu through its founder, it has reverted to being independent in 1991. An aggressive recruiter, Soka Gakkai has attained a modest following among young professionals in the United States and Great Britain.

6. All other schools belonging to the Individual Vehicle, of which the traditional number was established to be eighteen (including the Theravada) as early as three hundred years after the death of the Buddha, have long since disappeared.

7. The Metta Forest Monastery in Valley Center, California, is an example of a forest hermitage. The monk in charge is Thanissaro Bhikku.

8. The precepts are the refraining from (1) taking life; (2) stealing; (3) sexual misconduct; (4) lying; (5) drinking alcohol; (6) eating after noontime; (7) watching dancing, singing, and shows; (8) adorning oneself with garlands, perfumes, and ointments; (9) using a high bed; and (10) receiving gold and silver.

9. Available at http://www.Adherents.com.

10. Kosmin and Keysar, *Religion in a Free Market,* p. 27.

Chinese Religions: An Overview

Unlike the religions rooted in the Near East (Judaism, Christianity, Islam and Baha'i), which retain their individuality and uniqueness, China has made the three major religions—Confucianism, Daoism, and Buddhism—into one synthetic whole. Add to this mix Chinese folk religion, which resembles Buddhism and Daoism, and the general observation is that Chinese religions are an amorphous mass assimilated by the Chinese public. One might assert that all Chinese are socially Confucian and individually Daoist at the same time. These two native religions in turn influenced Buddhism in China in such a way that it is markedly different from the Buddhism practiced in South and Southeast Asia. China thus reflects a very different response to the multiplicity of religious traditions found in the West—a response based on accommodation and syncretism (religious mixing) rather than exclusion and isolation.

Some generalizations about Chinese philosophy, religion, and tradition might help to bring some order to what non-Chinese might consider a chaotic and incomprehensible mix of separate traditions:

1. Chinese religions and traditions are relatively practical in approach to the affairs of the living. They are more centered on the concerns of the individual in this world of the living and less concerned with the metaphysical or spiritual world. Generally speaking, the state is more important than religious establishments, and humanistic concerns take precedence over divine concerns or speculation. A creator god, for instance, simply is not discussed to any great extent nor is such a being considered important enough to affect one's way of life.

2. Chinese religious activity centers around a wisdom that orientates individuals to living a fulfilled and harmonious life here and now.

3. The achievement of a fulfilled and harmonious life is discussed and practiced in Confucianism, Daoism, Buddhism, and folk religion. All follow a *Dao* (Way) that leads one to the fulfilled life, but their respective ways of achieving this goal are fundamentally different.

16

Confucianism

Confucianism, or the Way of Confucius, is primarily moralistic or ethical in tone, emphasizing tradition, human relationships, rituals, and reason. The ultimate purpose was to construct a society that exemplified the *Dao*. In the sense that Confucianism emphasizes tradition, it has preserved those practices and viewpoints that, over the centuries, help to define what it means to be Chinese. For example, ancestor worship has a history of practice that goes back at least 3,500 years. Furthermore, acceptance of a Supreme Being or purposeful force (Heaven) that regulates the cosmic order has been and is part of Confucianism, as was the role of the Emperor as Son of Heaven who controlled the human order. As envisioned today, Confucianism is more a way of life or philosophy than a religion, for it is a systematic and reflective deliberation on living in this world. Confucian temples do exist, but they are not equivalent to the churches, synagogues, or temples of other religions. They were built with the intention of providing a place to honor Confucius, not to worship the gods. His birthday is commemorated September 28 at Taipei's Confucian Temple. Befitting Confucius as the greatest of Chinese teachers, this day is also Teachers' Day in the Republic of China.

Daoism

Daoism, on the whole, is opposed to the Confucian perspective. The *Dao*, as understood in Confucianism, had been perverted by reason and society according to the Daoists. The *Dao* instead was to be found in nature. This perspective, therefore, emphasizes not the intellectual and moral side of humanity but rather the emotional. Whereas Confucianism emphasizes social living and obligations, Daoism emphasizes the presocial individual; whereas conformity is expected in Confucianism, dissent and free will are emphasized in Daoism. It is not uncommon, therefore, for one to picture the artist, poet, and hermit as Daoist, or to associate the esoteric and bizarre as more closely associated with Daoism.

Unlike Confucianism, Daoism is more than a philosophy. In fact, the roots of Daoism appear in early Chinese history with the practice of shamanism and all that it entails (see the chapter "Daoism"). During the fifth or sixth century B.C.E. and later, philosophical Daoism appeared, beginning with Laozi's book, *The Way and Its Power*. This was followed by the more speculative thinking in the book *Zhuangzi* (presumably by the author of the same name), which led to later expressions in literature, painting, and reclusive behavior.

Later still, probably around the second century C.E., came an increasing concern for the attainment of immortality by various practices, as well as the concoction and drinking of elixirs. The alchemical side of Daoism in attaining transcendence of the limitations of life through breath control, sexual hygiene, dietary regimens, and elixirs became common. Also, the establishment of a religious Daoism, with the inclusion of a pantheon of various entities (nature gods, folk heroes, sages, and generals) originated at about the same time.

Buddhism

Buddhism, although a non-Chinese religion, adjusted to Chinese culture in the centuries following its introduction into China as early as the second century B.C.E. Unlike Daoism, however, which taught that life was valuable and should be enjoyed, Buddhism viewed all life as suffering. If Daoism was life-affirming, Buddhism sought to transcend life in this world. The crossbreeding of Buddhist, Confucian, and Daoist teachings occurred in the third and fourth centuries through the Chinese intelligentsia familiar with the literature of the three traditions. Daoism especially was considered to be similar to the Buddhist philosophy and certain Buddhist practices, mostly because of influences brought to bear on Buddhism by Daoism and vice versa. For instance, Daoist terms were employed by scholars to translate Buddhist concepts into Chinese. This was called *ge-yi* Buddhism: the use of Chinese indigenous ideas and terms, usually but not exclusively from the Daoist tradition, to explain Buddhist concepts. Daoism, in turn, was influenced by Buddhism and began to perceive itself as possessing a systematic body of doctrines contained within a literature. The making of statues also was taken over from the Buddhists. Even the biography of Laozi was based on that of the Buddha. Some people even claim that Laozi traveled to India and was none other than the Buddha. Also, the Neo-Daoist teaching of the Mystery (fourth to sixth century C.E.), involving the notion of being empty and nothing, appealed to some Buddhist scholars because of its similarity to the Buddhist emphasis on liberating oneself from all excessive and wrong desires.

Confucian differences with Buddhism lay in the Buddhist emphasis on the spiritual and its refusal to venerate the king or emperor (such veneration was a fundamental trait of state Confucianism). Yet a poet in the fourth century C.E. suggested that Confucius and Buddha were simply teaching from differing points of view: the outside (the Confucian emphasis on corruption in society) and the inside (the Buddhist stress on underlying truth). The eventual outcome in China was accommodation of both of these philosophies. By 500 C.E., Buddhist rites were practiced, Buddhist monasteries and temples proliferated, and Buddhist monks and nuns were numerous and respected. Daoism borrowed from Buddhism, and Confucian families, especially women, embraced Buddhism.

Part of the success of Buddhism in China was because of the translating activities of Chinese and non-Chinese scholars over the centuries, resulting in the eventual dissemination of popular teachings. Among the teachings in the more popular and devotional Mahayana Buddhist tradition (see the chapter "Buddhism") were those of the celestial Bodhisattvas (figures who delayed their entry into full *Nirvana*, or bliss, in order to help others achieve it) and the Pure Land doctrine. Regarding the latter, one strove to be reborn in the Pure Land (paradise) to achieve final liberation with greater facility.

Folk Religion

Folk religion is mainly part and parcel of a number of secular and social institutions. Consisting of numerous gods and goddesses, folk religion emphasizes the establishment of relationships with these divine beings. Although similar to Daoism in this respect, many of the divinities in folk religion are not included in Daoism. Like Buddhism, salvation in Chinese folk religion is open to all who follow the religion. In Taiwan (the Republic of China), the divinities that are of particular importance are the God of Heaven, who is associated with order and justice; the Earth God, to whom numerous temples are dedicated; and the House God, who receives offerings when the family moves into a new home. Other popular divinities include the patron goddess of fishermen, Matsu, as well as a number of divinities who were originally human including the healer Huatuo, who lived sometime between the first and third centuries C.E., and the warrior Guanyou, who lived during the period of the Three Kingdoms (221–280 C.E.). Also part of the folk religion are the Wangye of Taiwan, celestial spirits who protect humanity from evil spirits and epidemics. Some Chinese (mostly of *Hakka* descent) also worship the Three Kings of the Mountains.

In addition to worship of these divinities, geomancy (a form of divination involving lines and figures) and physiognomy (divination based on facial features or judging human character based on facial features) are practiced.

—J.S.

Further Reading

Adler, Joseph A. *Chinese Religious Traditions.* Upper Saddle River, NJ: Prentice Hall, 2002 [London: Laurence King Publishing, Religions of the World, Series Editor: Ninian Smart].

Allison, Robert E., ed. *Understanding the Chinese Mind: The Philosophical Roots.* Hong Kong: Oxford University Press, 1989.

Ch'en, Kenneth. *Buddhism in China.* Princeton, NJ: Princeton University Press, 1964.

Ching, Julia. *Probing Chinas's Soul: Religion, Politics and Protests in the People's Republic.* San Francisco: Harper and Row, 1990.

Ching, Julia. *Chinese Religions.* Maryknoll, NY: Orbis Books, 1993.

Cua, Antonio S., ed. *Encyclopedia of Chinese Philosophy.* New York: Routledge, 2003.

de Bary, Wm. Theodore, Wing-Tsit Chan, and Burton Watson, comps. *Sources of Chinese Tradition.* Vol. 1. New York and London: Columbia University Press, 1960.

Eliade, Mircea, ed. "Daoism," In *The Encyclopedia of Religion.* Vol. 14. New York: Macmillan, 1987, pp. 288–317.

Overmyer, Daniel L. *Religions of China: The World as a Living System.* Prospect Heights, IL: Waveland Press, 1986.

Robinet, Isabelle. *Taoism: Growth of a Religion.* Phyllis Brooks, trans. Palo Alto, CA: Stanford Univesity Press, 1997.

The Texts of Daoism: Part I (*The Tao Te Ching of Lao Tzu; The Writings of Chuang Tzu*) (Books I–XVII); Part II (*The Writings of Chuang Tzu*) (Books XVIII–XXXIII); *The T'ai Shang Tractate of Actions and Their Retributions; Appendices I–VIII (Part II)*. New York: Dover Publications, 1962 [reprint of the 1891 edition, published in the *Sacred Books of the East Series,* Volumes 39 and 40].

Watson, Burton, trans. *The Complete Works of Chuang Tzu.* New York: Columbia University Press, 1968.

Yao, Xinzhong. *An Introduction to Confucianism.* Cambridge, England: Cambridge University Press, 2000.

Web Sites

http://www.chinaknowledge.de/Literature/Religion/religions.html

http://www.gio.gov.tw/taiwan-website/5-gp/brief/info04_19.html

http://www.csupomona.edu/~plin/folkreligion/chinesefolkrel.html

http://www.fccj.edu/library/chi-reli/chi-defi.htm

http://www.adherents.com/Religions_By_Adherents.html#Chinese

Falun Gong: http://website.leidenuniv.nl/~haarbjter/falun.htm

Notes

1.   This essay is intended to explain the unique mix of religions in Chinese history. For practical data on Buddhism, Confucianism and Daoism as they relate to the classroom, see the separate entries on these three traditions.

The bust of Confucius/Master K'ung is the traditional symbol of Confuscianism.

Confucianism

Origins

The origins of Confucianism are found in the sixth and fifth centuries B.C.E. in the person of Confucius (Kongfuzi, Kongzi, or "Master Kong"; 551–479 B.C.E.). Born to a soldier father, he might have been an illegitimate child but nevertheless belonged to the aristocracy. He was educated, trained in archery and music, and held minor offices as a young man, although he never succeeded in the political realm. Confucius was concerned with the burning issue of the day the protracted decline of the social order that started in the eighth century B.C.E. and led to a long period of civil warfare that was not to end until the third century B.C.E. In such an age of decadence and warfare, the overriding issue of the time among philosophers was how to restore the social order and overcome the instability rampant in China.

Confucius was born in the state of Lu, which considered itself the custodian of Zhou culture. (The Zhou dynasty ruled China from 1122 to 256 B.C.E. but had only nominal control from the eighth century B.C.E. on). His solution to the turmoil of his time was to return to the ancient traditions established in the early days of the dynasty that were now being neglected. Taken in this context, Confucius did not consider himself an innovator but rather a transmitter of the teachings of the ancients.

Beliefs

What we have left of Confucius' teachings are a series of brief sayings and observations recorded in the *Analects*. His role was to preserve the social order and its ideals encompassed in the traditional civilization. This took its definitive form during the Zhou dynasty. Confucius did so by shaping the moral habits of the dynasty's leaders and, by the example of the leaders, their subjects. The essence of his teaching was to provide a system of right conduct that operated on three planes: individual, social, and political. The outcome of right conduct resulted in the building of individual character, the discharging of social obligations, and the administering of moral government.

In the Chinese context, the standard of conduct, the *Dao* (Way), was an ideal way of life for both the individual and the state. The individual who strove to reach this standard was known as the Gentleman, or person of noble character, and the individual who actually accomplished the goal of putting the *Dao* into practice was known as the Sage.

The specific virtues and values that underlay the three planes were as follows:

1. *li* [lee]—conduct: The rules of conduct and responsibility that governed all human modes of civilized relationship, including one's relations with parents during their lifetime (filiality) and after their death (ancestral worship), and with superiors, from simple rules of etiquette to formal court ritual.

2. *ren* [ruhn]—benevolence, affection, or humanity: The performance of actions that manifest what we might perceive as humanity or humaneness. The written Chinese character for *ren* signifies "two" and "man," suggesting the basis of humanity and human relationships.

3. *yi* [yee]—the sense of rightness or appropriateness of action.

The three virtues are interrelated. For instance, *ren* must conform to what is right (*yi*); *yi*, which is performed with the spirit of humanity (*ren*), is executed through conduct (*li*). Confucius also mentions other virtues. For instance, in *Analects* 17:6 he observes that courtesy, generosity, honesty, persistence, and kindness comprise *ren*. It is clear, therefore, that Confucius emphasized the human sphere, not the divine; this present life and not the future life; moral action based on traditional customs and not ritual or ceremonial action for the sake of empty convention.

Developments did occur after his death. For one, the divine sphere became increasingly important, with the Emperor, as the Son of Heaven, responsible for the proper functioning of the social and natural order through ritual action and retaining the Mandate of Heaven (divine or providential blessings). Confucianism under the Han dynasty (206 B.C.E.–220 C.E.) became the state ideology. The Confucianist emphasis on the bureaucracy, the family system, the civil service examination system, and study of the Five Classics were paramount. These and later developments help to define the Confucianist way of life. As a way of life, as an ethic, and in some aspects as a religion (such as ritual and myth), Confucianism helps to define the Chinese character in much the same way that the so-called Civil Religion of the United States helps to define the American character or Hinduism the Indian character.

The following observations can be made about Confucianism:

1. Confucianism is regarded more as a philosophy, a way of life, and a scholarly tradition than a religion, but in the past it included a political or royal ideology that included the ritual duty of the Emperor.

2. The inner life of the Confucian is governed by such virtues as humanity and rightness.

3. The outer expression of the Confucian is manifested by the rules of conduct that govern an individual's life and that are primarily but not exclusively encompassed in filial piety and ancestral worship. Filial piety, which was expanded in the *Doctrine of the Mean* (see "Sacred Books/Scriptures" below) to include the fivefold relationship between minister and ruler, son and father, wife and husband, younger and elder brother, and friends, is considered the foundation of virtue and the root of civilization. In other words, the family is the foundation of society.

4. Confucianists (and Chinese culture in general) place great stress on education. As early as the Han dynasty, mastering the Five Classics was the means of entering civil service and served as the basis of the state cult. Education was viewed as the primary means to success.

5. The *Doctrine of the Mean* stresses that human nature should be in harmony with the larger universe. It states:

    What Heaven [the early Zhou dynasty name for the Supreme Being who watched over the conduct of humans and the laws of nature] imparts to man is called human nature. To follow our nature is called the Way. Cultivating the Way is called education.

    The emphasis on achieving harmony with Heaven's will or mandate becomes the basis of political philosophy in the role of the Emperor and in the role of the Gentleman.

6. The Confucian strives to achieve harmony in personal conduct and convictions. In other words, one must be in harmony with one's nature as well as with the dictates of Heaven.

7. Connected to the role and the goal of harmony was the early (third century B.C.E.) inclusion of the *yin-yang* (literally, "shady [*yin*] and sunny [*yang*] side of the hill") —the concept of dual powers that permeate the universe: female and male, cold and heat, darkness and light, passivity and aggression, rest and activity, withdrawal and expansion. Maintaining harmony of the twofold nature of reality was to be of supreme importance to the Emperor in the performance of rituals. It also took on importance in other areas outside the specific philosophical range of Confucianism, such as medicine.

In conclusion, the Confucianism of Confucius was primarily concerned with the human sphere, especially moral conduct that derived its worth from its association with Heaven's will. Later, more emphasis was placed on the workings of the cosmos and its relationship with the human sphere. In so doing, Confucianism adopted teachings from non-Confucian philosophies and practices. This sharing of teachings with other major philosophies, Daoism included, has led the Chinese to take a nonexclusive view of their religious life. Confucianists—whether Chinese, Korean, or Japanese—may also profess to practice elements identified with Daoism, Buddhism, Shintoism,[1] or Christianity without denying the Confucian orientation that exists within their culture.

Sacred Books/Scriptures

Writings especially prestigious to Confucians in particular and Chinese in general are the Five Classics and Four Books. The Five Classics are the *Book of History* (which includes the reports and speeches of early Chou rulers), the *Book of Odes* (about 300 poems from early Chou times), the *Book of Changes* (a book on divination), the *Book of Ritual*, and the *Spring and Autumn Annals*, an account of Lu (the Chinese state) from 722 to 481 B.C.E.

The Four Books are the *Analects* of Confucius, the *Doctrine of the Mean* (which describes the duties of the Gentleman, social obligations, and the virtues of moderation and balance), the *Great Learning*, and the *Book of Mencius* (Mengzi [371–288 B.C.E.] who was the second greatest Confucian philosopher).

Practices

Practices performed by the populace (and not the formal state ceremonies that were once performed in China and Korea) include those involving four important life-cycle rituals: birth, maturity, marriage, and death.

Ceremonies surrounding birth include the protection of the mother-to-be by the Spirit of the Fetus (*taishen*), the disposal of the placenta, the mother resting for a month and being given a special diet, and the baby being supplied with all necessary items on the anniversaries celebrated in the first, fourth, and twelfth months.

The ceremony of reaching maturity is rarely celebrated today. When performed, the young adult is served chicken at a gathering celebrating the event.

The marriage customs involve the proposal, the engagement, the dowry (which is carried to the groom's home in a procession), the giving of gifts to the bride (generally equal to the dowry), the visit of the groom to the bride's home, the groom taking the bride to his home, the marriage and reception, and the bride's serving breakfast to the groom's parents the morning after the marriage.

The ceremonies surrounding death involve a number of actions required of the family. The body is washed, dressed, and placed in a coffin. Usually a Daoist or Buddhist officiant performs the ritual. Liturgies are held on the seventh, ninth, and forty-ninth days after the burial and on the first and third anniversaries of the deceased.

Ancestral worship, which involves an elaborate set of practices, is performed each year. One practice includes a number of events taking place over a fifteen-day period, among which are the preparation of the family shrine, where offerings and homage are made; and the hiring of priests (if the family can afford them) to announce the dead to deities, read scriptures to help in the ancestors' proceeding to the Western Heaven of Happiness, and perform the "burning of the bags" (*shubao*) ceremony for the ancestors (bags containing silver ingots bear the name of the male ancestor and his wife).

Main Subgroups

Because Confucianism is not a religion in the same sense as Christianity or Buddhism, there is no orthodox Confucian church, nor are there sects. It is primarily the cultural and traditional sides of society with inclusion of significant rituals (such as ancestral rites) that provide its defining characteristics.

Perhaps the best way to view Confucianism is through a historical perspective. From the teachings of Confucius developed the state ideology of the Han dynasty that included not only the Confucian (i.e., Confucius and later philosophers such as Mencius or Mengzi and Xunzi) teachings of human behavior, nature, society, and government but also cosmological teachings and divination practices that were not originally Confucian. Neo-Confucianism emerged much later, during the Song dynasty (960–1279 C.E.) as a response to Han dynasty Confucianism, which was chiefly interested in collecting ancient texts. Neo-Confucianism emphasized the value of life, a response to the "metaphysical" and perceived nihilist ideas of Buddhism. It also reacted to Daoism with its emphasis on a metaphysical approach to understanding human nature and the human condition. Both Confucianists and Neo-Confucianists accepted the following four ideas:[2]

1. The reality of humanity and the cosmos is affirmed.

2. A moral principle runs through both. This principle is a power known as Way (*Dao*), Principle (*li*), heaven (*tian*), Supreme Ultimate (*taiji*), or Great Harmony (*taihe*).

3. The goal of humanity is to achieve harmony with the cosmos and humanity.

4. Neo-Confucianists, together with Confucianists, accepted the notion that education or moral discipline is the chief means of attaining one's full potential.

Unlike Confucianism, Neo-Confucianists emphasized metaphysical speculation, developed the notion that an underlying principle (*li*) prevailed throughout the cosmos and in humanity and that a vital force or primordial substance (*qi*) permeates the cosmos, thus explaining the process of change therein.

New Confucianism has its origins in the twentieth century with the 1958 New Confucian manifesto and a subsequent attempt to rejuvenate Chinese culture and characterize Confucianism as its basis. Although influenced by Neo-Confucianism, it is not Neo-Confucianism but rather an independent movement whose motto is: "The spirit of Confucianism as substance and the Western culture as applications." In other words, it is an attempt to "Confucianize Western culture."

Common Misunderstandings and Stereotypes

Although Confucianism itself may not be well known in the United States, it should be noted that the East Asian cultures have all been significantly influenced by the Confucian ethic. It is typically understood to be a philosophy with political, social, ethical, and somewhat metaphysical overtones coupled with ritual and ceremonial practices. In popular culture, sometimes humorous remarks beginning with "Confucius say . . ." often take on negative racial overtones that demean the Chinese and their culture. Furthermore, the strong emphasis on education in Chinese culture sometimes leads to the misguided impression that the Chinese (and Asians in general) are genetically predisposed to general intellectual and mathematical skills.

Classroom Concerns

It is suggested that teachers emphasize at opportune times (e.g., the Chinese New Year) or along with the study of Chinese history or religions the significant contributions to civilization made by the Chinese. Contributions include numerous inventions (printing, paper, and explosives, to name but a few); the Great Wall of China; and the importance of the family, elders, education, and literacy in Chinese culture.

Population Data

Only about 26,000 Confucians live in the United States, based on the figures given in the sources used in the Website *Adherents.com*. It is not clear how this figure was determined, however, and thus it can only be a rough estimate of the actual number.

—J.S.

Further Reading

Confucius. *The Analects of Confucius.* Arthur Waley, Trans. Introduction by Sarah Allan. New York: Knopf, 2000 (Originally published in 1938; New York: Macmillan).

Creel, Herrlee Glessner. *Confucius, the Man and the Myth.* London: Routledge & Kegan, 1951.

Huang, Siu-Chi. *Essentials of Neo-Confucianism: Eight Major Philosophers of the Song and Ming Periods.* Westport, CT: Greenwood Press, 1999.

Oldstone-Moore, Jennifer. *Confucianism: Origins, Belief, Practices, Holy Texts, Sacred Places.* New York: Oxford University Press, 2002.

Shun, Kwong-loi, and David B. Wong. *Confucian Ethics: A Comparative Study of Self, Autonomy, and Community.* New York: Cambridge University Press, 2004.

Xinzhong Yao. *An Introduction to Confucianism.* Cambridge: Cambridge University Press, 2000.

Web Sites

http://plato.stanford.edu/entries/confucius/

http://confucius.org

http://encyclopedia.thefreedictionary.com/Confucius

http://www.sacred-texts.com/cfu/index.htm

http://philtar.ucsm.ac.uk/encyclopedia/confuc/

Notes

1. Shintoism/Shinto is the native religion of Japan that stresses the presence of divine powers, *kami* [KAH-mce], in nature (e.g., Mount Fujiyama). Shinto is not covered in this book because there are few practitioners in the United States.

2. Huang, *Essentials of Neo-Confucianism,* pp. 5–6.

The yin-yang symbol indicates how such opposites as dark (yin) and light (yang), passive and active, winter and summer, and female and male interact and complement each other.

Chinese Religions

Daoism

Origins

Unlike many other religious traditions, Daoism[1] has neither a single origin (like Christianity or Islam) nor an indistinct origin (like Hinduism). Instead two distinct sources exist for what we know today as Daoism: (1) the philosophers of the Warring States (civil war) period (403–221 B.C.E.) who followed a "Way" (*Dao*) of Nature rather than a *Dao* of society, and (2) the shamans [SHAW-muns] and magicians who, since the Shang dynasty (1523–1027 B.C.E.) and perhaps earlier, played an important role in the life of the ordinary Chinese population. Further developments in philosophical Daoism and shamanistic (or popular) Daoism resulted in what is known as religious Daoism.

Philosophical Daoism

The earliest of the philosophers associated with the Dao philosophy was Laozi, who lived either in the sixth century B.C.E. or, according to some Western scholars, during the Warring States Period, sometime during the fourth or third century B.C.E. Little is known of his life, and there is much discussion regarding whether the legendary Laozi was confused with a historical personage actually responsible for writing the *Daodejing*—namely, Li Er. It may be also that the *Daodejing* of Laozi was not the product of one person but actually a compilation of sayings by several teachers, all assuming the name Laozi.

29

The second great philosopher of the Warring States period was Zhuangzi [JWAHNG-dzuh] (369–286 B.C.E.), whose book of the same name reflects the teaching of the *Daodejing* but is more mystical, intuitive, and complex in its outlook.

Popular Daoism

The other roots of Daoism lay in the activities of shamans and magicians. Shamans are religious persons found worldwide who exhibit a number of unusual traits: magical flight, that is, communicating with spirits by traveling to their abode; magical healing by serving as mediators between spirits and humans; and the ability to enter into trance states for the purpose of journeying to the spirit world. Shamans in China typically were associated with the expulsion of evil spirits through magical healing and engaged in magical flights to heavenly and demonic regions. Furthermore, they used dancing, juggling, and tricks to induce the descent of the spirits. Chinese shamans were known either as *wu* (wizard, witch, magic; dancing) or *fangshi* (magician or scholar of magical recipes). Both men and women were shamans, with women perhaps being the more numerous. Female shamans were explicitly directed to exorcise the spirits at certain times of the year; to dance in times of drought or to perform certain gestures to encourage rain; to heal; and, in times of trouble, to entreat the spirits and engage in wailing and chanting. The association of women is significant because the Daoist ideal society is connected with matriarchal memories, femininity, and, later, an emphasis on sexual techniques. For instance, female *wu* represented the *yin* (female, water) element in nature when rain rituals were enacted.

Religious Daoism

Besides the philosophical Daoism engendered by Laozi and Zhuangzi, a number of developments occurred over the centuries that became subsumed under what is generally known as religious Daoism. The connection between the philosophical and the religious was maintained, however, in the primary objectives of Daoism: longevity, vitality, and a harmonious life. The regimen that took hold in religious Daoism included such techniques as alchemy, breath control and hygiene, magic, elixirs, and sexual techniques not unlike those of Buddhist Apocalyptic (Vajrayana) Buddhism.

Although the ultimate origins of Daoism as a religion are partly located in the ancient tradition and context of shamanism, the more immediate origins occurred during the first century B.C.E. Originating during this period was a popular movement dedicated to the culture hero Huangdi (the legendary Yellow Emperor) and Laozi. Known as the Huanglao philosophy, this movement divinized Laozi and raised to prominence the practices mentioned earlier, as well as those of astrology and divination. Many deities, including the divinized Laozi, were also introduced. This movement was formally organized by the religious leader Zhang Daoling in the second century C.E. As the first to be given the title of Heavenly teacher—a hereditary title that persists to the twentieth century with the Zhang family—Zhang Daoling is regarded as the historical founder of the Daoist religion. The Zhengyi sect claims connection with him.

Beliefs

The philosophy of Daoism in the *Daodejing*, which is regarded as a political treatise for the ruler, may be summarized as follows:

1. The *Daodejing* is a vision of reality or the order of nature known as the *Dao* (Way).

2. The *Dao* is regarded as an infinite whole that cannot be measured by human standards. Scattered throughout the *Daodejing* are descriptions of the *Dao* as being empty, invisible, formless yet complete, eternal, and existing prior to heaven and earth. The *Dao* is spontaneous, simple, and natural.

3. The highest embodiment of *Dao* is *De* [DU] (Power—the internalized *Dao*); it is the *Dao* dwelling in objects causing them to be what they are, a concept that resembles the notion of potentiality.

4. As the embodiment of *Dao*, *De* embodies effortlessness and spontaneity. Thus, the highest *De* is nonaction (*Wuwei*).

5. The Daoist philosophy is a corrective to excessive deliberation, excessive activity, excessive passion, and artificiality—in short, a corrective to the increasing complexity of living.

6. The solution in life is to return to the *Dao*, to conform to the *Dao*, to move like the *Dao*. In other words, the solution is to return to simplicity, to plainness, to a state of infancy, and to the practice of nonaction (i.e., to perform a minimum of action) and to become more natural or to follow nature.

7. The suggestion in the *Daodejing* is to correct the imbalance that has arisen in the world. Thus the theme of the *Daodejing* is to loosen one's hold on the conventional, the socially acceptable, and the so-called normal and "keep to the center." Scattered throughout the text are admonitions to adhere to the feminine rather than the masculine, the passive rather than the active, nondesire rather than desire, unselfishness rather than selfishness, and so on.

Incorporated in Daoist philosophy were the complementary principles of *yin* and *yang*. Although not unique to Daoism, they were employed in the *Daodejing* as the harmonious duality in the cosmos. The complementary natures of sun and shade, heat and cold, and summer and winter are examples of *yin* and *yang* operating in nature. Humans—men and women—have both masculine and feminine principles within them, and maintenance of harmony between the masculine and feminine is essential to physical and mental health.

The second great book of philosophical Daoism, the *Zhuangzi*, agrees in part with the *Daodejing*. For instance, it regards the *Dao* as the indescribable equivalent of the natural or cosmic order, and it emphasizes the unity and spontaneity of nature. Furthermore, the *De*, the virtue or power (natural ability) that makes us what we are, is the movement of the *Dao*. An underlying theme of the teaching in the *Zhuangzi* is that all beings should follow their nature, for to follow nature is to follow *Dao*. Anything that is not natural—the artificial, the nonspontaneous—only leads to misery. Thus, the

Zhuangzi states: "Emptiness, stillness, limpidity, silence, inaction [are] the substance of the *Dao* and its *De*."

One area of difference between the two books is that the *Daodejing* is a political text concerned with the action and proper rule of the sage-king, whereas the *Zhuangzi* is designed for the private individual.

Sacred Books/Scriptures

As already noted, the two most important philosophical books in Daoism are the *Daodejing* and the *Zhuangzi*. Scholarship has determined that the writer Li Er may actually be responsible for compiling the *Daodejing* and that it was not the product of one person but rather a compilation of sayings by several teachers, all assuming the name Laozi. The *Zhuangzi* was most probably compiled in the third century C.E. by the commentator Guoxiang.

Religious Daoism possesses a large number of sacred books that are specifically associated with the various Daoist movements or sects. Many of these are not open to the public but are reserved for initiates or those judged ready to receive the teachings.

Practices

Practices designed to promote health and longevity include alchemical practices (see "Origins" above), breathing exercises, movement exercises designed to circulate the *qi* (vital breath), and meditation. Divination with the Yijing (the Classic on Changes; also known as the I Ching), interpreted in a Daoist context, is also popular. Social Daoism resulted in the development of sects and religious communities that included priests and, later, monastic institutions and monks. The latter two developed from Buddhist influence. The presence of priests and monastic institutions resulted in the introduction of ritual practices to celebrate the birthdays of gods, to ward off misfortune, to attain or maintain peace and prosperity, to promote the successful building of a house, and to ordain priests.

Main Subgroups

Daoist religio-political communities date from the second century C.E. with the appearance of the Tianshidao ("Way of the Heavenly Masters") under its first and foremost Heavenly Master, Zhang Daoling (also considered the founder of the Daoist religion), and the Taibingdao ("Way of the Great Peace").

1. The first and most prominent sect developed into a religious movement under the Heavenly Master that is still prominent in Taiwan. An important ingredient of the practice of the school's priests is healing the sick with exorcism or faith healing.

2. The second sect, founded by Zhang Jiao, was a dissident movement that was millenarian (oriented to a future golden age) in nature. Zhang Jiao had the reputation of a great healer, but he is known for teaching that 184 C.E. was to be the beginning of a new era. His followers, Yellow Turbans, wore such turbans as a distinctive sign of the sect. The insurrection was, however, brutally suppressed.

3. Established in the fourth century C.E. was thc Maoshan (Mount Mao) sect. It reacted to the Buddhist monastic organizations by forming its own community that was designed to perform the Daoist practices of meditation and of external and internal alchemies, as well as mediumistic practices and communication with deities through visualization.

4. The Lingbao (Marvelous Treasure) sect of the fifth century introduced the worship of the Tianzun (Heavenly Worthies).

5. In the twelfth century, the Quanzhen (Completely Real) sect was founded by Wang Zhe (1112–1170). It advocated the amalgamation of Daoism, Confucianism, and Buddhism. It emphasized meditation as the major practice to achieve the Daoist goals.

Today, the Quanzhen and Zhengyi sects, the latter originating from the Way of the Heavenly Master through Zhang Daoling, still exist. Another group, from Taiwan, the Yiguandao (Great Dao), has recently made its appearance in California. This is an international movement that emphasizes more outreach to the general populace.

Common Misunderstandings and Stereotypes

Because many people in the United States have never heard of Daoism, stereotypes are not common. However, those who are familiar with Daoism in some way might consider it magical or superstitious. Although magic is an element of popular Daoism, it certainly does not apply to the tradition as a whole.

Classroom Concerns

It is suggested that teachers emphasize at appropriate times (e.g., the Chinese New Year) or in connection with the study of Chinese history the many contributions to civilization made by the Chinese (printing, paper, explosives, etc.); the Great Wall of China; and the importance of the family, elders, education, and literacy in Chinese culture. Teachers might also explain how the Daoist emphasis on living in accord with nature can be beneficial both to one's health and the environment.

Population Data

There is no way to determine the actual number of Daoist adherents. According to one source,[2] however, China has more than 1,600 temples and more than 25,000 priests belonging to the Quanzhen and Zhengyi sects. No estimate of lay believers is given. It has been estimated that 10 million members of the 55 minorities of China are Daoists. Outside China, the number of Daoists is considered to be around 32 million. Kosmin and Keysar's study found 40,000 adult believers in the U.S.[3]

—J.S.

Further Reading

Laozi. *A Translation of Lao Tzu's* Tao Te Ching *and Wang Pi's Commentary.* Ann Arbor: Center for Chinese Studies, University of Michigan, 1977.

Miller, James. *Daoism: A Short Introduction.* Oxford, England: Oneworld, 2003.

Pas, Julian F. *Historical Dictionary of Taoism.* Lanham, MD; London: Scarecrow Press, 1998.

Wang, Yi'e. *Daoism in China.* Zeng Chuanhui, trans. Beijing: China Intercontinental Press, 2004.

Web Sites

AskAsia.org: http://www.askasia.org/teachers/essays/essay.php?no=40/

Religion and Ethics—Taoism (British Broadcasting Corporation Web site): http://www.bbc.co.uk/religion/religions/taoism/

Notes

1. Older textbooks spelled Daoism with a T: Taoism, but the D spelling is more accurate phonetically.

2. Yi'e Wang, *Daoism in China,* pp. 204, 208–9.

3. *Religion in a Free Market,* p. 27.

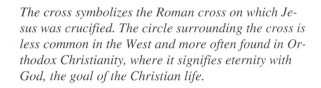

The cross symbolizes the Roman cross on which Jesus was crucified. The circle surrounding the cross is less common in the West and more often found in Orthodox Christianity, where it signifies eternity with God, the goal of the Christian life.

Christianity: Common Elements

Origins

Christianity (from *Christos,* the Greek term for "Messiah") began with the birth of Jesus of Nazareth/Jesus Christ and developed over the first 75 years of the first century C.E. into a religion distinct from Judaism. Jesus, after a period of preaching and healing, was arrested by Pontius Pilate, head of the Roman occupation government of Judea, on suspicion that he might lead a revolt against the Romans and on complaints from the Jewish High Priest and some of his associates, who objected to certain religious teachings of Jesus. He was crucified by the Romans. After the crucifixion, Jesus' followers proclaimed that God had raised Jesus from the dead and that he had appeared before some of them. Most Jews did not accept the message about Jesus,[1] even though the very earliest Christians were all Jewish. The Apostle Paul and other missionaries began spreading the teachings of Jesus to the non-Jewish population of the Greco-Roman world. They found an immediate response among many gentiles, especially those from the lower ranks of society. The new faith was declared illegal by the Roman government, and there was severe persecution under the emperors Nero and Diocletian. However, Emperor Constantine legalized Christianity in 313, and by 381, it had become the official religion of the Roman Empire.

This chapter is intended to explain what is common to Christianity. For particular data on African American Christianity, Christian Science, Mormonism/Church of Jesus Christ of Latter-Day Saints, Orthodox Christianity, Jehovah's Witnesses, Protestant Christianity, Roman Catholic Christianity, and Seventh-day Adventists as they relate to the classroom, see the separate chapters on these religions.

Beliefs

Christianity proclaims that Jesus is the Messiah, first spoken of in Judaism, and also God's son who redeemed or rescued humankind from its sinful condition. He possesses both a human and a divine nature, and in his divinity, he is one in his very essence with God the Father, the deity of the Jewish people. In addition, the Holy Spirit (or Holy Ghost), mentioned in the Gospels (see "Sacred Books/Scriptures" below), is also considered a divine being coequal with God the Father and Jesus. The Christian Godhead is called the Trinity because there are three personal manifestations of the one God—Father, Son, and Holy Spirit. Christians believe that Jesus will return to earth at some future point to defeat the powers of evil completely and to judge the living and the dead. Those who are redeemed will live forever with God in heaven, and those who are not redeemed will be condemned to hell, the absence of God.

Sacred Books/Scriptures

Christians accept both the Old Testament (identical to the Hebrew Bible of Judaism) and the New Testament as the revealed word of God. The Old Testament has three major divisions: Law/Torah (Genesis, Exodus, Leviticus, Numbers, Deuteronomy); Prophets (Former Prophets: Joshua, Judges, 1–2 Samuel, 1–2 Kings; Latter Prophets: Isaiah, Jeremiah, Ezekiel; and the twelve minor prophets); and Writings (Psalms, Proverbs, Job, Song of Songs, Ruth, Lamentations, Ecclesiastes, Esther, Daniel, Ezra-Nehemiah, 1–2 Chronicles). The New Testament consists of twenty-seven books: four Gospels (Matthew, Mark, Luke, and John), the account of Jesus' life and teachings; one historical book (Acts of the Apostles); one so-called apocalyptic writing (Book of Revelation), urging Christians suffering under Roman persecution to remain steadfast and describing the end of time and the afterlife; and twenty-one letters to churches, more than half of which are attributed to Paul.

Practices

The vast majority of Christians practice two rituals or sacraments, baptism (the initiation rite) and the Lord's Supper/Holy Communion/Eucharist (the consuming of bread and wine, which represent the presence of Jesus Christ).

With the exception of the Seventh-Day Adventists, Christians observe Sunday as the Sabbath, the day most worship services take place and workday activities are avoided. Other principal holy days include the following:

Advent—A four-week period of spiritual preparation for the coming (advent) of Jesus at Christmas. It begins on the Sunday nearest November 30.

Christmas—A celebration of the birthday of Jesus Christ: December 25 for Roman Catholics and Protestants and January 7 for Orthodox Christians. Some Orthodox Christians in this country celebrate Christmas on December 25 as an accommodation to Catholic and Protestant practice.

Lent—A forty-day period of penitence in February and March in preparation for Easter. Roman Catholics and Protestants mark the start of Lent with Ash Wednesday.

Good Friday (called Holy Friday by Orthodox Christians)—A commemoration of the day Jesus died by crucifixion that occurs two days before Easter. Many Christians attend services on the afternoon of Good Friday at about the time Jesus is thought to have died.

Easter Sunday—A celebration of the resurrection of Jesus. Its timing is based on a lunar calendar and varies from year to year. (See "Calendar of Religious Holidays," Appendix B.)

Ascension Day—A commemoration of Jesus' ascent into heaven to sit at the right hand of God the Father, occurring forty days after Easter.

Pentecost Sunday (from Greek *pentecosta*, fiftieth [day])—A celebration marking the descent of the Holy Spirit upon Jesus' apostles after his ascension into heaven, occurring on the seventh Sunday after Easter. Also known as Whitsunday.

With the exception of Advent and Christmas, the dates of these holy days are determined by the lunar calendar and thus vary from year to year. Because Orthodox Christians use a different calendar, they observe Holy (Good) Friday, Easter, and Ascension Day on different dates than Roman Catholics and Protestants. (See "Calendar of Religious Holidays," Appendix B.)

Main Subgroups

(Eastern) Orthodox. This traditional form of Christianity originated in the Middle East and Eastern Europe and is organized along national lines (Greek Orthodox, Russian Orthodox, etc.).

Roman Catholic. This, the largest branch of Christianity, began in Rome under Peter, the first bishop there, and accepts the authority of his successors, the popes.

Protestant. This most recent branch of Christianity began in western Europe in the sixteenth century as a protest against perceived abuses in Roman Catholicism and now includes numerous subdivisions (Anglicans/Episcopalians, Baptists, Lutherans, Methodists, Presbyterians, etc.).

Common Misunderstandings and Stereotypes

Because of Christianity's cultural acceptance and because the chapters on Catholic, Orthodox, and Protestant Christianity discuss misunderstandings specific to each, only one issue will be considered here. The term *Christian* is often used by evangelical and fundamentalist Christians (see the chapter "Fundamentalism") to describe themselves (as in the expression "When I became a Christian . . ."). Evangelical and fundamentalist Christians (or "born-again" believers), like all people, have every right to identify themselves in whatever way they wish. Many feel that they were only nominally Christian before their born-again experience or that their previous religious commitment was not authentically Christian. However, such people need to realize that the term Christianity is also a generic description for anyone who accepts some form of the religion in its Catholic, Orthodox, Protestant, or other expressions. In other words, people other than evangelical and fundamentalist Christians also have the right to call themselves Christians.

Classroom Concerns

In light of the cultural dominance of Christianity in the United States (which is about 77 percent Christian and comparable in Canada), there is the potential for teachers to assume that everyone in class is a Christian of some sort and to proceed accordingly. However, the approximately 20 percent of children in the United States who are not Christian include several million whose parents are Jewish, Muslim, Buddhist, Hindu, Sikh, or followers of other religions—or of no religion. Their beliefs and sensibilities must also be considered and respected. However, because Christianity has played a decisive role in the founding and development of this country, a study of the history and culture of the United States is incomplete without a study of Christianity.

Population Data

The recent exhaustive survey by Kosmin and Keysar cited in the introduction indicates that about 77 percent of the adult population of the United States (159.5 million) is Christian.[2] There are about 2.1 billion Christians in the world.[3]

—*B.H.*

Further Reading

Miles, Margaret. *The Word Made Flesh: A History of Christian Thought.* Oxford: Blackwell, 2005.

Olson, Roger E. *The Story of Christian Theology: Twenty Centuries of Tradition and Reform.* Downer's Grove, IL: Intervarsity Press, 1999.

Placher, Wiliam C. *A History of Christian Theology.* Philadelphia: Westminster Press, 1983.

White, L. Michael. *From Jesus to Christianity (How Four Generations of Visionaries & Storytellers Created the New Testament and Christian Faith).* San Francisco: Harper, 2005.

Notes

1. See the chapter Judaism under "Common Misunderstandings and Stereotypes" for an explanation of Jewish nonacceptance of Jesus.

2. *Religion in a Free Market*, pp. 24, 26.

3. Available at http://www.adherents.com. Retrieved June 6, 2006.

Christianity

African American Christianity

Origins

Africans enslaved in the New World were introduced to Christianity by southern clergy and by slave owners as a system of slave control. However, Africans interpreted the faith in ways unique to them by emphasizing (1) the Exodus experience of the Hebrew slaves who finally gained their freedom (as black slaves hoped to do); (2) an application of the teachings of Christianity to the experience of the slaves (and free blacks) through the interpretation of biblical stories, symbols, and events to fit the day-to-day lives of black people; and (3) a distinctively African tradition in worship services through the use of rhythmical preaching, upbeat, inspirational and stirring music, drums, moving, dancing, and an emotional intensity (particularly in sermons) as means of escape from an impossible situation. Furthermore, African American Christians saw themselves as restoring the church to its original purity.

In colonial times, many blacks belonged to the Methodist and Baptist denominations, which today are predominantly composed of whites. For example, in 1758 the African Baptist or "Bluestone Church" was founded on the William Byrd plantation in Mecklenburg, Virginia—the first known black church in North America. Still, many African Americans had experiences such as that of black Methodist pastor Richard Allen. In the middle of a prayer service, he was asked to move to the balcony of a Methodist church in Philadelphia in 1787. This resulted in his founding the African Methodist Episcopal Church and in the formation of other predominantly black churches in subsequent years.

Beliefs

There is little difference in the theology of African American churches as compared to their Protestant or Catholic counterparts. The Bible, however, is interpreted quite literally by most black Protestants, and the emotional aspects of worship are emphasized.

41

More important, preachers dispense oracles rather than convey information based on interpretation of Scripture. What is more, the Pentecostal movement began in Los Angeles in 1906 under the leadership of African American minister William Seymour who stressed speaking in tongues (believed by Pentecostals to be foreign languages of divine inspiration unknown to the speaker) as the final step in human sanctification. The so-called Holiness Churches also originated in the African American community with emphasis on the conversion experience as freeing one from sin and ensuring salvation.

Sacred Books/Scriptures

Black Christians accept the same Bible as other Christians.

Practices

There are no significant differences in such practices as Baptism and the Lord's Supper/Holy Communion or in the order of the worship service compared with most, mainly white Christian churches. There is, however, a different emotional tenor in black churches compared with white churches: more music (often with a rhythm and blues motif), more singing, more responsiveness on the part of congregants, more hand clapping, and other overt expressions of one's religious feelings.

Kwanzaa [KWAHN-zuh] (Kiswahili for "first fruits of the harvest") is a distinctively black holiday. Although not religious as such, it has a quasi-religious spirit and consists of a seven-day celebration of African American values and traditions and their continued validity. The celebration occurs from December 26 to January 1, with a different virtue stressed each day: unity, self-determination, collective work and responsibility, cooperative economics, purpose, creativity, and faith. Day six is the highlight of the festival, with a communal feast, music, speeches, and the honoring of elders.

Main Subgroups

As noted under "Population Data," most African Americans belong to one or another Protestant group, with most in one of the historically black denominations: the National Baptist Convention—U.S.A., the African Methodist Episcopal Church, the Progressive National Baptist Convention, the African Methodist Episcopal Zion Church, and the Christian Methodist Episcopal Church.

Common Misunderstandings and Stereotypes

There are many stereotypes about blacks that center on cultural rather than religious misunderstandings. However, there is some overlap in stereotypes:

"Blacks are lacking in moral discipline and self-control."

In fact, churchgoing African Americans tend to be quite strict with their children and very conservative on moral issues such as abortion, gay rights, and pornography. Moreover, they are the most religious segment of American society on the basis of church membership and religious (vs. secular) outlook.[1]

> *"Black churches are hotbeds of political activity in violation of federal law regarding tax-exempt organizations."*

Although it is true that African American churches have been a focal point for educational and organizational efforts to obtain civil rights, black preachers are not substitute precinct workers advising their congregants how to vote.

Classroom Concerns

It is important to recognize the distinctiveness of African American Christianity and its role in strengthening black culture and combating white racism over the past three hundred years.

Both Kwanzaa and the birthday of Rev. Martin Luther King, Jr. (January 15) are significant events for African Americans. On these days (as well as during February, Black History Month), teachers are encouraged to discuss the many contributions made by blacks to the history and culture of the United States.

Population Data

About 78 percent of the 21.7 million African American adults in the United States are Protestant, 6.6 percent Catholic, and 1.1 percent Muslim; 1.2 belong to new religious movements (such as Rastafarianism and Santería), 10.7 percent have no religion, and 2.4 percent did not know or refused to respond to the Kosmin-Keysar survey.[2]

—B.H.

Further Reading

Lincoln, C. Eric, and Lawrence H. Mamiya. *The Black Church in the African American Experience*. Durham, NC: Duke University Press, 1990.

Paris, Peter. *The Social Teachings of the Black Churches*. Philadelphia: Fortress Press, 1985.

Raboteau, A. J. *Canaan Land: A Religious History of African Americans*. New York: Oxford, 2001.

Notes

1. Kosmin and Keysar, *Religion in a Free Market,* pp. 243–44.

2. Kosmin and Keysar, p. 243.

Christian Science/ Church of Christ, Scientist

Origins

The Church of Christ, Scientist was founded by Mrs. Mary Baker Eddy (1821–1910) in 1879 in Boston, Massachusetts. Mrs. Eddy wrote *Science and Health with Key to the Scriptures,* a textbook of spiritual healing and a key for understanding the Bible. She reorganized her church in 1892 as the First Church of Christ, Scientist. There is only one Church of Christ, Scientist, which includes the Mother Church in Boston and its branches around the world. She began publishing an international newspaper, *The Christian Science Monitor,* in 1908.

Beliefs

God, who is Spirit, and his spiritual creation (which is an expression of God) constitutes the only reality. Believing in "matter" is a limited, temporal, and incorrect view of present reality. God and His creation are good, and sickness, sorrow, death, evil, and sin are not ordained or sustained by God. Christian Scientists make a distinction between "human beings," which is the worldly, material view, and "man," which is the spiritual reality seen from the point of view of God. This spiritual reality is much more than can be grasped through the senses. Because of the limitations of the senses, human beings come to believe in a mind apart from God. However, when the human mind yields to God—the divine Mind—sin and sickness are overcome, and human beliefs give way to "man" in the image and likeness of God, whole and perfect. The spiritual reality is immortal and free from evil, whereas human minds are subject to beliefs in sin, sickness, and death. This physical sense of life is a counterfeit of God's spiritual creation. Healing, therefore, is mental and, if needed, involves repentance and regeneration. Medical treatment of illness that does not take into account the mental nature of disease and the need

45

for regenerating the human mind does not reach the real problem that needs healing. Although in reality there is no death, humans "pass on" from one place of existence to another until regeneration effects the needed change.

The Trinity—Father, Son, and Holy Spirit—represents to humanity the divine nature: Life, Truth, and Love. God is immortal Mind (often called Father-Mother God) understood as Spirit, Soul, Life, Truth, Love, and Principle. Jesus was the human embodiment of Christ, the divine idea of sonship with God. He is revered as the Way-shower and master Christian healer. The Holy Spirit is God's own understanding of his relationship to his beloved creation.

Sacred Books/Scriptures

Christian Scientists accept the Bible as their guide to eternal life. Mrs. Eddy said she wrote *Science and Health* under divine inspiration. As its title indicates, it is a key to unlocking the spiritual treasures of the Bible and a resource for spiritual healing. It is considered to be the impersonal "pastor" of the church, together with the Bible.

Practices

The Sunday worship service of Christian Scientists is led by two people (usually a man and a woman)—the First Reader, who conducts the service and reads from *Science and Health,* and the Second Reader, who reads from the Bible. The sermon, which consists of references from the Bible and correlative passages from *Science and Health,* is prepared by the Mother Church and is the same for all branches. Church members read and study this sermon each day of the week prior to the Sunday service and listen to it read as a sermon on Sunday. There is no choir, but the congregation sings hymns reflecting Christian Science theology. At Wednesday evening meetings, members give testimonials of Christian Science healing.

There is no ordained clergy. Instead, there are readers, teachers, and practitioners. Although teachers are relatively few, almost all branches have one or more practitioners. They are professionals who devote their full time to the healing ministry. Practitioners do not give advice or provide personal counseling but treat the patient through prayer endeavoring to bring to light the patient's true spiritual status as the loved child of God. There is an extensive system of instruction in Christian Science, and classroom instruction is often a requirement for holding many positions in the church. A board of lectureship provides free public lectures throughout the world, sponsored by branch churches. There are also public reading rooms associated with each branch church where anyone may browse the library and read or purchase the Bible, *The Christian Science Monitor,* or other Christian Science publications.

Christian Scientists do not rely on inoculations or vaccinations for preventive cures. (See "Classroom Concerns" below.) They endeavor to reach disease in its incipient stage, which is seen as being mental, and thereby prevent its physical development. However, situations may arise in which they submit to inoculations or vaccinations while appealing to Christian Science to avoid any possible negative results. Christian

Scientists sometimes accept certain surgical practices, the medical setting of broken bones, dental work, and corrective eyeglasses, although all these conditions have been recorded as being healed through prayer. Christian Scientists report what appear to be infectious or contagious diseases to the health department but usually rely on Christian Science treatment for healing. Decisions about health care are left to individuals. When relying on Christian Science treatment for healing, God is understood as being the only healer, but if members decide to seek medical treatment, they are not abandoned by their church.

Just as God, the divine Mind, is pure and free from error, so one should maintain good moral practices by avoiding liquor, tobacco, and other harmful substances. With their attention to health and their emphasis on spiritual virtues, Christian Scientists generally have an optimistic view of life and participate fully in social, civic, and economic affairs of their communities.

Main Subgroups

There is only one Church of Christ, Scientist—the Mother Church—located in Boston, Massachusetts, and all local churches throughout the world are branches of the Mother Church.

Common Misunderstandings and Stereotypes

Note: Christian Science should be distinguished from Scientology. Scientology is a twentieth-century movement founded by L. Ron Hubbard that is a system of applied religious philosophy. (See the chapter "Scientology.") Christian Science should also be distinguished from the Church of Religious Science. (See the chapter "New Age Religion.")

"Christian Scientists avoid all medical treatment."

As a rule, this is true, but sometimes Christian Scientists might choose to use medical treatment until their understanding of God's care grows stronger.

"Christian Scientists would rather let their children die than seek medical help."

Cases of this sort have been reported in the press from time to time, and the public often responds with horror and outrage at the insensitivity of parents. But Christian Scientists love their children as much as any parents, and they choose Christian Science treatment not from insensitivity to their children's welfare but because they believe this form of treatment to be the most effective. The death of a child is always tragic and is never seen as the outcome of the way the child was treated. For many, Christian Scientists as well as others, the ability to love their children is grounded in faith. Christian Scientists try to live the very best life they can and to raise their children the best way they know. Legally, the issues concerning the health care choices parents make for their children are complex and have not been completely resolved.

Classroom Concerns

Christian Scientist parents will often present a form at the beginning of the school year requesting accommodations provided by state law with regard to physical examinations, courses of study or parts of courses dealing with certain aspects of health, and immunizations that are contrary to their religious tenets and practices. This form includes directions for treatment other than first aid in the event of illness or injury.

Children may ask to be excused from some classes, especially health courses that include disease symptomatology and medical instruction. This accommodation usually can be provided quietly and privately. Teachers often require these students to do an alternative assignment. Sometimes teachers have asked Christian Science students and parents to share how they deal with health issues, and they are generally happy to do so. This also provides an opportunity to explore how different worldviews affect people's understanding of health and illness.

Up to age twenty, children are given instruction in Sunday School in the practice of Christian Science. Although education is valued by Christian Scientists, human knowledge is of relative worth when compared with the truth they claim they find in the Bible and its interpretation in *Science and Health*. If this claim should be expressed in class, it would be an opportunity to explore the multiplicity of truth claims among religious traditions and how people should learn to live together even though they have different religious beliefs.

When a child is injured or appears ill, teachers should consult the school nurse or the parents, who usually have established a plan for care together.

Population Data

No official statistics are released by the Church of Christ, Scientist, but it is known that there are approximately 2,400 branch churches around the world. Kosmin and Keysar[1] found that there are 194,000 adult Christian Scientists in the United States.

—J.H.

Further Reading

DeWitt, John. *The Christian Science Way of Life*. Boston: Christian Science Publishing, 1971.

Gill, Gillian. *Mary Baker Eddy* (Radcliffe Biography series). New York: Perseus Books Group, 1999.

Gottschalk, Stephen. *The Emergence of Christian Science in American Religious Life*. Berkeley: University of California Press, 1973.

Peel, Robert. *Christian Science: Its Encounter with American Culture*. New York: Holt, Rinehart & Winston, 1958.

Schoepflin, Rennie B. *Christian Science on Trial: Religious Healing in America*. Johns Hopkins University Press, 2002.

Wilson, Bryan R. *Sects and Society: A Sociological Study of the Elim Tabernacle, Christian Science, and Cristadelphians*. Berkeley and Los Angeles: University of California Press, 1961.

Web Sites

Christian Science Home Page: http://www.tfccs.com/index.jhtml

The Mary Baker Eddy Library: http://www.marybakereddylibrary.org/home/home.jhtml;jsessionid=ZQP1MURSZ5KXBKGL4L1SFEQ?_requestid=31841

Ontario Consultants on Religious Tolerance: http://www.religioustolerance.org/cr_sci.htm

The Religious Movements Homepage Project@The University of Virginia: http://religiousmovements.lib.virginia.edu/nrms/chrissci.html

Note

1. *Religion in a Free Market*, p. 27.

Christianity

Jehovah's Witnesses

Origins

Charles Taze Russell (1852–1916), called Pastor, was the general organizer (Jehovah's Witnesses recognize no human founder) and first president, but it was in 1931 under the second president, Joseph F. Rutherford (1869–1942), called Judge, that the name Jehovah's Witnesses was first used. Russell calculated from evidence in the Bible that the world was in the last days before the Battle of Armageddon. The work of the Witnesses is to prepare the world for the consequences of this event. Their headquarters and printing factories are at Bethel in Brooklyn, New York, where they carry on an extensive publishing effort, producing works such as *The Watchtower, Awake!*, *Our Kingdom Ministry,* and other pamphlets, books, and brochures. They use these publications for evangelical and doctrinal purposes. The Watchtower Bible and Tract Society of Pennsylvania is incorporated and represents Jehovah's Witnesses legally. The president of the society, together with a group called the Governing Body, determine doctrine and practice.

Beliefs

Jesus Christ, the son of Jehovah[1] God and His first creation, was a perfect human being who died and was raised as an immortal spirit person. During his earthly life and ministry, he began to select the 144,000 "faithful and discreet slave" class (also called the Bride of Christ). They will rule with him during the thousand-year period called the Millennium. In a certain sense, that period has already begun, for Christ's presence can be recognized even now. Satan has been cast out of heaven and currently rules the world, working his perfidious will through such human institutions as religion, business, and government. Soon, the Battle of Armageddon will take place, when Satan and his following will be cast into the abyss. The dead, who have been in a state of unconsciousness, will be resurrected and given a second chance. At the end of the Millennium, Satan will return to earth to "deceive the nations" (Rev. 20:8). Then, together with all those who have continued to be willfully wicked, he will be utterly destroyed by fire. The faithful, who resist Satan's assaults, will be granted everlasting life in the flesh on paradise earth, and Christ will return the rulership of the world to his father, Jehovah.

Dates have been set for these events (Pastor Russell began this process). The most important one is 1914, when the "times of the Gentiles" (which started in the biblical period) ended and the "times of the end" began. Many of the events predicted by Russell and others did not take place, but leaders have been ready and willing to admit their mistakes. They do not claim to be prophets but say that the chronological order is an imperfect tool that is constantly undergoing reevaluation. Nevertheless, they maintain that we are even now in the times of the end.

Sacred Books/Scriptures

The Bible is the sole basis of belief. Its interpretation and application is the responsibility of the Governing Body. It is the revealed will of Jehovah God. There is no other creed, dogma, doctrine, or tradition that carries authority, although the many publications, pronouncements, and guidelines of the leaders are consulted regularly as aids to understanding the biblical message.

Practices

Jehovah's Witnesses consider themselves a society, not a denomination or sect, and they meet in Kingdom Halls, not churches. They are organized as a theocracy (a society governed by God), with Jehovah and Christ as the principal rulers, and the president of the Watchtower Bible and Tract Society, together with the Governing Body, as the main governing agents. Local congregations are organized into larger units called circuits, and these in turn are organized into regions. Each congregation is served by a body of elders under the supervision of a circuit overseer. There is no separate clergy, but all members are expected to participate in evangelical ministry. Active members are called publishers. They distribute the Society's literature, witness from door to door, and evangelize those who are not Jehovah's Witnesses. There are also ministerial servants, who work as clerks and attendants, as well as pioneers, who dedicate themselves to full-time evangelical activities.

Baptism is by immersion and is considered a public sign of dedication. Once a year, Jehovah's Witnesses observe the Lord's Supper, or the Lord's Evening Meal, as a memorial. They use no images in their services and pray directly to Jehovah through Christ. Their main activity, as the name implies, is to preach to those who are not Witnesses the "Good News" that God's original earthly paradise will return and those who are saved will receive everlasting life.

Jehovah's Witnesses try to maintain a neutral attitude toward worldly affairs because they believe that the world is controlled by Satan. They keep themselves apart by observing a number of special practices. Although they observe weddings, anniversaries, and funerals, they do not celebrate holidays or birthdays, hold elective office, salute the flag of any country, sing nationalistic songs, or serve in the military, and they are discouraged from voting. They follow the Bible in not accepting whole-blood transfusions.

The Bible says blood is life, a gift of God, and is not to be "eaten" (Lev. 17:10–14), which Jehovah's Witnesses have understood to mean *consumed* in any way, as, for example, by transfusion. There is now an effort to modify this practice and allow *components* of blood to be used.[2] They are submissive to all laws not in conflict with God's law, but they are firm in their conviction that the Bible is the sole authority and model for practice.

Main Subgroups

The main subgroups include Assemblies of the Called Out Ones of Yah, Assemblies of Yah, Assemblies of Yahweh, Assembly of Yahweh, Church of God (Jerusalem), New Life Fellowship, Scripture Research Association, and Yahweh's Assembly in Messiah.

Among other groups that share millennial and separatist views are Seventh-Day Adventists, Dawn Bible Students Association, Layman's Home Missionary Movement, and Advent Christian Church.

Common Misunderstandings and Stereotypes

"Jehovah's Witnesses are unpatriotic because they do not salute the flag or perform military service."

Witnesses do not mean to be disrespectful toward any nation, but they believe saluting the flag is an idolatrous act (i.e., the worship of something other than God). Military service, voting, holding public office, and participating in patriotic celebrations are not in keeping with God's law, which admonishes them to stay apart from the world. They have been severely persecuted, punished, and martyred for their attitude toward worldly powers. Yet they have had a major influence on constitutional law and broadening the exercise of civil liberties such as freedom of speech, worship, and the press.

"Door-to-door proselytizing is an annoying invasion of personal privacy and a misguided attempt to force religion on people."

Some people feel that encounters with Jehovah's Witnesses at their front doors are annoying. However, Jehovah's Witnesses are trained in personal evangelizing and believe that their message must reach as many individuals as possible to prepare them for the final struggle. They recognize that people cannot be forced to accept their views, but they are prepared to pay the consequences of affronting some as the price of their dedication and efforts. In fact, they are exercising constitutional freedoms that should be respected as much as any other rights.

"Jehovah's Witnesses are inconsistent, expecting the imminent return of Christ but planning to live in the world at the same time."

Although they have been disappointed a number of times, Jehovah's Witnesses believe and have been assured there will be a Second Coming of Christ. They rely on their leaders to provide as accurate an account of these anticipated events as possible, recognizing that all such calculations are subject to human error. In the meantime, they avoid contact with worldly institutions that they believe remain under the influence of Satan—other religions, the business world, and government—while following the biblical injunction to provide for themselves and others.

Classroom Concerns

Children of Jehovah's Witnesses are expected to follow biblical practices and avoid saluting the flag, pledging allegiance, standing for the pledge (if by standing they give evidence of participating in the observance), marching in patriotic parades, singing patriotic or school songs, participating in school politics, observing holidays (whether national, religious, or local), celebrating birthdays, participating in extracurricular activities and sports (especially where cheerleading and homecoming activities are involved, or martial arts such as boxing and wrestling are practiced), or taking part in lotteries, games of chance, or gambling. They are also to be carefully selective when asked to join a club or take part in school plays. These and other restrictions are based on moral and religious principles. Therefore, accommodations should be made for their observance. Jehovah's Witnesses do not mean to be disrespectful, even though other children may ridicule them. It is important that Jehovah's Witnesses not be made to feel left out because of their convictions. If a student is noticed by other students to be following these practices, the teacher could turn this occasion into an important lesson on constitutional rights and freedoms.

Jehovah's Witnesses do not give or accept whole-blood transfusions. School nurses usually are acquainted with the particular preferences of Jehovah's Witnesses families regarding the kind of medical treatment to be administered to their children.

The views of Jehovah's Witnesses regarding Christian history, the nature of God and Jesus Christ, and what will happen in the future may not be the same as other Christian or non-Christian views. For Jehovah's Witnesses, their history is a sacred, true, and meaningful account of the world that includes an understanding of the nature of human life and its ultimate destiny as the Bible has foretold. If this difference should come up in class, teachers might use the occasion to teach cultural diversity and toleration of different viewpoints.

Population Data

Kosmin and Keysar[3] report an adult population of 1,331,000 Jehovah's Witnesses in the United States. There about 5.9 million Witnesses worldwide according to adherents.com.[4]

—J.H.

Further Reading

Beckford, James A. *The Trumpet of Prophecy: A Sociological Study of Jehovah's Witnesses*. Oxford: Basil Blackwell, 1975.

Harrison, Barbara G. *Visions of Glory: A History and a Memory of Jehovah's Witnesses.* New York: Simon & Schuster, 1978.

Penton, James. *Apocalypse Delayed: The Story of Jehovah's Witnesses.* Toronto: University of Toronto Press, 1998.

Web Sites

Ontario Consultants on Religious Tolerance: http://www.religioustolerance.org/witness5.htm

Religious Movements Homepage Project @The University of Virginia: http://religiousmovements.lib.virginia.edu/nrms/Jwitness.html

Watchtower—Official Web Site of Jehovah's Witnesses: http://www.watchtower.org/

Notes

1. "Jehovah" is the Jehovah's Witnesses' rendering of the Hebrew YHWH, the unique name for God in the Old Testament/Hebrew Bible. Because the original Hebrew text did not have vowels, the exact pronunciation of YHWH remains uncertain.

2. New Light on Blood: Official Web site of Associated Jehovah's Witnesses for Reform on Blood: http://www.ajwrb.org/. Accessed July 25, 2006.

3. *Religion in a Free Market*, p. 27.

4. www.adherents.com/Na/i_j.html. Accessed July 28, 2006.

Mormonism/The Church of Jesus Christ of Latter-day Saints

Origins

Joseph Smith, Jr. founded the Church of Jesus Christ of Latter-day Saints in 1830 in Fayette, New York. Smith said that he was visited by God the Father and his Son Jesus Christ, who commanded him to "restore" the ancient church, which was originally established by Jesus Christ. Smith and his followers faced persecution because of their beliefs and left their original homes, moving first to Ohio, then Missouri, and finally to Illinois. There, Smith and a brother were murdered while in protective custody. Under a new leader, Brigham Young, a major branch of Mormons moved west to Salt Lake Valley, Utah, and in 1847 established the headquarters of the Church of Jesus Christ of Latter-day Saints. Although accustomed to the appellation "Mormon," most followers refer to themselves as "Latter-day Saints" or, more informally, "Saints."

Beliefs

Mormons accept the basic beliefs of Christianity. Their understanding of the "restored gospel" is that the Godhead consists of three separate, distinct beings: God the Father and his son Jesus Christ (who are beings of flesh and bone) and the Holy Ghost. There is no concept of original sin. Humans are individually responsible for their actions, and transgressions will be punished. All except a few "sons of perdition" will be saved and will go to one of three kingdoms (Celestial, Terrestrial, Telestial). However, only those who are faithful in all things will be exalted to the Celestial kingdom. To be faithful, one must perform works, gain knowledge, repent, receive baptism by immersion for remission of sins, and receive the laying-on of hands for the gift of the Holy Ghost. Mormons believe they were born as spirit children to Heavenly Parents before they are born on earth to mortal parents. Therefore, those who die faithful will progress spiritually until they become like their Heavenly Parents. To be like them requires that mortal men and women be sealed in marriage for all eternity, an act that can be performed only in a Mormon temple. This practice reveals the enormous importance of the family for Mormons. Those who are not married may qualify themselves for the Celestial Kingdom, but—unlike those who are married—they cannot become like their Heavenly Parents.

For Mormons, history begins with the creation of the world, and the events of the past two hundred years are part of that ongoing history. God continues to reveal himself, formerly to the prophet Joseph Smith and subsequently to the Church presidents.

According to Smith's *Articles of Faith,* Mormon belief also includes the gift of tongues, visions, and healing; being subject to the laws and government of their country; the free exercise of conscience and the right of all people to worship as they choose; being honest, true, chaste, benevolent, and virtuous; and doing good to everyone.

Sacred Books/Scriptures

Latter-day Saints believe *The Book of Mormon* to be equal in status to the Bible as the revealed word of God. It is the record of a sacred history that began in 600 B.C.E. when a prophet in Jerusalem named Lehi led his followers to North America under God's direction. Soon after their arrival in North America, the followers of Lehi began to keep records on metal plates. Subsequently, conflict ensued, which divided Lehi's expanding offspring into two groups, one of which is among the ancestors of the Native Americans. From the time of Lehi to Christ's crucifixion, the Savior's birth and atonement were explicitly prophesied in the Book of Mormon. Christ, after his resurrection, visited North America (the New World) and established his church there. The Book of Mormon ends at about the year 420 C.E. with Moroni [muh-ROHN-eye], a descendant of those who survived the final destruction of his people. Moroni received from his father, Mormon, an abridgment of the plates begun under Lehi and eventually buried them at a place in New York state called Hill Cumorah. Then, in the "latter days," Moroni returned as an angel and revealed their location to Joseph Smith, who translated them as the Book of Mormon. For Mormons, the Book of Mormon is a "second witness" of the divinity of Jesus Christ. Because revelation is continuous, the scriptural canon is not closed. At present it includes *The Holy Bible, The Book of Mormon: Another Testament of Jesus Christ, The Doctrine and Covenants,* and *The Pearl of Great Price.*

Practices

Deseret (meaning "honeybee"), Utah's original name in *The Book of Mormon,* aptly describes the Mormon Church, which is a beehive of activity. It is run by the president, who is called Prophet, and several bodies of officers who counsel, supervise, and preside over its various parts. There is no official clergy, but every male is eligible to hold either the Melchizedek (higher) or the Aaronic (lesser) priesthood. All officers serve without pay, except those few in full-time leadership positions. At age twelve, boys are ordained to a priesthood office and are expected to assume duties of service to the church.

Activities include the following:

Family Life—The family is the most important unit of the church. A notable activity of family life is the moral and spiritual education of the children. Monday is Family Home Evening, a time for education, discussion, and recreation. Children are taught to refrain from tobacco, alcohol, tea, and coffee; to observe a healthy diet; to abide by church dress codes; to engage in regular exercise; and to act with moderation. Careful attention is paid to sexual morality because of the example set by the Heavenly Parents: in giving birth to preexistent human beings, they established marriage as the perfect and only context for sexual activity.

Families donate one-tenth of their annual income to the church. In addition, they make a fast offering each month and donate to the needy the cost of the two meals not eaten. Families are urged to provision themselves with at least one year's supply of the basic needs of food, clothing, and shelter.

Women serve central roles as wives and mothers, although they are active in other areas of the church as well. After baptism, at age eight or so, sons accompany their fathers to meetings and begin taking an active role in the church.

Mission—At about age nineteen, young men are called to serve missions; young women may serve missions as well. In pairs, the missionaries are sent to various parts of the world—including locations in the United States—for a period of two years, bringing the Mormon message to those who are willing to listen (those who are "honest in heart").

Ward Activity—The church is divided into areas, regions, stakes (geographical divisions), and wards (local churches or parishes). Ward activities include weekly worship, social events, classes, and welfare projects. The church sponsors and encourages participation in many cultural events (the Mormon Tabernacle Choir is justly famous). The church is committed to doing good throughout the world and is active in charities and international welfare projects. It is organized to meet all the needs of its members, having its own newspaper, television station, real estate services, banks, insurance companies, and department stores.

Temple Work—Temples are not places for Sunday worship; they are reserved for marriage, baptism, and other forms of church work, such as baptism for the dead. After a temple is dedicated, it is closed to all but Mormons in good standing who have been approved by their bishops.

Genealogy—Those who have died without hearing the restored Gospel may receive vicarious baptism, which is carried out by members who stand proxy for them. Because the dead must be identified individually, an extensive genealogical library in Salt Lake City has come into existence where searches can be made. However, baptism does not guarantee salvation because even the dead are free to choose whether to accept it.

Main Subgroups

Although the Church of Jesus Christ of Latter-day Saints is the largest body of Mormons, there are several groups that differ from it doctrinally or practically. These are the Church of Christ (Temple Lot); Church of Jesus Christ (Bickertonites); Church of Jesus Christ of Latter-day Saints (Strangite); and Reorganized Church of Jesus Christ of Latter-day Saints, as well as others.

Common Misunderstandings and Stereotypes

"Mormons practice polygamy."

In 1852, the church admitted the practice of polygamy, calling it celestial or plural marriage. The purpose was a religious one: to raise a righteous generation to greet Jesus Christ at the Second Coming. Polygamy was not against federal law until 1862 and, even after that, it was defended as a religious right under First Amendment protection. After much persecution, the church officially discontinued plural marriage in 1890, although some dissenting groups—not recognized by the LDS—continue the practice. This decision was coincident with a new turn in church history, whereby millennial and separatist views were given up in favor of participation in the larger community.

"Mormons do not allow African Americans to be members of the priesthood."

Although this was true in the past, in 1978 it was revealed and ruled that the "long-promised day" had come: every faithful, worthy man in the church could receive the holy priesthood, with power to exercise its divine authority.

"Mormons are not Christian."

Mormons believe that salvation depends upon knowing Christ. They understand themselves to be Christians and their church to be the only legitimate church of Jesus Christ. However, the Mormon understanding of salvation and cosmic history is sufficiently distinct that some consider them another branch of Christianity in addition to Protestant, Catholic, and Orthodox Christians.

"The story of Joseph Smith translating gold plates found on Hill Cumorah cannot be proved."

As an instance of sacred stories, the existence of the plates can be no more (or less) proved than many other religious "facts." For Mormons, their history is a sacred, true, and meaningful account of the whole of creation, including the nature and destiny of human and divine life and the historical and eternal relationships among all human beings, living and dead. These considerations supersede questions of proof.

"Door-to-door proselytizing is an annoying invasion of personal privacy and resented for its attempt to force religion on people."

Mormons on mission understand their efforts to be educational, and the householder always has the choice of accepting the message or not. That people may resent being evangelized is something Mormons accept as the price they must pay for their efforts.

Classroom Concerns

Mormons look after the moral and spiritual education of their children with great care. If Mormon students sometimes appear unresponsive when sex education or other morally sensitive topics are taught, it is not out of disrespect or lack of interest but because they already have been taught at home. The teacher could use this as an opportunity to explore the plurality of ethical codes.

Some Mormon students may want to be excused from evening activities such as homework or school events, particularly on Monday, which is Family Home Evening. Because active participation in church life is expected, students need to organize their weekly schedule so that homework, for example, can be done during those times when they are not busy with church activities.

Mormon understanding of history may not be the same as other Christian or non-Christian views. If this difference should come up in class, teachers may use the occasion to teach cultural diversity and toleration of different viewpoints.

Population Data

Adherents.com estimates a worldwide LDS population of 12.5 million. Kosmin and Keysar[1] list the adult Mormons in the United States at 2,787,000. Including children, this would translate into a total U.S. Mormon population of 4 to 5 million.

—J.H.

Further Reading

Arrington, Leonard, and Davis Bitton. *The Mormon Experience: A History of the Latter-day Saints*. New York: Alfred A. Knopf, 1979.

Bushman, Richard L. *Joseph Smith and the Beginnings of Mormonism*. Urbana: University of Illinois Press, 1984.

Moore, Laurence. *Religious Outsiders and the Making of Americans*. New York: Oxford University Press, 1986.

Shipps, Jan. *Mormonism: The Story of a New Religious Tradition*. Urbana and Chicago: University of Illinois Press, 1985.

Web Sites

The Church of Jesus Christ of Latter-day Saints: www.lds.org

Ontario Consultants on Religious Tolerance: http://www.religioustolerance.org/lds.htm

Religious Movements Homepage Project @The University of Virginia: http://religiousmovements.lib.virginia.edu/nrms/mormon/mormon.html

Notes

1. *Religion in a Free Market,* p. 27.

Christianity

Orthodox Christianity (Eastern Orthodoxy)

Origins

The Orthodox ("right doctrine/worship") Church traces its origins to the churches founded by the apostles in the Middle East and the Balkans in the first century. Additionally, the church's roots are in the Christianity of the Byzantine or Eastern Roman Empire. As the church developed in the early centuries, seven ecumenical or all-embracing councils were held at which the bishops of the entire church assembled to discuss and clarify matters of belief and practice. These seven councils were held at cities in what is now Turkey: Nicaea (325 C.E.), Constantinople I (now Istanbul) (381), Ephesus (431), Chalcedon (451), Constantinople II (553), Constantinople III (680), and Nicaea II (787). The councils determined the basic creed of Christianity on such points as the nature of Jesus as both God and man; the nature of the Trinity of Father, Son, and Holy Spirit (three persons in one God); and the role of Mary as Mother of God (Greek *theotokos*, God-bearer). Although other councils were held later, they involved only the Latin Catholic Church and are therefore Orthodox Christians are not affected by them.

Beliefs

Like other Christians, the Orthodox affirm the role of Jesus as Messiah (Hebrew *Mashiach* ["anointed one"] whose Greek equivalent is *Christos* [Christ]) who sanctified or redeemed the human race from its estrangement from God. Orthodox Christians believe that Jesus is the Son of God whose life, death, and resurrection confirm his status as both fully human and fully divine. They affirm the doctrine of the Trinity whereby the three Persons—Father, Son, and Holy Spirit—share the divine nature of the one God. They believe as well in the doctrine of Christ's triumphant return to judge living and dead at the end of time and in an afterlife with God for the righteous and of permanent estrangement from God for those who reject God's love. Orthodox theology puts more stress than does Roman Catholic or Protestant thought on Christ as victor over sin, death, hell, and the devil. Human nature was not wounded by Original Sin, as the Western church teaches. Consequently, the goal of human existence is to become more like God rather than to repent for sinfulness. The Western church emphasizes Christ as the sacrificial lamb who atones for the world's sins by his death and resurrection.

The Orthodox Church considers itself (1) the one true, visible church (a belief also held by Roman Catholicism) and (2) a fellowship of churches that developed in the Byzantine Empire, originally under four patriarchates (or rule by church fathers): Constantinople, Alexandria, Antioch, and Jerusalem. There was a fifth, Rome, but it separated from the Eastern patriarchates in 1054.[1] (The reasons for the split or schism are complex but centered mainly in the claim of the pope or bishop of Rome to be the head of the entire church rather than simply one of the five patriarchs.) Despite the separation, Orthodox and Catholic Christians usually recognize the validity of each other's sacraments and call each other "sister churches."

There is no one individual leader in Orthodoxy comparable to the pope in Roman Catholicism. Instead, there are various patriarchates and self-governing churches (of which there are now fifteen; see "Main Subgroups" below). The patriarch of Constantinople does have "primacy of honor" within the church, but this is not a primacy of authority. The structure of the Orthodox church, like that of the Roman Catholic church, is hierarchical: the bishop leads his community—the body of Christ—in teaching true doctrine, administering the sacraments, and making eternal salvation possible. In other respects, the Orthodox Church resembles Roman Catholicism and Protestantism in its basic beliefs, as these three principal branches of Christianity all accept the decrees of the first seven church councils (see "Origins" above).

Sacred Books/Scriptures

Orthodoxy, like Roman Catholicism and Protestantism, accepts the Old and New Testaments but uses the Septuagint or Greek version of the Old Testament as its official text. It contains a number of books not found in the Hebrew version used by Jews and Protestants. These additional books in the canon of the Old Testament are: Tobit, Judith, the Additions to the Book of Esther, the Wisdom of Solomon, Ecclesiasticus or the Wisdom of Jesus Son of Sirach, Baruch, the Letter of Jeremiah, the Prayer of Azariah and the Song of the Three Jews, Susanna, Bel and the Dragon, First and Second Maccabees (all of which Catholics also accept as scriptural); and four other books (not accepted by Catholics): 1 Esdras, the Prayer of Manasseh, Psalm 151, and 3 Maccabees.

Practices

Orthodox Christians practice seven sacraments (the same as Catholics): baptism, chrismation (confirmation), Eucharist (Liturgy/Holy Communion), confession, holy orders (the ordination ritual of deacons, priests, and bishops), marriage, and the anointing of the sick. Orthodox Christians baptize by a triple immersion of the child in water (unlike Catholics, who usually baptize by pouring water on the child's forehead, although immersion is also permissible). Chrismation occurs immediately after baptism (for

Catholics, confirmation usually occurs no earlier than age six). The Eucharist is central to Orthodoxy and is offered in three different rites or forms of prayer, with that of St. John Chrysostom the most popular. The other Eucharistic styles—which do not differ significantly from that of St. John Chrysostom—are those of St. Basil (used during the Sundays of Lent) and of Gregory the Great or the Pre-Sanctified which is actually a communion service for Lenten weekdays. The Eucharistic ceremony includes abundant use of incense, candles, chanting, and the wearing of ornate vestments by the priest.

Orthodoxy (unlike Roman Catholicism) permits divorce as a last resort but never a fourth marriage. Priests may marry (unlike Roman Catholicism) but must do so before their ordination; otherwise, they must take monastic vows and remain celibate. Bishops may not marry and are usually chosen from the ranks of the monastic communities (who are celibate by virtue of their vow of chastity). Since the fourth century, monasticism (the disciplined life of monks or nuns) has been very important to the church. Unlike Western monasticism, there are no religious orders but rather individual communities with their own rules. Orthodox Christians venerate icons (two-dimensional paintings) as a way of honoring Christ, Mary, and the saints. Orthodox churches, as well as Bibles and religious writings, contain such icons. Orthodox Christians celebrate Christmas on January 7 because they follow a calendar different from that of Catholics and Protestants. The date of Easter sometimes coincides with the date observed by Catholics and Protestants but not always, because the Orthodox stipulate that Easter must always come before the start of the Jewish festival of Passover. The Orthodox New Year is September 1 and marks the start of the cycle of holy days for the church year. Additionally, many Orthodox customarily celebrate the New Year on January 1.

Main Subgroups

Orthodoxy consists of fifteen self-governing churches: Constantinople, Antioch, Alexandria, Jerusalem, Russia, Serbia, Georgia, Romania, Bulgaria (all headed by patriarchs); and Greece, Cyprus, Albania, Poland, the Czech Republic, and the United States (headed by archbishops/metropolitans). There are also so-called autonomous churches in Japan, Finland, and Crete that lack full independence. In the United States, Orthodox Christians from many of these national churches have formed an umbrella organization, the Standing Conference of Orthodox Bishops of America.

Two Eastern Christian churches, which some might even consider to be fourth and fifth branches of Christianity, are closely allied with the Orthodox Christianity: the Assyrian Church—with its patriarch in Baghdad—that stresses the humanity of Jesus (to the detriment of his divinity, in the view of the other Christian churches); and the Oriental Orthodox Church, which stresses Jesus' divinity (to the detriment of his humanity, say the other Christian churches). The Oriental Orthodox Church includes Coptic/Egyptian, Ethiopic, Armenian, and Syrian subdivisions. The Assyrian Church accepts only two ecumenical councils as valid (versus the seven accepted by Orthodoxy proper), whereas the Oriental Orthodox accept only the first three.

Common Misunderstandings and Stereotypes

"All Orthodox Christians in the United States are Greek or Russian in origin."

Orthodox Christians come from many countries (see "Main Subgroups" above). Moreover, many persons of other ethnic and religious backgrounds have converted to Orthodoxy, and so Orthodoxy today is an American religion, although with historical ties to various European or Asian mother churches.

"Orthodox Christians are foreigners with little interest in this country."

Americans of many ethnic and national backgrounds—including Greeks, Russians, and others who are Orthodox—have a natural interest in the countries from which they or their ancestors came. Still, they chose to come to the United States and are as loyal as any other Americans. (This stereotype is applicable to many of the religions discussed in this book.)

"Orthodox Christians worship icons."

As explained in "Practices" (above), icons are only symbolic representations meant to inspire devotion to Christ, Mary, and the saints. The icons themselves are not worshipped.

Classroom Concerns

It is suggested that teachers familiarize themselves with the dates of the Orthodox holy days (see Appendix B for a calendar). Because Roman Catholicism and Orthodoxy are similar in so many respects, it is important to clarify the distinctions when teaching about Christianity.

Population Data

Kosmin and Keysar report 645,000 adult Orthodox adherents in the United States.[2] There are about 350 million Orthodox Christians worldwide, along with 36 million Oriental Orthodox and 3.3 million Assyrian Christians (see Main Subgroups, above).[3]

—B.H.

Further Reading

Harakas, Stanley S. *The Orthodox Church: 455 Questions and Answers.* Brookline, MA: Holy Cross Orthodox Press, 1988.

Meyendorff, John. *The Orthodox Church.* Crestwood, NY: St. Vladimir's Seminary Press, 1981.

Pelikan, Jaroslav. "Orthodox Christianity in the World and in America." In *World Religions in America,* Jacob Neusner, ed. 3rd ed. Louisville, KY: Westminster John Knox Press, 2003.

Ware, Timothy. *The Orthodox Church.* New York: Penguin Books, 1983.

Notes

1. Some scholars consider the real break to have occurred in 1204 when the crusaders, on their way to liberate the Holy Land, sacked Christian Constantinople and briefly established a Latin empire. Still others point to 1755 when the patriarch of Constantinople said Latin baptisms were invalid.

2. *Religion in a Free Market,* p. 26.

3. Available at http://www.adherents.com. Accessed on September 6, 2006.

Christianity

Protestantism

Origins

There is no "Church of Protestantism" but rather a group of churches that trace their origins to the Protestant Reformation. Thus, Protestantism began in the sixteenth century as a reform movement within the Roman Catholic Church. Although there had been previous reforms, Martin Luther (1483–1546), a German priest, was the first Protestant reformer. He wanted to change the Church's beliefs and practices. For him, humans were sinful and incapable of achieving their own salvation. He accused the Church of corruption because of its stress on sacraments and the sale of indulgences[1] as means of achieving salvation. Luther's reformulation led to the separation of Protestant churches from the Roman Catholic Church. The Reformation's second most important figure was John Calvin (1509–64) whose teachings resembled Luther's but with greater stress on God's sovereignty.

Under King Henry VIII, the Church of England (Anglican Church) also separated from the Roman Catholic Church. Then Puritans, in their turn, wanted to cleanse the Anglican Church itself of *all* vestiges of Catholicism. Even further, Separatist or Independent Puritans concluded that reformation from within was impossible, and they created their own churches. They fled England for Holland, and then America, where, as Pilgrims at Plymouth Colony, they signed the Mayflower Compact uniting church and state "for the glory of God." Nonseparating Puritans also came to America looking for a purified Church of England, but in the long run created their own (Congregational) churches. The separatist spirit appeared also in Rhode Island, where Baptists reacted strongly against church-state union. Anglicans, Quakers, Mennonites, Presbyterians, and Dutch Reformed settled in other colonies. The Great Awakening, a revival movement beginning in the eighteenth century, preached a message of personal salvation. Methodism, at first an evangelical effort within the Anglican Church in the eighteenth century, became a separate church in America and contributed to the revivalist spirit.

69

Stimulated by the disestablishment of churches and the consequent freedom of religious choice, Protestant movements in the United States continued to proliferate in the nineteenth century. In addition to the major denominations, Protestantism included nondenominational Christian churches and other movements as well: Transcendentalism and Unitarianism, occult and spiritualist groups, Mormonism and Christian Science, African American churches, Millennialists (who expected the imminent return of Christ), and utopian communities (Shakers, Oneida Community). In the twentieth century, Social Gospel, Pentecostal, fundamentalist Christian, New Age, and Charismatic movements have added to the complexity of the religious scene in the United States.

Beliefs

Like other Christians, Protestants affirm the role of Jesus as the Messiah (Hebrew *Mashiach* ["anointed one"], whose Greek equivalent is *Christos* [Christ]) who redeemed the human race from its estrangement from God. Protestants believe that Jesus is the Son of God whose life, death, and resurrection confirm his status as both fully human and fully divine. They affirm the doctrine of the Trinity whereby the one God is experienced in three Persons—Father, Son, and Holy Spirit. They believe as well in the doctrine of Christ's triumphant return to judge the living and the dead at the end of time and, for the righteous, an afterlife with God but permanent estrangement from God for the wicked.

Most Protestants also subscribe to the following beliefs, which distinguish them from Catholic and Orthodox Christians:

- Salvation is by the grace of God through faith alone, rather than by human effort.

- The Bible is the sole authority for faith, rather than church traditions or rituals.

- God is sovereign and chooses who will be saved.

- Humans are sinful and cannot achieve salvation by their own efforts.

- All believers have direct access to God without the mediation of the church.

- All life and work is a sacred Christian vocation, in addition to the work of the church.

- God alone is worthy of worship, nothing in the world.

Sacred Books/Scriptures

The Christian Bible contains the Old Testament (equivalent to the Hebrew Bible) and the New Testament, a collection of narratives, letters, and writings about the life of Jesus and his Apostles. Some Protestant denominations recognize the Apocrypha or "hidden" books as being scriptural. The Apocrypha includes 1–2 Esdras, Tobit, Judith, the Additions to Esther, Wisdom of Solomon, Ecclesiasticus (Sirach), Baruch, Letter of Jeremiah, Prayer of Azariah and Song of the Three Young Men, Susanna, Bel and the Dragon, the Prayer of Manasseh, and 1–2 Maccabees. Certain groups—such as Mormons and Christian Scientists—supplement the Bible with their own writings. There are at least three Protestant views regarding the origins of the Bible: (1) it was created by humans but under God's direct inspiration; (2) it contains the literal words of God, recorded without error by human hands; or (3) it is the work of fallible humans struggling to write a divine story in limited human language. There are numerous English translations of the Bible from the original Hebrew and Greek. Each denomination uses a version that reflects its particular understanding of God and history.

Practices

Most Protestants participate in weekly or semiweekly congregational worship, observe the major Christian holy days, and permit clergy to marry. Worship may be elaborate and liturgical (e.g., Lutherans) or simple and without ritual (e.g., Quakers). Most Protestants recognize only two sacraments, baptism and the Lord's Supper (Eucharist). Some Protestants believe that the sacraments are sources of divine grace, whereas others believe them to be memorials of the redemptive work of Christ.

The weekly worship service usually includes the following: congregational and choral singing, prayer, Bible readings, preaching, confession of faith, sacraments (baptism, Lord's Supper/Eucharist), and collection of tithes and offerings.

As the word *protestant* suggests, in principle there is a critical tension between Protestants and the social status quo. For some, the world is corrupt and will be saved only by the return of Christ to earth. They take little part in social and political matters. Others believe the world is in a constant state of renewal at the hand of God. Their task is to help bring about this renewal by working actively in society.

Main Subgroups

Subgroups, with typical examples, include the following:

Adventist (Seventh-day Adventists; Jehovah's Witnesses)—Strong conviction that the end of the world will occur in the very near future and that they must be prepared for this event. (See the chapters "Seventh-day Adventists" and "Jehovah's Witnesses" for more detail.)

Baptist (Christian Church [Disciples of Christ]; Baptist)—Practice adult baptism. Stress complete separation of church and state, with emphasis on religious freedom and personal conscience (not to be confused with Anabaptists of the Radical Reformed tradition; see below).

Christian Science (Church of Christ, Scientist)—Believe God is Spirit, and human beings are immortal and free from evil. It is only when human beings believe in a mind apart from God that they become subject to sin, sickness, and death. Treatment by prayer is preferred to medical treatment. (See the chapter "Christian Science" for more detail.)

Communal (Amana Community; Amish; Shakers)—Communities exist entirely apart from the larger society and often include a strong leader, a strong system of social control, and economic self-sufficiency.

Episcopal (called the Episcopal Church in the United States; the Anglican Church in Canada, England, and elsewhere)—Similar to Roman Catholic in that it stresses the Bible, tradition, and reason but different in that it is ruled by bishops rather than the pope. The Book of Common Prayer contains the major doctrines and guidelines for worship.

Evangelical-Fundamentalist (Plymouth Brethren; Independent Bible Churches)—Believe in a personal experience of salvation through Jesus Christ; biblical inerrancy; obligation to proclaim the Gospel; different historical ages or dispensations during which God renews his efforts to save the world; imminent return of Christ (Second Advent); strict ethical practices in contrast to laxness of modernity; restoration of purity of early church independent of denominations; and the church as a fellowship of the saved.

It is noteworthy that since 1990, the number of self-identified adult Evangelicals in the United States has grown from 242,000 to 1,032,000, while the number of self-identified Protestants has decreased from 17,214,000 to 4,647,000. Evangelicals, as well as many who disclaim denominational affiliation, believe in the ongoing ministry of the Holy Spirit. They also believe the Bible is the sole authoritative account of the Holy Spirit. Consequently, they tend to call themselves "Christians" without any further designation that would limit or specify the Holy Spirit. This may account for the fact that the number of people who self-identify as "Christian" also increased during this same period, from 8,073,000 to 14,150,000. Why this change in the appearance of Christianity in America has taken place is something still under investigation. A partial explanation may be that many Americans, nurtured on ideals of individualism, want to be free to choose their own religion, or to choose none, in accordance with the guarantees of the First Amendment. Evangelicals believe modern secular life lacks a moral anchor and puts too much trust in reason alone. Many choose the guidance of the Holy Spirit.

Various Christian groups have emerged to give collective expression to these choices. They include Calvary Chapels, Vineyard Ministries, Charismatic groups, Pentecostal Churches, the Jesus Movement, and the Latter Rain Movement, among others. Evangelical groups usually move away from elaborate ceremonial liturgies toward simpler, more casual, participatory forms of worship. This is generally understood as a return to the earliest, and therefore purest, form of Christianity, when signs of the Holy Spirit such as prophecy, miracles, faith healing, and speaking in tongues were acknowledged. (See also the chapter "Fundamentalism.")

Holiness (Church of the Nazarene; Churches of God)—Reject worldliness and advocate a strict code of behavior. Believe in "second blessing": after being born again, one grows in grace until perfected in holiness or sanctification.

Liberal (American Ethical Union; Unitarian Universalist)—Believe that human ability and intelligence is able to bring about a better world; the Bible is understood through modern methods of history, literary criticism, and archaeology; acceptance of scientific, evolutionary view of origins of the world; toleration of many views of salvation and various Christian doctrines. (See also the chapter "Unitarian Universalism.")

Lutheran (American Lutheran Church; Lutheran Church—Missouri Synod and Wisconsin Synod). Because of human sinfulness, salvation is not merited and cannot be earned; salvation is by the grace of God through faith alone, rather than faith and works, as the Catholic Church teaches; bread and wine of the Eucharist are not replaced by the body and blood of Christ (transubstantiation), as in Catholic practice, nor is the Lord's Supper considered a symbolic remembrance, as in other Protestant practices, but Christ is present everywhere, His body and blood being especially present along with the bread and wine in the Eucharist (consubstantiation).

Methodist (United Methodists; African Methodist Episcopal)—Orderly organization and living are combined with emphasis on direct religious experience; all people can receive the grace of God and are eligible for sanctification, that is, freedom from sin.

Mormon (Church of Jesus Christ of Latter-day Saints)—Mormons believe that their founder, Joseph Smith, discovered sacred tablets in 1830 that comprise the Book of Mormon. Equal in status to the Bible, it is the record of a sacred history dating to 600 B.C.E. when Lehi, a prophet in Jerusalem, led his followers to North America under God's direction. Mormon theology differs in several respects from that of other Protestants. (See the chapter "Mormonism" for more detail.)

Pentecostal-Charismatic (Assemblies of God; Church of God)—Believe in personal ecstatic experience of the Holy Spirit; manifestations of Holy Spirit through speaking in tongues and healing; biblical inerrancy; baptism of the Holy Spirit subsequent to conversion; imminent return of Christ.

Radical Reformed (Mennonites; Society of Friends/Quakers)—Mennonites and other Anabaptists practice adult baptism; oppose taking oaths, military service, or holding public office; believe in strict separation from the state, strict adherence to the Bible, and the fellowship of believers. Quakers are free of church organization, creed, doctrine, and sacrament; God is a real presence within each person; and worship typically consists of silent fellowship punctuated by individual witness or prayer.

Reformed-Presbyterian (Presbyterian; United Church of Christ; Reformed Church in America)—Presbyterians are governed by elected elders or presbyters; believe humans are sinful and saved only by God, who chooses those he wants for eternal life; faith and a good life are the fruits of salvation. The United Church of Christ (Congregational) is governed by the consent of the people, and in theology is similar to Presbyterian. Two other offshoots of Presbyterianism are the liberal Christian Church (Disciples of Christ) and the conservative Church of Christ.

Protestantism in Canada–Protestantism in Canada parallels its U.S. counterpart denominations with one important exception: In 1925, the Methodist Church in Canada, the Congregationalist Union of Canada, 70 percent of Canada's Presbyterians, and the General Council of Union Churches joined together to form the United Church of Canada (UCC). In 1968, they were joined by the Evangelical United Brethren.

Common Misunderstandings and Stereotypes

"All religions, Christian or non-Christian, have a framework similar to Protestant Christianity."

In this uncritical view, to be religious means to practice weekly worship of God in a church, in hope of salvation from sin and with the promise of eternal life. It includes the exercise of moral conscience, free choice regarding which church to attend, the freedom to believe in religion even though others may not (or not to believe even though others may), and, often, a deeply emotional experience of salvation. Although this is certainly true of Protestant Christianity, one can find among the religions of the world those that either have no weekly worship, no God, no church, no idea of salvation from sin, no notion of eternal life, no religiously based moral conscience, no freedom of choice, or no emotion (or several of these together), yet they are religions and should be respected as such.

"Christians are different from Catholics."

Some Protestants avoid labels altogether, wishing only to be called Christian. Because Protestants are different from Catholics, it may seem that Christians also are different. Yet Catholics *are* Christian. The distinction should be between *Catholic* and *Protestant* Christians.

"Protestants and Catholics are at loggerheads on many issues."

Since the Second Vatican Council (1962–65), relations between these two principal branches of Christianity have improved significantly. Although differences remain on such issues as the pope's leadership, veneration of Jesus' mother Mary, and justification by faith, these are less pronounced. The two communities are in broad agreement on basic theological tenets and the need for programs to alleviate hunger, homelessness, drug addiction and other sources of human suffering.

"Protestants know what they believe. People who don't know what they believe can hardly be called religious."

Because many Protestant churches are confessional, having written statements of belief and practice, knowledge of these verbal codes may appear as the essence of the religion. Therefore, when followers of other religions are asked what they believe and sometimes are unable to answer, an erroneous conclusion is that they do not know their own religion. However, religions are composed of stories, myths, rituals, and symbols, as well as beliefs, and it is impossible to reduce all of these to linguistic formulae.

Classroom Concerns

With more than three hundred branches, Protestant Christianity may appear confusing. Common to all, though, is a concern with ultimate values and a critical attitude toward popular morality. Exploring how Protestant Christianity has dealt with society is one way of teaching critical thinking.

The various Protestant groups approach the Bible differently. Some believe in divine inspiration, whereas others treat it as they would any other book. Controversy over the Bible should not be an excuse to avoid teaching about it. Of course, as a topic of study in the classroom, the Bible must be used for educational, not religious, purposes. It should be treated fairly, as one would treat any sacred book, whether the Qur'an of Islam or the Bhagavad-Gita of Hinduism.

Some Protestants may not want their children to salute the flag, and others may practice vegetarianism. For particular restrictions, see the chapters "Jehovah's Witnesses," "Seventh-day Adventists," "Christian Science," and "Mormonism."

Some Protestants advocate prayer in schools. This is a difficult issue, because it pits the principle of separation of church and state against that of freedom of worship. Current practice allows prayer when it is not disruptive or does not compel others to participate. (See Appendix A: "Ramona Unified School District Policy Instruction: Recognition of Religious Beliefs and Customs.")

Some Protestants advocate teaching Creationism (treating the biblical creation story as scientific theory) or Intelligent Design (treating the universe as too complex to have happened merely by chance) along with evolution. This is also a difficult issue because of ambiguities in defining words such as *fact, science, design,* and *theory.* Current practice, based on recent court decisions, allows teaching Creationism and/or Intelligent Design in comparative religion or history/social studies classes, but not in science.[2]

Population Data

As noted earlier, there are more than three hundred Protestant churches and denominations in the United States, with more than 72 million adult members. According to Kosmin and Keysar,[4] the largest (in millions) are as follows: Baptist, 34; Methodist, 14; Lutheran, 9.6; Presbyterian, 5.6; Episcopal, 3.4; Mormon, 2.8; Churches of Christ, 2.6. Kosmin and Keysar estimate the combined adult population of Protestants (i.e., the total of all adult Protestants from all denominations) to be about 106 million.

—J.H.

Further Reading

Almond, Gabriel A., R. Scott Appleby, and Emmanuel Sivan. *Strong Religion: The Rise of Fundamentalisms around the World* (The Fundamentalism Project). Chicago: University of Chicago Press, 2003

Brown, Robert McAfee. *The Spirit of Protestantism.* New York: Oxford University Press, 1961.

Gaustad, Edwin. *Religious History of America.* New York: Harper & Row, 1974.

Marty, Martin E. *The One and the Many: America's Struggle for the Common Good.* Cambridge: Harvard University Press, 1997.

Mead, Frank S. *Handbook of Denominations in the United States, New Tenth Edition.* Revised by Samuel S. Hill. Nashville, TN: Abingdon Press, 1995.

Rosten, Leo, ed. *Religions of America.* New York: Simon & Schuster, 1975.

Web Sites

First Amendment Center: Religious Liberty: http://www.firstamendmentcenter.org/rel_liberty/index.aspx

Religion Online. An encyclopedic source of books and articles about religion, especially Christianity: www.religion-online.org

Religious Movements Homepage Project@The University of Virginia: http://religiousmovements.lib.virginia.edu/nrms/fund.html

Notes

1. An indulgence is the pardoning by God of some of the temporal punishment due to sin, thereby lessening the time a soul would have to remain estranged from God in purgatory before reaching heaven. It results from the performance of an activity such as prayer, church attendance, or a pilgrimage. The selling of indulgences to aid the release of loved ones from purgatory was outlawed by the Roman Catholic Council of Trent in the mid-sixteenth century.

2. *Kitzmiller v. Dover Area School District et al.* (WL 578974 MD Pa. 2005).

3. *Religion in a Free Market,* p. 27.

Christianity

Roman Catholicism

Origins

Roman Catholics (from the Greek *catholicos,* "universal") trace their origins to Jesus' disciple Peter, first bishop of Rome, and to his successor bishops who became known as the Holy Father (Italian: *papa*: English: "pope") or "Vicar of Christ on Earth." Although there were other important bishops in the early church in such Eastern Mediterranean cities as Jerusalem, Antioch, Alexandria, and Constantinople (now Istanbul), the Roman bishop was the clear leader among the Western bishops. Gradually his authority grew in both the ecclesiastical (church) and secular spheres, and he became recognized in the West—and to a lesser extent in the East—as the "first among equals." The Eastern (Orthodox) Church ceased to recognize his authority in any sense after 1054 C.E., when the pope and the patriarch of Constantinople mutually excommunicated each other and the Orthodox Church and Roman Catholic Church separated. (These excommunications were lifted by mutual agreement in 1964.)

Beliefs

The essential beliefs of Roman Catholic Christians are similar to those of the two other major divisions of Christianity, Orthodox and Protestant; there is more agreement than disagreement. Like other Christians, Catholics affirm the role of Jesus as Messiah (Hebrew *Mashiach* ["anointed one"] whose Greek equivalent is *Christos* [Christ]), who redeemed the human race from its estrangement from God. Catholics believe that Jesus is the Son of God whose life, death, and resurrection confirm his status as both fully human and full divine. They affirm the doctrine of the Trinity whereby the one God is experienced in three Persons—Father, Son, and Holy Spirit. They believe as well in the doctrine of Christ's triumphant return to judge living and dead at the end of time and in an afterlife with God for the righteous and of permanent estrangement from God for the wicked. Differences appear mainly on matters of Church governance and specific practices, such as the following:

1. Only Catholics recognize the pope's leadership of the college of bishops and his role as Christ's representative (vicar) on earth. They also believe that when he speaks officially on a matter of faith or moral teaching, he cannot err (the doctrine of papal infallibility).

2. Only Catholics continue to convene the bishops of the entire church for ecumenical councils to discuss matters of belief and practice. There have been twenty-one such councils in the Catholic Church's history, the most recent being the Second Vatican Council (1962–65). Eastern Orthodox Christians and many Protestant denominations recognize the first seven of these councils.

3. Catholics, like Orthodox Christians, accept the authority both of the Bible and of tradition (i.e., the traditional teaching of the church by the pope and/or the bishops, or as found in the documents of the ecumenical councils).

4. Only Catholics require that priests remain celibate (Orthodox Christianity requires celibacy solely of its bishops. Protestant clergy are universally permitted to marry).

5. Only the Catholic Church forbids an ecclesiastical divorce under any circumstances (although the practice of granting annulments—a declaration that no marriage existed in the first place, enabling a civilly divorced couple to remarry—has become widespread over the past forty years).

6. Like the Orthodox but unlike Protestants, Catholics revere the Virgin Mary, mother of Jesus, with great fervor. In the doctrine of the Immaculate Conception, they believe that she was conceived without "original sin" (a sort of alienation from God caused by Adam and Eve's original disobedience). There are holy days in her honor (see "Practices") and shrines at locations in several countries commemorating appearances by her to devotees (e.g., Lourdes, France; Fatima, Portugal; Guadalupe, Mexico).

7. Catholic and Orthodox Christians recognize seven sacraments (baptism, the Eucharist, confirmation, reconciliation/penance, matrimony, holy orders, anointing of the sick); most Protestants accept only baptism and the Eucharist. Catholics take a strict view of Christ's presence in the Eucharistic bread and wine. Referred to as the "real presence" or transubstantiation, this doctrine holds that the entire substance of the bread and wine is changed into the body and blood of Christ. Orthodox Christians simply say that Christ is present in the Eucharist with no further philosophical distinctions. Protestants have held several positions on the Eucharist from consubstantiation (Christ is present in, with, and under the presence of bread and wine) to a symbolic presence where the bread and wine remain but symbolize Christ's presence. Baptism is performed either by immersion or, more commonly, sprinkling water on the candidate's forehead. Confirmation is often administered at the beginning of adolescence, although frequently at age seven outside the United States.

Sacred Books/Scriptures

The Bible used by Catholics is virtually identical to that used by other Christians. The exceptions are twelve deuterocanonical (added later to the canon or official list) books, or parts of books, accepted as canonical by Catholics: Tobit; Judith; the Additions to the Book of Esther; the Wisdom of Solomon; Ecclesiasticus or the Wisdom of Jesus, Son of Sirach; Baruch; the Letter of Jeremiah; the Prayer of Azariah and the Song of the Three Jews; Susanna; Bel and the Dragon; and 1st and 2nd Maccabees. (These writings are known to Protestants as the Apocrypha or "hidden" books.) Orthodox Christians also accept these books as scriptural, along with a few others found in neither the Catholic nor Protestant canons.

Practices

In addition to the solemn festivals surrounding the Easter Triduum (Good Friday, Holy Saturday, Easter Sunday), and to Christmas and some other holy days, Catholics celebrate several feast days in honor of the Blessed Virgin Mary. The two principal ones are:

> **Assumption**—A holy day celebrated August 15 commemorating the Assumption of Mary bodily into heaven.

> **Immaculate Conception**—A commemoration on December 8 of the conception of Mary without original sin.

Latino/Hispanic Catholicism

Because Latino Catholics now comprise about a quarter of the adult Catholic population,[1] it is important to mention several religious holidays unique to them:

> **El Dia de los Muertos** (the Day of the Dead), November 2—This holiday is equivalent to All Souls' Day.

> **El Dia de los Reyes Magos** (the Day of the Magi Kings), January 6—Equivalent to the Feast of the Epiphany (usually occurring on the Sunday between January 2 and 8), this is the day (rather than Christmas) when Latino children receive gifts.

> **Feast of Our Lady of Guadalupe**—Celebrated December 12, this is probably the most important of Latino Catholic holidays and commemorates the appearance of the Virgin Mary to a Mexican Indian peasant, Juan Diego, in 1531.

> **Las Posadas** (the Wayside Inns)—A commemoration of the difficulty Mary and Joseph had in journeying from Nazareth to Bethlehem and finding a place to stay prior to Jesus' birth. It is celebrated from December 16 to 24 with pageants, the lighting of candles, and the praying of the rosary (a devotional prayer using prayer beads that focuses on the Virgin Mary).

> **Lent** is a forty-day period during which Catholics abstain from meat on Ash Wednesday (the first day of Lent when ashes are placed on the foreheads of Catholics symbolizing the need for repentance) and on all Fridays of Lent; they also fast on Ash Wednesday and Good Friday. (Fasting for Catholics means eating only one full meal and two smaller ones.)

Catholics celebrate the Mass or Eucharist daily, although attendance is not mandatory, whereas most other Christians celebrate the Lord's Supper/Holy Communion/Eucharist weekly at most. Catholics are obliged to attend Mass only on Sundays and major holy days.

Although not as frequently as before the Second Vatican Council (1962–65), Catholics confess their sins privately to a priest in the sacrament of penance, or reconciliation. (They must do so at least once a year if they have sinned seriously and wish to receive Holy Communion.) The priest absolves them of the guilt involved, although not from possible future punishments in the afterlife in Purgatory (see below).

Catholics, like Orthodox Christians, accept the concept of Purgatory, a purifying experience in the afterlife for those who have lived a basically righteous life but have committed sins for which they must repent. The punishment or purgation consists of a painful longing for God during a period corresponding to the sins committed on earth.

Main Subgroups

There are no branches within Catholicism. A relatively small number of "Eastern rite" Catholics whose belief system is identical to those in the Roman system but whose celebration of the sacraments is slightly different, live in the United States. (In the countries of origin of these Eastern rites, such as Lebanon, priests may marry but not if they reside in the West.)

Common Misunderstandings and Stereotypes

"Catholics worship the Blessed Virgin Mary."

Although Catholics venerate Mary as the most important of the saints—and even pray to God through her—she is not considered divine but simply the holiest person, besides Jesus, who ever lived.

"Catholics accept the teachings of the pope as being without error and the pope himself as incapable of sinning."

The pope is only considered as capable of teaching without error (infallibly) when he makes an official pronouncement on a matter of belief or morality in his official role as head of the church. Moreover, Catholics do not receive instructions from the pope or their bishops about whom to vote for, although the pope or the United States Conference of Catholic Bishops publish statements instructing Catholics on matters of morality (abortion, assisted suicide, etc.). The pope, although usually a person of high moral character, is as capable of sinning as any other human being.

Classroom Concerns

On Ash Wednesday and the Fridays of Lent, non-meat dishes should be available in the school cafeteria. Also on Ash Wednesday, some Catholic students (and staff) may come to school with ashes on their foreheads. The ritual for that day includes the priest's placing ashes in the form of a cross on the forehead.

Anti-Catholic stereotypes about a Catholic's absolute allegiance to the pope on political matters or about worship of Mary, which still persist to some degree, should be corrected if and when they are expressed by students.

Finally, it would be worthwhile to point out to students—especially those from conservative or evangelical backgrounds—that Catholics have much more in common with other Christians than the doctrinal differences separating them. In particular, with the recent rise in the numbers of those preferring to call themselves "Christians" rather than "Protestants," some of them might think that Catholics are not Christians a some what understandable category mistake but one that needs correction.

Population Data

There are about 51 million adult Catholics in the United States (making Catholicism the largest single denomination or individual church in the country)[2] and more than 1 billion worldwide.[3]

—B.H.

Further Reading

Catechism of the Catholic Church. Vatican City: Libreria Editrice Vaticana, 2nd ed., 2000.

Doyle, Dennis M. *The Church Emerging from Vatican II: A Popular Approach to Contemporary Catholicism.* Mystic, CT: Twenty-Third Publications, 1992.

McBrien, Richard P. *Catholicism, New Edition.* San Francisco: HarperCollins, 1994.

New Catholic Encyclopedia. 2nd ed. Washington, DC: Catholic University of American Press, 2003.

The Official Catholic Directory. New Providence, NJ: P.J. Kennedy & Sons, 2005.

Web Sites

Official site of the U.S. Catholic Bishops: http://www.usccb.org

Official site of the Roman Catholic Church/Vatican: http://www.vatican.va

Notes

1. Kosmin and Keysar, *Religion in a Free Market,* pp. 26, 247. They also report that 59 percent of the adult Latino population is Roman Catholic compared with 66 percent in the 1990 survey by Kosmin and Seymour P. Lachman in *One Nation under God: Religion in Cotemporary American Society.* New York: Harmony Books, 1993.

2. Kosmin and Keysar, p. 26.

3. *Statistical Yearbook of the Church.* Vatican City: Vatican Publishing, 2002.

Christianity

Seventh-day Adventists

Origins

The Seventh-day Adventist Church grew out of the Great Disappointment, when the Millerite expectation of the return to Earth of Jesus Christ on October 22, 1844, did not take place. William Miller, a New England Baptist preacher, had based his calculations on the Bible—specifically, the Book of Daniel. By the spring of 1845, Miller and most of his followers abandoned the time calculations concerning the Second Advent (Second Coming of Christ). However, a few retained their confidence in the time calculations, contending that Christ, instead of coming to Earth, had entered a new phase of ministry in the heavenly sanctuary. Some of the followers, including James and Ellen White, began keeping the seventh-day Sabbath. Mrs. White inspired the movement with her visions, prophecies, and writings. She was also influential in establishing educational, publishing, and medical missionary programs. The name Seventh-day Adventist Church was adopted in 1860 to distinguish the church from other Protestant churches and to highlight its missionary thrust.

Beliefs

Based on the Bible, especially the books of Daniel and Revelation, Seventh-day Adventists believe that their mission is to help prepare for the Second Coming of Christ by preaching the "everlasting gospel" to all the world as an antidote for increasing wickedness. When the Gospel has been effectively preached to all the world, Jesus Christ will return to Earth, resurrect the faithful dead (who are in a state of unconsciousness), grant them immortality, and take them back to heaven for the thousand-year reign of Christ, called the Millennium. This is the first resurrection. At this time, Satan will be bound and cast into the bottomless pit. At the end of the Millennium, during the second resurrection, Satan will be unbound and will return to earth, where he will deceive the nations. At the same time, all those who have died sinners will be raised. They will review their own

83

roles in the rebellion against God. They will confess that God is loving and just, but they do not want to exist under the conditions of his kingdom. God will cease sustaining their lives and they will cease to exist, as will Satan. Then the Holy City, with all the saints, will return to earth, which will regain its original purity and become the eternal abode of the saints.

Christ's return will be very soon, although no exact date can be set. Still, current events can be read as signs of the times, revealing that the return is close at hand. In preparation for this event, all biblical principles must be restored. Because the Ten Commandments are central to Christ's high priestly ministry in the heavenly sanctuary, it is necessary that believers follow them. The fourth commandment is to keep the Sabbath day, Saturday, as a memorial of creation, for God rested on the seventh day (Exodus 20: 8–11). It therefore signifies that, through faith, human beings will live righteously. As a sign of the coming new creation, restoration of the Sabbath is necessary for Christ's return.

Sacred Books/Scriptures

The Bible alone is sacred and authoritative. Interpreting its message of the Second Advent of Christ is central to the church. The Bible predicts that the Second Advent will begin a thousand-year, or millennial, period. After the Great Disappointment, a reinterpretation of the Bible led to the principles that are central for Seventh-day Adventists today. Mrs. White's prophecies and writings are next in importance to the Bible in their spiritual authority.

Practices

The church operates as a representative democracy, with delegates meeting periodically to set policies regarding their missionary, educational, benevolence, health, and publishing activities. Local churches are independent, and many operate their own schools. Pastors are trained in Adventist seminaries and assigned to local churches.

Adventists practice the ordinances of baptism by immersion (a symbol of conversion) and the Lord's Supper (preceded by foot washing). They accept the gifts of prophecy and treat the Bible as an infallible guide and rule for faith and practice.

In keeping with their view of the nearness of Christ's return to earth, Adventists do not conform to the world. They consider the body a temple of the Holy Spirit and avoid habits or practices that would defile it. They do not use alcohol, tobacco, or narcotics; avoid gambling and dancing; and observe proper decorum and modesty in dress. They are opposed to war but prefer to serve as conscientious cooperators in the medical corps rather than conscientious objectors.

In keeping with their emphasis on habits of health, Adventists maintain hospitals and provide medical services, not only for themselves but as a missionary outreach to non-Adventists as well. Mrs. White incorporated health reform into her theology and considered it an important dimension of religious experience. Healthful living is a part of the biblical principles to be restored before the return of Christ. Hence, health is a moral and spiritual virtue. It prepares one for that moment when the mortal body will be translated to immortality. Mrs. White also emphasized vegetarianism, in keeping with mid-nineteenth-century health reform practices. Because the earth is to be restored to the perfect conditions of the Garden of Eden before the Fall, Mrs. White reasoned that one ought to follow the practices of the first inhabitants, who ate only of the fruits, nuts, and grains that grew there. In addition, eating meat, which causes pain and death of animals, is the result of the Fall into sin and was not part of God's original plan.

Some Millerites discontinued evangelism after October 22, 1844, because they thought that, at that time, Christ had ceased his intercession for sinners, and therefore new conversions were impossible. At first, Sabbath-keeping Adventists adopted this view, but Mrs. White and others gradually modified the position by emphasizing the need to preach the preparation for the Second Advent. Through their understanding of the importance of the Ten Commandments, and especially of the Sabbath, they stressed the need to tell all non-Adventists that the biblical principles, including the Sabbath, must be restored before Christ's return.

Main Subgroups

Some of the main subgroups are Branch SDAs; General Association of Davidian Seventh-day Adventists; People's Christian Church; The Registry; Seventh-day Adventists Church, Reform; Seventh-day Christian Conference; and Unification Association of Christian Sabbath Keepers.

There are several Adventist groups in addition to Seventh-day Adventists: Jehovah's Witnesses; Advent Christian Church; Davidian Seventh-day Adventists Association; Church of God, International; General Conference of the Church of God; Worldwide Church of God; Assemblies of Yahweh; and a number of small, local groups.

Common Misunderstandings and Stereotypes

"Seventh-day Adventists are not Christian because they follow the Jewish practice of worshipping on Saturday."

It is true that there is a strong emphasis placed on the Hebrew Bible, especially the book of Daniel and the Ten Commandments. However, Adventists, like many other Christians, read and follow both the Old and New Testaments. By the second century, the Catholic Church had adopted the first day of the week, Sunday, as the chief day of worship, because it was on this day that Christ was raised from the dead. However, by giving priority to Biblical, rather than Church, authority, and to the Ten Commandments in particular, Seventh-day Adventists became convinced of the need to return to the Sabbath, which they took as a sign of everlasting devotion between God and his worshippers.

> *"Seventh-day Adventists are not entirely consistent, expecting the imminent return of Christ but working to improve the world at the same time."*

Following the Ten Commandments and observing the Sabbath are understood as expressions of faith in Jesus Christ. In addition, Mrs. White encouraged the establishment of hospitals and emphasized habits of healthy living (the church has a well-deserved reputation for its medical services). However, none of this contradicts the anticipation of Christ's imminent return. After the Great Disappointment, a reinterpretation of the Bible revealed that humanity was to be purified and true worship restored in preparation for the return. All members of the church are considered missionaries and contribute to the worldwide work of proclaiming this theme of restoration.

Classroom Concerns

Adventist students may want to be excused from school-related Saturday activities because this day is their Sabbath, and they are expected to participate in Adventist observances. Teachers might help these students organize their weekly schedule so that homework, for example, can be completed when they are not busy with church activities.

Some Adventist students follow a vegetarian diet. This is a religious practice, so provision should be made to accommodate their dietary requirements.

The Seventh-day Adventist view of history and the Sabbath may not be the same as other Christian or non-Christian views. For Adventists, their history is a sacred, true, and meaningful account of the world that includes an understanding of the nature of human life and its ultimate destiny as the Bible has foretold. If Adventist views are expressed in class, teachers might use the occasion to teach cultural diversity and toleration of different viewpoints.

Practices that set Adventists apart from the world, such as not eating meat and observing Saturday as the day of worship, should not make Adventist children feel left out. When such practices are noticed by other students, teachers might use the occasion to develop a lesson on religious freedom, the exercise of conscience, and toleration of different practices.

Population Data

Kosmin and Keysar[1] list 724,000 adult SDA members in the United States. Latin America, Africa, and Russia have experienced rapid membership gains in the past few years. The church operates 5,700 preschools, primary and secondary schools, as well as colleges, universities, seminaries, and medical schools throughout the world. It also runs 152 hospitals and sanitariums.

—J.H.

Further Reading

Dick, Everett N. *William Miller and the Advent Crisis 1831–1844.* Berrien Springs, MI: Andrews University Press, 1994.

Doan, Ruth Alden. *The Miller Heresy, Millennialism, and American Culture*. Philadelphia: Temple University Press, 1987.

Gaustad, Edwin, ed. *Rise of Adventism: Religion and Society in Mid-Nineteenth Century America*. New York: Harper & Row, 1974.

Numbers, Ronald L., and Jonathan M. Butler, eds. *The Disappointed: Millerism and Millenarianism in the Nineteenth Century*. 2nd ed. Knoxville: University of Tennessee Press, 1993.

Pearson, Michael. *Millennial Dreams and Moral Dilemmas: Seventh-day Adventism and Contemporary Ethics*. New York: Cambridge University Press, 1990.

Spalding, Arthur W. *Origin and History of Seventh-day Adventists*. 4 vols. Washington, DC: Review & Herald Publishing, 1961.

Web Sites

Ontario Consultants on Religious Tolerance: http://www.religioustolerance.org/sda.htm

Seventh-day Adventist Church: http://www.adventist.org/

Religious Movements Homepage Project @The University of Virginia: http://religiousmovements.lib.virginia.edu/nrms/sevn.html

Notes

1. *Religion in a Free Market*, p. 27.

The Church of Scientology

Origins

Of all the new religious movements, the Church of Scientology has been the most consistently controversial in the eyes of the general public. The usual charges—that it is a cult; that it engages in criminal activities such as fraud, tax evasion, false imprisonment, and brainwashing; that it lies and practices undue influence and deceit; and that it attacks free speech by engaging in intimidation and threats against its opponents—are common in the media and on the Internet. Yet nothing exists in the teachings and practices of the Church and its earlier iteration, Dianetics, that would warrant such charges.

Like the traditional religions, Scientology views humanity as defective and dysfunctional. It offers solutions like other religions, with the problems of humanity described in terms similar to those of the Yogacara philosophy in Mahayana Buddhism, the New Thought Movement, and its cousin, Christian Science. If Buddhism is sometimes touted to be the most scientific of the traditional religions because of its emphasis on the mind, the teaching of Dianetics and Scientology might be viewed similarly as the most scientific of new religious movements. Although Scientology suggests "science" and "scientific religion" in the modern sense of the term, "scient-" (from *scire,* to know) is defined as "knowing in the fullest sense of the word." Also, the "Glossary for Scientology and Dianetics" describes Scientology as a "study of" (-logy *logos*) and "handling of the spirit in relationship to itself, universes and other life. In itself the word means literally *knowing how to know.*"[1] Nonetheless, the implication that this religion is scientific bears some truth. Scientologists describe the concepts and components of Scientology in precise terms by using technical language devoid of any connotation except what Scientology intended. Furthermore, Scientologists claim that the teachings in Dianetics and Scientology are not faith-based nor revealed by higher powers but were accessed through observation and experimentation.

Still, many investigators conclude that Scientology is not and cannot be a science according to the strictures of scientific methodology. Certainty, neither doubt nor uncertainty, curiosity nor ignorance is its starting point. Rather, absolutes and meta-empirical goals are stressed, both of which have no place in science. Thus, some researchers consider Scientology to be a pseudo-science. It acts as if it were subjecting the human condition to scientific inquiry, stressing the rational and empirical, and avoiding the trappings of spiritual, emotional, and religious terminology. Its goal, however, is neither materialistic nor physical. It reaches beyond the physical, thus exhibiting a "secularized system of belief which rejects emotion and emphasizes reason."[2] Furthermore, Scientology, unlike science, provides a direct and almost certain means of gaining the ultimate goal promised by the religion: *Clear* in Dianetics and *Operating Thetan* in Scientology (see "Beliefs," below).

The person responsible for both Scientology and its predecessor, Dianetics, is L. (Lafayette) Ron Hubbard (1911–86). All teachings and practices in both are credited to him. No other member of the Church of Scientology or the practice of Dianetics can lay claim to an original doctrine or practice. As a result, Hubbard's influence and charisma have been retained within the church despite his demise in 1986. A hagiography has been established that assures his special status, and by implication, the status of the edifice that he founded and developed. It is no accident that the L. Ron Hubbard Life Exposition was established, in 1991, near the heart of the movie industry on Hollywood Boulevard in Los Angeles.

Some question whether Hubbard's life as represented in the Life Exposition or narrated in the official biography is totally accurate. Many question the implication that Hubbard is more than an ordinary human being, perhaps transcending even the likes of a Buddha. The bare essentials include his birth in Tilden, Nebraska; his becoming acquainted with a Blackfoot Indian medicine man after his family moved to Helena, Montana, and being initiated as a blood brother of the Blackfoot Indians at age six; his involvement with the Boy Scouts after his family moved to Washington State and becoming the nation's youngest Eagle Scout (1924); his travels to the Orient from 1927 to 1929; his enrollment at George Washington University in 1930 to study engineering and atomic and molecular physics; his undertaking a scientific voyage in 1932 and 1933 to collect floral and reptile specimens; his embarking on a career of writing fiction and becoming a Hollywood scriptwriter; his commission in the U.S. Navy and recovering from war injuries at Oak Knoll Naval Hospital; his contributions to the development of Dianetics following his recovery over the next three years, with the publication of *Dianetics* in 1950; the significant discovery that humans are spiritual, not physical beings (1951), leading to the establishment of Scientology in 1954; and his subsequent research and continued development of Church teachings and their applications until his death.

The outcome of an incredibly productive life has led to a fully developed movement and religion that combines ancient teachings with modern technology designed to guarantee a liberation or salvation for seekers who follow the regimen as defined by Hubbard and the Church. Liberation, according to Dianetics and Scientology, is freedom of the mind to function without impediment. Perhaps the best example of such a person is L. Ron Hubbard himself. His accomplishments resemble those of the Renaissance man: an educator, music maker, photographer, aviator, explorer, artist, sea captain, yachtsman, horticulturalist, administrator, filmmaker, philosopher, and science fiction writer, among other accomplishments.

Beliefs

The beliefs of the Church of Scientology fall under the following categories: (1) the Creed, (2) therapy and purification of the mind, and (3) applications.

The Creed of the Church was composed in 1954, the year when Scientology was constituted as a religion:

We of the Church believe:

That all men of whatever race, color or creed were created with equal rights;

That all men have inalienable rights to their own religious practices and their performance;

That all men have inalienable rights to their own lives;

That all men have inalienable rights to their sanity;

That all men have inalienable rights to their own defense;

That all men have inalienable rights to conceive, choose, assist or support their own organizations, churches and governments;

That all men have inalienable rights to think freely, to talk freely, to write freely their own opinions and to counter or utter or write upon the opinions of others;

That all men have inalienable rights to the creation of their own kind;

That the souls of men have the rights of men;

That the study of the mind and the healing of mentally caused ills should not be alienated from religion or condoned in nonreligious fields;

And that no agency less than God has the power to suspend or set aside these rights, overtly or covertly.

And we of the Church believe:

That man is basically good;

That he is seeking to survive;

That his survival depends upon himself and upon his fellows, and his attainment of brotherhood with the universe.

And we of the Church believe that the laws of God forbid man:

To destroy his own kind;

> To destroy the sanity of another;
>
> To destroy or enslave another's soul;
>
> To destroy or reduce the survival of one's companions or one's group.

And we of the Church believe:

> That the spirit can be saved and
>
> That the spirit alone may save or heal the body.[3]

The Creed was designed to define the Church of Scientology as a religion. The second category, therapy and purification of the mind, has its beginnings with the publication of *Dianetics,* which places emphasis on the mind, how it functions and dysfunctions, and how it can be cured and cleared. Its main purpose is to maintain survival. In Scientology, there are eight urges or impulses (labeled "dynamics") to survival. They include the urge to survival as or through (1) self, (2) sex and family, (3) groups, (4) all mankind, (5) living things (plants and animals), (6) the material universe, (7) spirits, and (8) infinity or the Supreme Being.[4]

There are two main parts that make up the mind: the analytic mind (the conscious mind which "thinks, observes data, remembers it and resolves problems") and the reactive mind (the unconscious mind which contains memories of negative experiences). The reactive mind helps explain why the mind sometimes operates counterproductively, that is, against survival. All negative experiences are retained by the reactive mind in mental images, which then exerts control over a person's awareness, thoughts, and actions. If an individual is struck unconscious, the reactive mind will continue to record all pain. All mental images are stored in the reactive mind and remain inaccessible to the analytic mind. They accumulate throughout a person's life in accordance with an exact time sequence. Known as "time track," it is compared to a photograph, but is more than a simple photograph because it "is a complete recording, down to the last accurate detail."[5] Such a mental image is called an "engram." The reactive mind is but an "engram bank" which functions as a stimulus-response mechanism.

The goal, known as *Clear,* is to get rid of engrams and the reactive mind. This is achieved through auditing (see under "Practices" below). A person who is Clear is free from fears and traumatic experiences that were products of the reactive mind. As a consequence, a person can function without the limitations imposed by these fears and traumatic experiences. Some of the attributes of the Clear are the abilities to be "freed from active or potential psychosomatic illness or aberration"; "self-determined; vigorous and persistent; unrepressed; able to perceive, recall, imagine, create and compute at a level high above the norm; stable mentally; free with his emotion; able to enjoy life; freer from accidents; healthier; able to reason swiftly; able to react quickly."[6]

Dianetics was associated primarily with this form of mental therapy. Yet shortly after the publication of *Dianetics*, in 1951, Hubbard announced that individuals actually lived previous lives. In other words, human beings are neither minds nor physical bodies; they are spirits. The spirit, called "thetan" in Scientology, is immortal and is not part of the physical universe composed of MEST (matter, energy, space, and time). Proof of the thetan's identification with the individual is the phenomenon of *exteriorization,* "the state of the thetan being outside his body with or without full perception, but still able to control and handle the body." In other words, when the thetan is *exterior,* the person is still aware of him/herself as a person, despite not being in the body. With the discovery of the thetan came the discovery of past lives, that is, a form of reincarnation, and the existence of levels above Clear known as Operating Thetan (OT), of which there are eight. These eight levels are all confidential, so that this aspect of the teaching is treated as esoteric. One definition of the OT is "a state of beingness," implying independence or freedom and an ability to control MEST, form and life. The implication is that the person is in control of his or her actions. The third category, Applications, is discussed under "Practices."

Sacred Books/Scriptures

The scriptures of the Church of Scientology consist of Hubbard's written and spoken words. The list is extensive: more than three thousand taped lectures, one hundred films, and more than five thousand writings including forty books—together comprising more than 500,000 pages.

Among the books considered especially significant are *Dianetics: The Modern Science of Mental Health; Scientology 0–8: The Book of Basics; Scientology 8–80; Scientology 8–8008; Scientology: A History of Man; Scientology: The Fundamentals of Thought; The Scientology Handbook;* and *What Is Scientology?* The publisher of all of Hubbard's books in the U.S. is Bridge Publications, Inc. (New Era Publications publishes outside the United States.)

Among the thousands of taped lectures, the 447 *Saint Hill Special Briefing Course Lectures* are the most comprehensive and organized regarding the philosophy and practice of Scientology.

Practices

Scientology, like Dianetics, regards auditing as the primary practice that can lead to Clear and states beyond. In addition to auditing, the application of the principles of Scientology to social reform, social betterment, and organizational and management models appear in such programs as the Citizens Commission on Human Rights, the National Commission on Law Enforcement and Social Justice (NCLE), and World Institute of Scientology Enterprises (WISE), which is an organization with international membership designed to administer the Hubbard Management Technology. The Association for Better Living and Education (ABLE) now administers those programs designed to alleviate society from drugs, crime, illiteracy, and immorality respectively through Narconon International, Criminon International, Applied Scholastics International, and The Way to Happiness Foundation International.

The main practice, *auditing,* is designed to delete the engrams from the reactive mind. The auditor, a minister or minister-in-training in the church, can follow a number of different processes, such as asking a series of questions designed to help the person being audited increase his or her self-knowledge, or engage in a word-association technique to elicit the respondent's reaction.

A device that is used during the auditing session is the e-meter or electro-psychometer. Its purpose is to record "electrical charges contained in the engrams of the reactive mind."[7] Because the mental images in the mind contain energy and mass, the experience of the image activates the two ingredients, thus causing a charge or harmful force. The needle movements of the e-meter allow the auditor to identify the emotional charge or engram and to discuss it. The result will be a lessening or elimination of the charge. When the e-meter registers no reaction, then the charge is cleared.

Associated Organizations

Auditing serves as the prototype for the applications cited above. If auditing frees or purifies the individual of the reactive mind and engrams, then Narconon serves a similar purpose when applied to drug rehabilitation, drug prevention, and the related educational program designed to bring about a drug-free environment. Narconon International was founded by William Benitez in 1966 while serving a prison sentence in Arizona State Prison. The practices established in Narconon are designed to rid the body of drug residue through an eight-step program which includes detoxification, a Learning Improvement Course, and a Way to Happiness course. The largest Narconon center is the Chilocco New Life Center in Newkirk, Oklahoma, and its international headquarters is in Los Angeles.

Related to Narconon is *Criminon International,* a program designed to address the causes of criminality and to provide a number of services such as drug detoxification and education to those in the Criminal Justice system.

Applied Scholastics International provides guidance and technical assistance to educational institutions, teachers, and students. The basis of learning and study is given in Hubbard's *The Technology of Study.* Known as Study Tech, this consists of three principles: (1) the use of visual material to aid in teaching abstract objects, (2) reduction of complex concepts to simple ideas, (3) definition of all unfamiliar terms. This technique is used throughout the world, including Canada, Colombia, Israel, Italy, and the Ukraine. There are dozens of schools in the United States that engage Applied Scholastics.

The *Way to Happiness Foundation International,* founded in 1984, is based on the book of the same title. In it, twenty-one precepts for successful living are introduced that provide a "non-religious moral code based entirely upon common sense" (Introduction to *The Way to Happiness*). Some of the twenty-one precepts include: "Take Care of Yourself" (no. 1), "Love and Help Children" (no. 4), "Set a Good Example" (no. 6), "Don't Do Anything Illegal" (no. 9), "Be Worthy of Trust" (no. 14), "Respect the Religious Beliefs of Others," (no. 18), "Try to Treat Others as You Would Want Them to Treat You" (no. 20).[8]

Among the other organizations associated with the Church is the *Citizens Commission on Human Rights.* This organization was cofounded in 1969 by the Church and Dr. Thomas Szasz, Emeritus Professor of Psychiatry, State University of New York (Syracuse). The purpose of the Citizens Commission is to expose the abuses of psychiatry by becoming an active opponent of the psychiatric profession. The Church views psychiatry as many critics view Scientology: a fraudulent organization. The CCHR's role is to offer outlets for such forms of activism as reporting psychiatric abuse, creating blogs, engaging in legislative campaigns, and writing to newspapers about the abuses and damage committed by the profession.[9]

The *National Commission on Law Enforcement and Social Justice* (NCLE) was established in 1974 in response to "civil rights violations stemming from false reports residing in government files." Much of the abuse was directed against the Church of Scientology, which damaged church operations in other countries. An outcome of its activities has been the passing of laws that open government documents to the public, and employing the Freedom of Information Act to uncover false and damaging documents. Although not formally associated with NCLE, the journal *Freedom,* published by the Church of Scientology, discusses many of the same issues associated with human rights that are under the purview of CCHR and NCLE.

The *World Institute of Scientology Enterprises* (WISE) provides a business organizational and management model based on L. Ron Hubbard's research to its membership. Details of the organizational format are contained in Hubbard's Organization Executive Course and the Management Series, a group of volumes containing some 2,500 policies. In addition, WISE established the Hubbard College of Administration "to provide the public with the knowledge and techniques they need to tackle every possible challenge that can be encountered in administering and running any group, company or organization."[10] Campuses are located in at least ten countries; in the United States, at Los Angeles, New York City, and Clearwater, Florida.

Main Subgroups

There are no subgroups within the Church of Scientology.

Common Misunderstandings and Stereotypes

"Scientology is a cult that involves brainwashing, coercion and other abuses."

Unlike other religions, Scientology is plagued not simply by a few misconceptions but by numerous controversies that involve academic, governmental, and private institutions as well as media personalities and private individuals who publicize their opposition to Dianetics and the Church of Scientology through blogs and fully developed anti-Scientology Web sites. Conversely, the Church does not take such attacks and criticism lying down. The conflict between Scientologists and its critics exists on a wide range of topics—brainwashing; recruitment practices; fraud; troubles with the Internal Revenue Service; extortion; coercion; illegally practicing medicine; and misrepresentation of its practices, programs, and the life of Hubbard. Controversy began with the disinterest or opposition of the American Psychiatric Association and the American Medical Association to Hubbard when he first introduced dianetic therapy and, later on, Scientology. Then there was the seizure of e-meters and church literature by the Federal Drug Administration in 1963, and open opposition to Scientology by Australian psychiatrists and psychologists from Melbourne University, and by other medical officials and members of the Australian Medical Association. This resulted in the suggestion in 1962 by Australian psychiatrist E. Cunningham Dax, chairman of the Victoria Mental Health Authority, to ban Scientologists from advertising.

Brainwashing has been a frequent and common charge against Scientologists. Thousands of Web sites cover this charge, but some scholars, notably J. Gordon Melton (*The Church of Scientology*, 54), argue that brainwashing had been discredited as early as the 1950s and again in the 1980s. Evidence is given in Massimo Introvigne's "'Liar, Liar': Brainwashing, CESNUR and APA" (http://www.cesnur.org/testi/gandow_eng. htm), citing the American Psychological Association's rejection in 1987 of "brainwashing or mind control theories applied to new religious movements on the ground that they were outside the field of mainline science." In the amicus brief submitted to the Supreme Court of the State of California in a case relevant for Scientology (*Molko and Leal vs. Holy Spirit Association for the Unification of World Christianity*), one statement stands out as particularly noteworthy:

> Denuded of its scientific legitimacy, the coercive persuasion theory, as applied in the Unification Church context, amounts to little more than a refusal to accept that persons could choose to adopt the belief system and way of life of that Church.[11]

If the validity of brainwashing or mind control does not meet scientific standards, then a similar charge has been set against Dianetics and Scientology. Because the subtitle of the book, *Dianetics* is "the modern science of mental health," it is obvious that Hubbard introduced Dianetics as medical science, as is also evident in his earlier *Dianetics: the Evolution of a Science.* To be called a science, Dianetic therapy would have to be examined under strict scientific methodology. According to the available evidence, Dianetics has not passed the science bar. An example is the 1953 report by Harvey Jay Fischer, *Dianetic Therapy: An Experimental Evaluation*, which concludes that in the three areas that dianetic therapy claims effectiveness (intellectual functioning, mathematical ability, and personality conflicts), "Dianetic therapy does not systematically, favorably or adversely influence the ability to perform."

"Scientology is not really a religion."

One difficulty in understanding Dianetics, Scientology, and its applications are their disparity with traditional religions. The Church of Scientology obviously calls itself a religion. One scholar of religion, Irving Hexham, has suggested that Scientology is genuinely a religion according to the definitions in Ninian Smart's "Meaning in and the Meaning of Religion," ("a set of institutionalized rituals identified with a tradition and expressing and/or evoking sacral sentiments directed at a divine or trans-divine focus seen in the context of the human phenomenological environment and at least partially described by myths or by myths and doctrines") and in Stark and Bainbridge's *Theory of Religion:* "Religion refers to systems of general compensators based on supernatural assumptions."[12] Scientology itself answers the question in this way:

Why is Scientology a religion?

Scientology meets all three criteria generally used by religious scholars when examining religions: (1) a belief in some Ultimate Reality, such as a Supreme Being or eternal truth that transcends the here and now of the secular world; (2) religious practices directed toward understanding, attaining or communicating with this Ultimate Reality; and (3) a community of believers who join together in pursuing the Ultimate Reality.

There is no reason to doubt Scientology as a religion if we assume a transcendental factor and a means by which a transformation can be achieved by a set of actions, practices, and/or mental exercise to realize, experience, or become the transcendent reality acknowledged in the religion. Auditing is such an action; the Supreme Being or Ultimate Reality is the transcendent; and the Operating Thetan is the state wherein the individual rises to eternity. To a large degree, Scientology shares some similarity to the Upanishadic teaching in Hinduism of the Atman and Brahman (note, too, that the letter "theta" is the first letter of the Greek words for God (*theos*) and soul (*thymos*). Such an equation may be deemed blasphemous by those in the Western religions, especially if the claim to liberation and perfection is gained not by spiritual means but by secular, if not purely scientific, means.

There are numerous reasons Scientology is attacked: some personal, wherein the aggrieved is convinced of an injustice. But an underlying cause of the institutional attacks on Scientology is reflective of a perceived threat to the institutions in question: those who view themselves as professionals and scientists (the fields of psychiatry and psychology) who view Dianetics as quackery and a threat to their profession, and those who represent true religion—fundamental and evangelical Christianity. The greatest crime that one can commit is blasphemy, that is, claiming the attributes of God. This may be the real reason for the animus against the Church of Scientology.

Classroom Concerns

In addition to the Church of Scientology's being primarily an adult-based religion, there is little or no data on second-generation scientologists. As a result, it is unlikely that parental-based issues will arise in the classroom. As a client-based group with practices akin to therapy, it is more likely the case that students may have contacts with the Church or Dianetics without parental guidance. For this reason, teachers should possess accurate information to answer the student's curiosity about both movements.

Population Data

According to Church figures, more than 5,100 churches, missions, and related organizations minister to eight million individuals worldwide.[13] Adherents.com, quoting Carlos Spartos of the *Village Voice*, puts Church membership at 3 million in the U.S. and 8 million overall. This figure includes those with dual religious affiliations or who are simply studying Scientology.[14] However, the 2001 Kosmin and Keysar survey resulted in a much smaller total of about 55,000 adult followers in the United States.[15]

—J.S.

Further Reading

Christensen, Dorthe Refslund. "Inventing L. Ron Hubbard: On the Construction and Maintenance of the Hagiographic Mythology of Scientology's Founder." In *Controversial New Religions,* ed. James R. Lewis and Jesper Aagaard Petersen. New York: Oxford University Press, 2005.

Hubbard, L. Ron. *Dianetics: The Modern Science of Mental Health.* Los Angeles: Bridge Publications, 1950 (reprint: 2000).

Melton, J. Gordon. *The Church of Scientology.* Torino: Signature Books in cooperation with CESNUR (Center for Studies on New Religions), 2000.

Petrowsky, Marc, and William W. Zellner. *Sects, Cults, and Spiritual Communities: A Sociological Analysis.* Westport, CT: Praeger, 1998.

What Is Scientology? Compiled by the staff of the Church of Scientology International. Los Angeles: Bridge Publications, 1992.

Wilson, Bryan R. *The Social Dimensions of Sectarianism: Sects and New Religious Movements in Contemporary Society.* Oxford, England: Clarendon Press, 1992.

Web Sites

http://www.scientology.org/

http://www.whatisscientology.org/

http://www.bonafidescientology.org/

http://www.scientologyreligion.org/

http://www.lronhubbardprofile.org/

http://www.xenu.net/archive/audit/ofpapers.html (Official reports and court judgments)

http://www.ultimatescientology.org

http://www.narconon.org/

http://www.criminon.org/

http://www.able.org/

http://www.wise.org/

http://www.appliedscholastics.org/

http://studytech.org/

Notes

1. Available at http://www.scientology.org/gloss.htm#s. Accessed September 3, 2006.

2. Bryan R. Wilson, *The Social Dimensions of Sectarianism.* Oxford: Clarendon Press, 1992, p. 274.

3. Available at http://www.ultimatescientology.org. Accessed September 3, 2006.

4. Available at http://www.scientology.org/gloss.html. Accessed September 5, 2006.

5. Available at http://www.scientology.org/gloss.htm. Accessed September 6, 2006.

6. Available at http://www.whatisscientology.org/Html/part02/chp04/pg0149.html. Accessed September 15, 2006.

7. Marc Petrowsky and William Zellner, *Sects ,Cults and Spiritual Communities: A Sociological Analysis.* Westport, CT: Praeger, 1998, p. 148.

8. Available at http://www.mrdata.net/books/twth/htm. Accessed September 3, 2006.

9. Available at http://www.cchr.com/. Accessed September 12, 2006.

10. Available at http://www.scientology.org/en_US/world/news/wise/pg005.html. Accessed September 8, 2006.

11. Available at http://www.cesnur/org/testi/molko_brief.htm#Anchor-INTEREST-4459lp.40. Accessed September 10, 2006.

12. Available at http://www.ucalgary.ca/~nurelweb/papers/irving/scient.html. Accessed September 16, 2006.

13. Available at http://www.bonafidescientology.org/Chapter/page00.htm. Accessed September 20, 2006.

14. Available at http://www.villagevoice.com/news/9904,spartos2,3687,1html. Accessed September 22, 2006.

15. *Religion in a Free Market*, p. 27.

Fundamentalism

Origins

There is no "Church of Fundamentalism" in the United States. Rather, there are Protestant churches that describe themselves as fundamentalist in orientation. Moreover, the terms *fundamentalism* and *fundamentalist* have been extended during the past thirty years (particularly since the Iranian revolution under the Ayatollah Khomeini in 1979) to include any follower of one of the world's religions who holds highly conservative views regarding his or her religion (e.g., forbidding unmarried adults of the opposite gender from having any contact unless accompanied by a chaperon).

The term itself was coined at the turn of the twentieth century when members of various Protestant denominations began to disagree over biblical interpretation. The more liberal among them accepted the scientific approach to interpreting the Bible, originating in Germany. The German biblical scholars used literary criticism, archeology, history, and other disciplines to interpret the meaning behind many "legendary" elements in the Hebrew and Christian Bibles (Old and New Testaments). Thus, for example, some of the miraculous events narrated in the Book of Exodus (the plagues upon the Egyptians, the parting of the Red Sea) or concerning Jesus' life (walking on water, multiplying loaves and fishes) were interpreted as symbolic rather than literally true.

By contrast, more conservative clergy and laypeople objected to what they saw as an attempt to water down the word of God. From 1910 to 1915, a group of biblical scholars at Princeton Seminary and elsewhere published "The Fundamentals," a series of pamphlets that defended the literal truth of the Bible and cited specific doctrines contained in the scriptures that had to be accepted as fact to be of the Christian faith. These included Jesus' divinity and virgin birth, his death as the atonement for the sins of humankind, his bodily resurrection and physical return, his miracles, and the literal truth and reliability of every word of the Bible.

Beliefs

Christian fundamentalists accept the basic creeds and ethical codes of traditional Christianity but interpret them very conservatively. In particular, every word of the Bible is considered true and accurate, not only as regards religious aspects but historically and scientifically as well. For example, the accounts of creation and the flood in the opening chapters of Genesis are considered fact. Thus, God created the world about six thousand years ago and did so directly and in this order: vegetation, fishes, birds, animals, insects, and finally humans. Evolutionary theories were expressly ruled out. Likewise, Noah literally took pairs of all animals into the ark in anticipation of the biblical flood.

Opposition to evolution led to the 1923 Scopes "Monkey Trial" in which a young Tennessee biology teacher, John Scopes, was accused of teaching evolution in violation of Tennessee law. Although Scopes was found guilty, his conviction was later thrown out by the Tennessee Supreme Court. The net effect of the trial was ridicule of fundamentalists, causing them largely to avoid involvement in political affairs until the late 1970s. Then, the Rev. Jerry Falwell's Moral Majority was founded and—on the coattails of the Reagan presidency—entered the political world, particularly over issues such as abortion, Creation Science (a movement defending the Genesis creation accounts by criticizing the theory of evolution and providing its own scientific explanation of human origins), assisted suicide, and prayer in public schools. (For a fuller discussion of the evolution issue, see the "Introduction," note 8.)

It is important to distinguish fundamentalists from evangelicals, a larger but more moderate grouping of conservative Christians (mainly Protestant). (**Although almost all fundamentalists are also evangelicals, the reverse is not true;** *evangelical* **is the more inclusive term for conservative Christians.**) Although sharing a reverence for the Bible with fundamentalists, evangelicals are somewhat more open to interpreting the Bible. For example, a strict fundamentalist might hold that Jesus literally cast out demons, while an evangelical would be open to the possibility that some of these exorcisms involved Jesus' healing of psychotics. Evangelicals are also not quite as suspect of the secular world. Along with a belief in the inerrancy of the Bible, the common threads of the two movements are (1) belief in the necessity of "believer's baptism," a mature commitment to Jesus Christ; and (2) dedication to evangelizing (converting others to Christianity).

The term fundamentalism has now been extended to include highly conservative— and sometimes fanatical—members of any religion. Although the word is still widely used to describe ultra-conservative members of any religion, Muslims in particular point to its Christian origins. As a result, many scholars and journalists have switched to the term *Islamist* to describe Muslims who follow an extremely orthodox interpretation of their faith and are critical of the Western lifestyle and U.S. foreign policy. This might, in some instances by marginalized groups, include the use of terror tactics and suicide attacks in the perceived defense of Islam.

The distinguished religion scholar Martin Marty[1] has created a profile of world-wide fundamentalism that includes the following characteristics:

1. an "us-versus-them," extremist viewpoint that is unwilling to compromise with moderates within one's own faith and finds other religions completely lacking in truth;

2. a defensive mentality that sees the outside world as massed against the true believers and trying to destroy them and their values, and that condemns certain nations or individuals (e.g., America as the "Great Satan" in the eyes of Iran's religious leaders and the followers of al-Qaeda and Hezbollah);

3. a literal reading of scriptures allowing for interpretation only on the basis of other passages in the sacred text (Bible, Qur'an, etc.) and not on the basis of outside scholarly sources;

4. a missionary zeal that seeks to bring new believers into the fold;

5. the desire to bring the state under the control of the fundamentalist religious community so that a theocracy—such as that in Iran—results;

6. a dominant role for men in all spheres of life so that the role of women is largely domestic;

7. a sense that the world is in a state of crisis, or that "the end is near," and that the true believers will play a dominant role in the events of the end times; and

8. a sophisticated use of the tools, but not the values, of modernity—especially the mass media and Internet—in achieving its aims.

Sacred Books/Scriptures

Fundamentalists accept the sacred texts of their respective religions (Bible, Qur'an, etc.) but use them in an absolutist way, as indicated above.

Practices

Fundamentalists observe the same holidays and rituals as traditional believers. What differentiates the two groups is that fundamentalists may use a holiday as an occasion for a political protest demonstration.

Main Subgroups

As noted in "Origins" above, fundamentalism is a philosophy operating within various religions and their subdivisions rather than a church unto itself. Thus, a significant portion of the country's 16 million Southern Baptists would consider themselves fundamentalists, as would some members of the Missouri and Wisconsin Synods (districts) of the Lutheran family of churches. One of the oldest Protestant centers of fundamentalism is Bob Jones University in South Carolina, which several years ago resisted federal efforts at forced racial integration, even at the cost of losing government funding.[2]

Common Misunderstandings and Stereotypes

"Fundamentalists are simply religious terrorists."

Although some fundamentalists have resorted to terrorism, as in the Middle East, most use nonviolent means to obtain their goals. In other words, a fundamentalist is not, by definition, a religious fanatic—someone who resorts to violent tactics to achieve goals. Examples of fanatical groups include the Haredi movement in Israel, which resorts to stone throwing on the Sabbath to prevent less religiously observant Jews from driving cars; HAMAS/Islamic Resistance Movement in the Palestinian territories, which has sent its members on suicide missions to kill Israelis; Hezbollah in Lebanon; the Church of Jesus Christ Christian, Aryan Nations, which is closely associated with the Ku Klux Klan; and Sikh separatists who have used terror tactics in seeking to gain independence from India for Punjab State.

"Fundamentalists are ignoramuses or 'Bible thumpers.' "

One may not agree with the idea of taking the Bible literally to solve all of life's problems. However, many fundamentalists are educated people who simply feel that there is a source of wisdom higher than humanity—God's revealed word. They reason, moreover, that once you begin to tamper with or interpret the Bible or Qur'an, there is no end to the process. You ultimately end up, they believe, with a book of fairy tales.

Classroom Concerns

Fundamentalists may object to having their children exposed to units on world religions and have the right to remove them during such instruction and request alternate assignments. Many fundamentalists consider Halloween a pagan holiday associated with witchcraft. Teachers might want to send a letter to parents to see how they feel about any activities planned for this holiday.

The teaching of evolution in biology and science classes presents problems for those families who reject it and espouse creation science (see "Beliefs" above). The Supreme Court ruled (*Edwards v. Aguillard*, 1987) that a Louisiana statute granting equal time to the teaching of creation science in science classes was unconstitutional. Creation science or Intelligent Design (see note 2) can, however, be discussed in world religions or social studies classes, and parents may remove their children from science classes when evolution is studied.

Sexuality education is another sensitive issue for conservative Christians, Jews, and Muslims. Some claim, for example, that information about birth control methods actually increases the incidence of teen pregnancy rather than preventing it. However, the State Court of Louisiana ruled in 1992 that Sex Respect, the sex education curriculum promoted by many conservative Christians, violated state law by promoting religious beliefs and disseminating inaccurate information. Here again, parents have the right to remove their children from programs they find objectionable. Discussions between parents and teachers may be helpful in clarifying a sex education curriculum.

A sensitive issue for some fundamentalist parents is the use of textbooks or other assigned readings found objectionable on various grounds: sexually explicit content, use of obscene language, allegedly pagan content, and so on. If a particular textbook has been problematic in the past, teachers might want to consult with parents about it.

Population Data

Kosmin and Keysar in *Religion in a Free Market,*[3] report that 61,000 adults self-identified as "fundamentalist." However, significant numbers of those in the survey who said they were Baptist, Christian, Pentecostal/Charismatic, Churches of Christ, Jehovah's Witnesses, Seventh Day Adventist, Assemblies of God, Holiness/Holy, Church of the Nazarene, Full Gospel, or Foursquare Gospel would hold a position on the Bible consistent with fundamentalism. As far as we know, there has never been a scientific survey of the number of fundamentalists in other religions. However, it appears from press reports that there are significant numbers in Judaism, Islam, Hinduism, and Sikhism.

—B.H.

Further Reading

Almond, Gabriel, R. Scott Appleby, and Emanuel Sivan. *Strong Religion (The Rise of Fundamentalisms around the World).* Chicago: University of Chicago Press, 2003.

Kimball, Charles. *When Religion Becomes Evil.* New York: HarperCollins, 2002.

Martin, William. *With God on Our Side: The Rise of the Religious Right in America.* New York: Broadway Books, 1996.

Ruthven, Malise. *Fundamentalism—The Search for Meaning.* New York: Oxford, 2004.

Web Site

Discussion of the violence that sometimes accompanies religious extremism: www.religioustolerance.org/relviol.htm

Notes

1. Martin E. Marty and R. Scott Appleby, eds., chap. 15, "Conclusion: An Interim Report on a Hypothetical Family." In *Fundamentalism Observed* (Chicago: University of Chicago Press, 1991).

2. Members of Pentecostal churches (see the chapter "Protestantism"), although different from fundamentalists, who tend to be uncomfortable with such practices as speaking in tongues and the laying on of hands, share with fundamentalism literal interpretation of the Bible and use of evangelism.

3. See p. 26.

The symbol of Hinduism is the sacred lett om (ohm)
*pronounced at the beginning and the end of prayers
and recitations from scripture. It is the seed of all*
mantras *(sacred utterances).*

Hinduism

Origins

Hinduism is generally considered to be the world's oldest continuing religion. It stems from other sources: aboriginal cultures; the Indus Valley Culture (2500–1700 B.C.E.) and its possible descendants in south India belonging to the Dravidian language groups; and the Sanskrit-based Aryan culture and religion—Brahmanism—as contained in the Veda or "Sacred Wisdom." The form of Hinduism familiar to Hindus today first appeared around 500 B.C.E. with the composition of the epic literature—Mahabharata and Ramayana—and the later Puranas or "Ancient Stories."

By definition, Hinduism does not refer to one religion but rather to numerous religious movements, philosophies, teachings, and practices that originated in India over the course of thousands of years and are part and parcel with the cultures of the Indian subcontinent. Indeed, the terms *Hindu* and *Hinduism* are artificial and overarching terms—etymologically identical with *India* and *Indian*—and attached to those religions that seem to be identified with the Indian worldview. Although Buddhism, Jainism, and Sikhism are also Indian religions separate from Hinduism, it appears that this sense of separateness is more the choice of these religions than of Hinduism. Sikhism, for example, originated out of a branch of devotional Hinduism and was considered Hindu until the Sikhs themselves selected a separate identity.

107

Beliefs

What holds this web of philosophical and religious movements together as Hindu is the acceptance by most adherents of certain doctrines and practices that are either unique to or closely identified with Hinduism. Chief among these is the view that the scripture called the Veda—especially the last part, the Upanishads—is the basis of all Hindu teaching and wisdom and is not of human origin. Two other compositions, the Mahabharata and Ramayana, hold such great honor and prestige among the population that they probably have as much or more authority among most Hindus of all walks of life. Furthermore, other compositions possess a somewhat lesser position of authority because they are concerned with more specific departments of knowledge. Examples of the latter are the Law Books (*dharma-sutras* and *dharma-shastras*), which define the manners and mores of the Hindu communities.

Other unifying factors are the celebration of a large number of festivals; the importance of pilgrimages to sacred sites for all Hindus; the acceptance of karma (any willed action produces an effect, good or bad, on the individual committing the action); acceptance of rebirth; the importance of the role of astrology in one's life; the presence of a large and bewildering number of divinities that are honored during certain festivals or in more private worship; the marriage ceremony as the most frequently performed of the life-cycle rituals; and caste or subsocieties that follow rules governing whom one may marry and eat with and, to a lesser extent, the occupation reserved for that group.

Sacred Books/Scriptures

The Veda is the central scripture. It consists of more than fifty separate works divided into four sections: (1) collections of hymns: Samhitas; (2) discussions of rituals and their contents: Brahmanas; (3) mystical discussions of selected rituals: Aranyakas; and (4) "secret knowledge" of the nature of the supreme force both within and beyond the universe: Upanishads. Whereas the first three sections are primarily concerned with attaining success in the world, the later portion of the Veda—the Upanishads—is concerned with realizing the nature of the absolute and with attaining salvation from this world of ignorance.

Additionally, as noted, the two great epics, the Mahabharata (which includes the Bhagavad-Gita; see "Main Subgroups" below) and the Ramayana, have great popular appeal.

Practices

The main practices are festivals, pilgrimages, worship, and life-cycle rituals. Other practices that are commonly accepted are nonviolence (at least in principle), vegetarianism, and the veneration of the cow as a sacred creature.

Festivals include fasting, worship, feasting, dramatic spectacles, entertainment, dance, music, and sometimes a procession in which the divinity is paraded on a chariot through the streets. Celebrations are usually centered on national epics or stories of the divinities. Thousands of festivals are celebrated throughout India, but the following are more widely observed worldwide. (The dates of festivals vary from year to year because Hinduism follows a lunar calendar. The months begin around the fifteenth day of the solar months, with the year beginning in the month of Chaitra [March/April]. See Appendix B for a calendar.)

Dassehra (Dusserah)—The festival lasting "ten days," reflecting the name of the celebration. This is perhaps the most popular of all festivals and is celebrated throughout the country for ten days in September/October. The first nine days are devoted to the worship of the goddess Durga in her nine guises; the 10th day is a celebration of the victory of Rama, hero of the Ramayana, over Ravana, demon king of Sri Lanka.

Dipavali (Diwali)—The festival of lamps. This celebration honors Lakshmi, the goddess of wealth and good fortune, over a five-day period in September/October or October/November. It also commemorates Rama's victory over Ravana and Rama's return to the city of Ayodhya.

Sri Ramakrishna Jayanti—This celebration, in February, marks the birthday of the great nineteenth-century mystic, Sri Ramakrishna.

Shivaratri (Night of Shiva)—Celebrated throughout India in February/March by all Hindus, regardless of caste or class, it is at this time that Shiva manifests himself in the form of the flaming *linga* (the phallus, characteristic symbol of Shiva) to shower his grace on his devotees.

Holi—One of the most popular of Hindu festivals, this two-day spring festival celebrated in February/March marks the end of winter.

Rama-navami—The birthday of Rama, celebrated in March/April.

Sri-Krishna-Jayanti—The birthday of Krishna, celebrated in July/August or August/September.

Pilgrimage to sacred sites such as cities or rivers is especially important not only for Hindus but also for Indians of other religions.

Worship (*puja*) of a deity in human or abstract form or any object considered sacred is performed publicly and privately within the home. It may be a simple offering or a sequence of services, each one accompanied by a *mantra* or sacred sounds in the form of formulae, syllables, phrases, or hymns. The idea of a *puja* is to honor the invited and invoked deity.

Life-cycle rituals include the birth ceremony, first feeding of the baby, giving of the baby's name, learning of the alphabet, initiation rite (the male child of the upper classes undergoes a spiritual rebirth and so becomes twice-born), marriage, and the funeral rite.

Main Subgroups

Traditionally, Hindus are grouped according to which deity is considered the chief divinity of devotion:

> **Shaiva Hindus** worship Shiva as their main divinity, together with divinities associated with him, such as the consort of Shiva, Parvati; Ganga, the deified Ganges River; the children of Shiva and Parvati: Ganesha and Skanda; and particular animals associated with Shiva: the cobra (*naga*) and Nandi, the bull.

> **Vaishnava Hindus** worship Vishnu or one of his incarnations. He is perhaps the most popular deity, especially in two earthly forms: (1) Krishna, who appears as the supreme lord-teacher of the popular scripture, the Bhagavad-Gita; as the impish child who steals butter and slays demons and who subdued the serpent Kaliya as an adolescent; and as the paramour of the *gopis* or cow-girls; and (2) Rama, the hero of the Ramayana who defeats the demon king of Sri Lanka, Ravana; and husband to the ideal of Hindu womanhood, Sita.

Many Hindus honor the Goddess (Devi) in one of her many manifestations representing the mother, life, and fertility. Sometimes referred to as *Shakta Hindus,* one of the most popular manifestations is Durga, the slayer of the Buffalo-Demon. Other goddesses include Annapurna, the beneficent goddess; Kali, the personification of the goddess's anger; and Sarasvati, the goddess of learning.

Many subdivisions of Hinduism also exist that follow the teachings of a great philosopher in the past, such as Shankara (788–820) or Ramanuja (1017–1137); or a leader of a devotional movement, such as Caitanya (1486–1533), the inspiration of the present-day Hare Krishnas; or a host of modern teachers or gurus, such as Sri Ramakrishna (1836–1886), the guru of Swami Vivekananda (Swami Vivekananda founded the Vedanta Society), and Aurobindo Ghose (1872–1950).

Common Misunderstandings and Stereotypes

What most non-Hindus know about Hinduism centers around certain popular misconceptions regarding cows, idol worship, rebirth, nonviolence, the caste system, and the almost incalculable number of divinities. Although based partly in fact, these misconceptions draw false conclusions and fail to recognize that Hindus are not unanimous in their own opinions of the above. Cows are venerated throughout India, but it is more a reflex or habit on the part of most Hindus, not conscious reflection. The cow is indeed venerated in some festivals such as Pongal, a festival held in southern India in January marking the end of the harvest season. The cow is extremely important because of its role in the agricultural areas of India and its close association with the earth.

Hindus use both anthropomorphic and abstract images of deities in worship, but this use is not idolatry in the strict sense. The image is not the object of worship but only the representative or container of the divinity during the period of worship. Many non-Hindus perceive Hindus to be nonviolent because of their notion of rebirth and suppose that, because a relative or family member can be reborn an animal or human, violence toward any animal or human might be directed at a former family member. Such opinions rarely arise among Hindus and are gross simplifications.

Caste does exist to this day, but many ideas about it were shaped from ancient writings or by generalizations no longer as prominent today. Although abuses exist, the attitudes toward caste are changing, especially in the cities such as Bombay (Mumbai), Calcutta, and New Delhi. Rural areas and villages, however, still retain some of the old conceptions of the hierarchical structure of caste. It is a complicated subject that defies generalization.

Finally, the number of gods is a problem for many who are not acquainted with Hinduism. Throughout India, there are thousands of names associated with the divinities, but, despite this number, Hindus are not necessarily polytheists in the strict sense. According to philosophical background and sophistication, the acceptance of many divinities and the acceptance of one underlying ground of existence or force are not mutually exclusive. For many Hindus, the divine, whether personal or impersonal, may be accepted as supreme and absolute, and the other divinities—and for that matter the whole of creation—as being only manifestations of that supreme being.

Classroom Concerns

It is recommended that teachers and other professionals avoid making generalizations and judgments about Hinduism. This religion is represented by a large number of diverse practices and teachings that defy sweeping statements. Students with an Indian background most likely will come from families that perceive and understand Hinduism through a specific tradition of a particular teacher together with the practice of certain festivals, rites, and accompanying stories of the divinities honored in the festivals. Some students may know enough to comment on whatever appears in classroom texts and should be called on to speak if they are comfortable with the situation. If not, parents or friends might be willing to give presentations on general aspects of Hinduism as they understand it. Such presentations lend an air of authenticity and are to be encouraged.

Population Data

Kosmin and Keysar's 2001 survey found 766,000 adult Hindus in the United States—a threefold increase from a comparable 1990 survey.[1] Based on recent Indian census data of 2001, the population of Hindus is slightly more than 80 percent (828 million) of the total population of India. The world population figure is over 900 million.

—*J.S.*

Further Reading

Basham, A. L. *The Wonder That Was India.* New York: Grove Press, 1954.

Flood, Gavin. *An Introduction to Hinduism.* Cambridge, England: Cambridge University Press, 1996.

Klostermaier, Klaus K. *A Survey of Hinduism.* 2nd ed. Albany, NY: SUNY Press, 1994. [Third edition expected in July 2007.]

Miller, Barbara Stoler, trans. *The Bhagavad-Gita.* Toronto: Bantam, 1986.

Mitchell, A. G. *Hindu Gods and Goddesses.* London: Her Majesty's Stationery Office, 1982.

O'Flaherty, Wendy Doniger. *Textual Sources for the Study of Hinduism.* Chicago: University of Chicago, 1990 [originally published by Manchester University Press, 1988].

Santucci, James. *Hindu Art in South and Southeast Asia.* Self-published. Fullerton: California State University, 1987.

Web Sites

http://www.adherents.com/

http://www.censusindia.net/religiondata/index.htm

http://www.bbc.co.uk/religion/religions/hinduism

http://www.sacred-texts.com/hin/index.htm

http://www.hinduwebsite.com/hinduism/hinduismatoz.asp

Notes

1. *Religion in a Free Market,* p. 27.

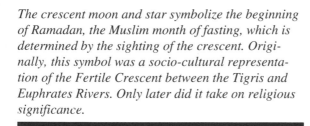

The crescent moon and star symbolize the beginning of Ramadan, the Muslim month of fasting, which is determined by the sighting of the crescent. Originally, this symbol was a socio-cultural representation of the Fertile Crescent between the Tigris and Euphrates Rivers. Only later did it take on religious significance.

Islam

Origins

Islam (meaning "peace through total submission to God's will") began with a series of divine revelations to Prophet Muhammad in about 610 C.E. in which he received his mission to bring belief in one God (monotheism) to the people of Arabia and humankind generally. However, the religion received its greatest impetus through the Hijrah [HEEJ-rah] in 622 C.E. (the year 0 in the Muslim calendar) when Muhammad was forced to flee for his life from Mecca in the Arabian peninsula to Medina, where he established the first Muslim community.

Beliefs

Muslims are monotheists who accept the same God as Jews and Christians but call the deity Allah [al-LAAH] (Arabic for "the God"). They revere the same biblical figures, including Noah, Abraham, and Moses. Jesus is also considered a prophet, but not the divine son of God, and Muhammad is the final prophet. Hence, the Muslim declaration of faith (creed) simply states: "There is no deity except Allah, and Muhammad is his messenger." Muslims believe in an afterlife of rewards or punishment.

Sacred Books/Scriptures

The Qur'an [koor-AAN] (less accurately spelled Koran) is the sole scripture of Islam. The Old Testament (Hebrew Bible) and New Testament are respected as earlier revelations from Allah, but errors and loss of material have rendered them less accurate over time. Consequently, they are not considered equal to the Qur'an, which is understood by Muslims as "setting the record straight" on particular points. It is the literal word of God revealed to Muhammad from age forty through the remaining twenty-three years of his life. He memorized the revelations and dictated them to various disciples, who also memorized and, in some cases, wrote them down. A few years later, Zaid ibn Thabit collected this material into what is now known as the Qur'an. The scripture, written in Arabic, consists of a series of 114 chapters (suras) arranged roughly in descending order of length.

Recorded sayings and deeds of the Prophet—as distinct from Allah's words in the Qur'an—are known as hadith and are found in various collections, six of which are considered most authoritive.

Practices

The Muslim way of life rests on the Five Pillars: the creed "There is no deity except Allah and Muhammad is his messenger"; prayer five times daily (at dawn, noon, afternoon, sunset, and night); fasting from dawn until sunset during the lunar month of Ramadan (no food, drink, or sexual relations); almsgiving (generally reckoned at 2.5 percent of one's savings); and a one-time pilgrimage (Hajj) to Mecca (or Makkah), Islam's holiest city, by all who are physically and financially able. The exact implementation of the pillars and other practices is dictated by the Sunnah [SOON-nah], the customary way Prophet Muhammad did things. For example, the Qur'an mandates that Muslims pray daily, and the Sunnah instructs one on the exact times and manner of praying.

The Muslim day of communal worship is Friday, when Muslim men are required to gather at noon in the mosque (*masjid*) for prayer and a sermon by the imam [ee-MOM], or prayer leader. (Women may also attend but are not obliged to do so.) Friday is not a day of rest in the Jewish or Christian sense, but some Muslims may take the day off—or part of it—where possible.

Muslim Holidays

All Muslims observe two holidays:

> **Eid al-Fitr** [eed ul-FI-tur] (Festival of Fast-Breaking)—The lesser of the two holidays, Eid al-Fitr occurs immediately after the Ramadan fast on the first day of the following month and is a time of feasting and gift giving.

> **Eid al-Adha** [eed ul-ad-HAA] (Festival of Sacrifice)—Eid al-Adha occurs on the tenth day of the twelfth lunar month when pilgrimages are made to Mecca. Besides being a festive time, Eid al-Adha is a period of sacrifice

commemorating the prophet Abraham's willingness to offer up his son Ishmael. Because Allah provided Abraham a ram instead, Muslims sacrifice an animal as part of the rites of the Hajj (pilgrimage) and give away one-third to needy families and one-third to friends.

A third holiday is celebrated by Shi'a Muslims:

Ashura [AA-shu-raah] (Martyrdom of Hussein)—This holiday is celebrated on the tenth day of the first lunar month and commemorates the defeat of Ali's son Hussein at Karbala (modern-day Iraq) while defending his Shi'a followers.

Because Muslims use a lunar calendar that is about eleven days shorter than the solar cycle, the solar date of Muslim holidays—and the month of Ramadan—move through the seasons in a thirty-two-year cycle. It is hoped that more and more secular and school district calendars will begin to list these holidays, as they do Christian and Jewish ones. This will make it much easier for schools with Muslim populations to avoid scheduling school events on these days.

Note that the majority of Muslims rely on the actual sighting of the new crescent moon on day twenty-nine of Ramadan to determine when the month of fasting has ended. If it is not sighted because of weather conditions, the fast is continued for one more day. Hence, the calendar date of Eid al-Fitr could possibly be one day premature. Further, all Muslim days begin at sundown (as in Judaism). Thus, when a non-Muslim calendar shows that a Muslim holiday begins on a particular day, be aware that it actually starts the evening before.

Dietary Rules

Muslims are forbidden to eat pork or pork derivatives, and meat must be slaughtered according to Islamic law. (Muslims in the West often eat Jewish kosher foods to be sure that no pork is present.) However, Muslims are permitted to eat in the homes of others "who have received the Scripture" (Qur'an, surah 5:5)—Jews and Christians—without worrying about the status of the food. Muslims must also refrain from consuming alcohol and other intoxicating substances.

Circumcision of male children is required, but female circumcision is neither required nor approved.

Main Subgroups

Sunni—About 85 to 90 percent of Muslims worldwide belong to this branch of the faith (Sunnah in Arabic means "customary practice," that is, the practice of the prophet Muhammad). Sunni Muslims rejected the notion that Prophet Muhammad's blood descendants should inherit his authority and opted instead for the election of their leader, or caliph.

Shi'a (or Shi'i)—The smaller branch derives its name from Shi'a (party of) Ali, the Prophet Muhammad's cousin and son-in-law. Shi'a Muslims venerate a series of Ali's descendants as imams, or revered leaders, the last of whom will return at the end of time to redeem the world. Shi'ism also holds that the Qur'an contains hidden meanings that refer to Ali. Iran, Iraq, Lebanon, Bahrain, and Azerbaijan are the countries where Shi'a Muslims constitute the majority.

Sufism—Not a branch as such, Sufism is a mystical movement within Islam dating from the eighth century that stresses Allah's immanence and the possibility of mystical union with him. It is popularly known through the "Whirling Dervishes" once prominent in Turkey but suppressed in 1925 by Turkish ruler Ataturk. Small Sufi communities now exist in North America.

In the United States, where Muslims are a minority religion, rivalry between Sunnis and Shi'is is minimal, and one's identity as a Muslim is foremost. Hence, inter-marriage between a Sunni and Shi'a Muslim is not problematic, as it is in some predominantly Islamic countries.

Some 300,000 African American adults are Muslims and comprise 27 percent of all U.S. Muslims.[1] However, Louis Farrakhan's Nation of Islam (with perhaps 20,000 adherents) is not considered a legitimate Islamic group by U.S. Muslim authorities. Still, the Nation of Islam's members follow most Muslim practices, such as the Five Pillars. They do not, however, accept the Muslim belief that people of all colors and ethnicities are equal in God's sight and thus may belong to Islam.

Common Misunderstandings and Stereotypes

"This religion is known as 'Muhammadanism.' "

Although this term is still found in some older books, it is completely inaccurate. Muhammad was not a divine being, according to Islam, but simply God's last and greatest prophet. Muslims stress that the religion consists of submission to God, not Muhammad. *Islam* (from a root word meaning to submit) is the name of the religion, and *Muslim* (more accurate phonetically than "Moslem") is the name for one who submits to God via adherence to this religion.

"Islam is a militaristic religion."

This idea springs in part from an oversimplified reading of history in which Islam is viewed to have spread initially by armed force. In fact, most people accepted Islam freely, consistent with the saying in the Qur'an that "there shall be no compulsion in religion" (surah 2:256). The charge of militarism also stems from a misunderstanding of the term *jihad*. It does mean "military struggle in defense of Islam," and some of Islam's principles for defensive warfare anticipated the current Geneva Accords on this issue. However, it does not mean "holy war." Moreover, the primary meaning of jihad is "spiritual struggle or striving to become a better Muslim." Acts of terrorism by a small minority of Muslims—especially in connection with the September 11 attacks and al-Qaeda global terrorism—have also caused some people to label all Muslims as fanatics or terrorists.

"Muslims condone suicide terror attacks in some circumstances."

Islam unequivocally forbids suicide (see surah 4:29) and attacks against civilian populations. Muslims who commit such acts are doing so from a twisted understanding of their religion, perhaps under the influence of real or perceived injustices against their coreligionists.

"Muslims are prudish and puritanical."

Although Islam stresses modesty and prohibits the use of alcohol, sexual love in marriage is considered a great blessing from God. Ironically, earlier Western views of Islam stressed its male licentiousness, as exemplified by Muhammad's having been married to several women (although only after his first wife Khadija had died) and the practice of polygamy (see below). This, too, is a caricature.

"Islam is a religion that suppresses women."

Most of the criticisms of Islam in this respect stem from local customs or practices in particular countries or regions and have no basis in Islamic doctrine. For example, Islam does not condone female circumcision, which predates the religion and is most widely practiced in sub-Saharan Africa where educated Muslims are trying to eliminate it. On the positive side, a woman after marriage retains whatever property or possessions she owns, has full rights over her property (to buy, sell, etc.) and wage earnings, and has specific inheritance rights guaranteed by the Qur'an. It is true that a woman may not serve as imam or prayer leader, but this prohibition parallels the refusal of Orthodox Judaism and Roman Catholicism to ordain women as clergy. Finally, a word about polygamy: it is permitted, but not encouraged. A man may marry up to four wives, but only if he can financially and emotionally support each wife, with equality—no small task.

Classroom Concerns

Teachers should familiarize themselves with the dates of the two principal Muslim holidays, Eid al-Fitr and Eid al-Adha, and with the Ramadan fast (see "Practices" above) and make allowances for students who must be absent from school (and, in the case of physical education classes, for those who are fasting). Teachers should also try to be sensitive to students who need to do their required prayer while at school.

Because Islam generally prohibits art that represents a human being, it is recommended that teachers provide alternative assignments in art classes. More important, though, teachers should discuss the matter with the student, because many Muslim authorities permit depiction under certain circumstances (e.g., anatomy diagrams, instructional illustrations, and figurative toys for children).

Islamic rules of modesty may require that Muslim students wear sweat pants (at least to the knees) and long-sleeved T-shirts in physical education classes. It is recommended that teachers permit this even if other students are wearing gym shorts. Also, some Muslim girls may wear a head covering (*hijab*), a symbol of modesty, in school. To avoid leaving such students open to ridicule, teachers might want to explain these customs to other students in the class.

Male and female students might wish to be seated among same-sex members of the class and should be given this option. Similarly, dating, mixed-sex dancing, and other forms of premarital intimacy are not permitted in Islam. Consequently, it is suggested that Muslim students not be urged to attend proms and other social activities that bring boys and girls together.

Because Muslims are not comfortable with some of the practices surrounding Halloween and Valentine's Day, care should be taken that they not be required to participate in classroom projects related to these days.

Although dogs may be used for hunting or security, they are normally not found inside Muslim homes. (Dog saliva is considered unhealthy by most Muslims.) Consequently, care should be taken to alert Muslim students ahead of time if a dog is to be brought to school as part of a school program or for some other purpose (e.g., a seeing-eye dog).

Finally, as is the case with observant Jewish students, school cafeterias should provide an alternative entrée for Muslim students if pork products are being served. Other food may be eaten.

Population Data

There are an estimated 1.3 billion Muslims worldwide, with large concentrations in the Arab world, sub-Saharan Africa, Iran, India, Pakistan, Bangladesh, and Indonesia.[2] Kosmin and Keysar report an adult Muslim population in the United States of 1,000,104. However, they note that "there is undercounting of religious minorities beyond our ability to weight the data on demographic variables" because of language problems and fear of answering personal questions regarding religion. So they also provide an "upper range estimate" of 2,200,000 adult Muslims.[3] Half of the Muslim population is married; if these couples have on average two children, we arrive at a total "upper range" population of 5,400,000—reasonably close to estimates within the Muslim community itself.

—B.H.

Further Reading

Armstrong, Karen. *Islam: A Short History.* New York: Modern Library, 2002.

Esposito, John L. *Islam: The Straight Path.* New York: Oxford University Press, 1991.

Hassaballa, Hesham A., and Kabir Helminski. *The Beliefnet Guide to Islam.* New York: Doubleday, 2006.

Nasr, Seyyed Hossein. *The Heart of Islam: Enduring Values for Humanity.* New York: HarperCollins, 2002.

Web Sites

http://www.islamicity.com

http://www.islam101.com

http://www.freemuslims.org

Notes

1. Kosmin and Keysar, pp. 264–65.

2. www.adherents.com

3. Kosmin and Keysar, pp. 262, 265.

The symbol of Jainism is that of a wheel on the palm of the hand. The wheel has twenty-four spokes representing the twenty-four Great Teachers in the Jain tradition; the five fingers of the hand represent the five Great Vows, and within the central portion of the wheel is the word ahimsâ *(nonviolence; not shown in this version of the symbol).*

Jainism

Origins

From a historical perspective, the religion we know as Jainism [JÎ-nism] was most probably established by Mahavira, "the Great Hero" (so called because he stands fast in the midst of dangers and fears and bears up under all hardships). An older contemporary of the Buddha, Vardhamana Mahavira was born most likely in 599 or 598 B.C.E. (dates vary) and died around 527 or 526 B.C.E. In Jain tradition, however, Mahavira was but the last of a long line of twenty-four Great Teachers known as *Tirthankaras* [Teer-TUN-karas] ("Ford-makers"), who reestablished the ancient spiritual path and truth. Of these twenty-four, the only other likely historical figure who may have had a hand in establishing a Jain movement was the previous Great Teacher, Parshvanatha (872 or 817–772 B.C.E.).

The name of the religion reflects the nature of the founders: Jain refers to a follower of a *jina* or (spiritual) victor. All the Great Teachers are *jinas* because they have acquired supreme knowledge and have overcome all inner imperfections such as greed and anger. They are Tirthankaras by virtue of their providing the means by which suffering can be conquered. As such, a Tirthankara is a teacher of salvation.

121

The life of Mahavira (and Parshvanatha) follows the pattern of the religious hero and, not unlike the life of the Buddha, includes miracles and marvels. Born in the northern Indian state of Bihar and raised in a family belonging to the second class of society (administrators, rulers, and protectors), he spent his first thirty years living among householders (who, coincidentally, were followers of Parshvanatha). He married Yashoda at sixteen and had a daughter (one sect of Jains, the Digambaras, deny both his marriage and fatherhood). Like the Buddha, Mahavira lived in a palace surrounded by opulence. At the age of thirty, he received permission from his elder brother and other authorities to leave the palace, his family, and possessions. He went to a park near his hometown, removed his ornaments, pulled out his hair in five handfuls, fasted for two and one-half days, and put on the robes of an ascetic (practitioner of penance) for a year. He then renounced clothing and entered the homeless, wandering life of a renunciant. After a period of twelve years of wandering, meditating, and fasting for long periods of time, he attained "complete, perfect or infinite knowledge," becoming omniscient. He thus knew completely the affairs of all living beings in the world and the previous and future births of gods, humans, animals, and demons. As a Tirthankara for the next thirty years, he became a wandering teacher attracting disciples from all walks of life, eventually organizing a community into a fourfold order consisting of monks, nuns, laymen, and laywomen. At age seventy-two, after giving a forty-eight-hour sermon to his followers, he died in the city of Pava (some 250 years after the liberation of Parshvanatha, according to tradition).

Beliefs

The goal of the Jain is the liberation of the soul from the bondage of this world of suffering, ignorance, pain, and rebirth. What causes bondage and rebirth is *karma* (action), so ultimately all action must be abandoned. Inherently connected to this goal is *ahimsa* (nonviolence), which is the very basis of Jainism. No living being is to be harmed, injured, oppressed, enslaved, or killed—including microorganisms, plants, insects, animals, and humans. Realistically, this goal can only be approximated by the ascetic and homeless monks and nuns, not by the lay community.

In addition, nonattachment to materiality is also important to the Jain practitioner. It is, therefore, to be expected that Jainism is a religion that is ideally practiced by ascetics, not by the lay community. At the inception of the religion, the attitude persisted that the laypeople could not help but perform violent actions or be attached to worldly things because of the needs of survival in this world. This attitude, however, has changed considerably over the millennia with the recognition that ascetics were dependent on lay support. Therefore, a place was found for the participation of laypeople in Jain practice, although the ascetic life is still the ideal.

Jainism today stresses religious tolerance, purity of action, and proper religious attitude. These are reflected in the Three Jewels of the religion: (1) Right insight allows one to see reality according to its true nature. (2) Right knowledge involves the intellectual understanding of the insight. (3) Right conduct is the action necessary to realize this insight.

Liberation or freedom is achieved when all actions (*karma*) are destroyed. *Karma* itself refers not only to actions and their results but also to material residue that associates itself with the soul. There are many varieties of *karma*: Some karmic actions can be destroyed by the knowledge and practice revealed by Mahavira and the Great Teachers who came before him. Some karmic actions cannot be altered by practice or knowledge. One's gender, length of life, species (human or nonhuman), family, and personality, for instance, are all determined by past *karma*s. However, if a person is liberated, there will be no return to this or any other world of suffering. The soul will then rise to the top of the universe, where only liberated souls reside, beyond the lower, earthly and heavenly worlds of the unliberated. Those souls not liberated will be reborn in a body (human or nonhuman) and location appropriate to the *karma* performed in their previous lives.

Sacred Books/Scriptures

The Jain canon formerly consisted of about sixty books, divided into three sections. The first section, known as the *Purva* ("Previous" or "Ancient"), consisted of fourteen texts that supposedly date back to the time of Parshvanatha. Although lost, the subject matter is listed in later works. Subjects such as astrology and methods of attaining occult and psychic powers were included in the *Purva* texts.

The other two sections of the canon that comprise the present canon are the *Angas* ("Limbs")—twelve in number though the last work, the *Drishtivada*, is lost—and the *Angabahya* ("Outer Limb"), which in turn is subdivided into the twelve *Upanga* ("Subsidiary Limbs"); the seven (one of which is lost) *Cheda-sutras* ("Aphorisms or Scriptures on the Reduction of a Monk's Seniority," in other words, monastic discipline); the four *Mulasutras* ("Root Scriptures"); the ten *Prakirnaka-sutras* ("Mixed or Miscellaneous Scriptures"); and the *Culika-sutras* ("Appendix").

The forty-five texts comprise the canon for most Shvetambara [shvay-TUM-ba-ra] Jains, more specifically, the Image Worshipping Assembly (see "Main Subgroups" below), as opposed to the aniconic (image-denying) subgroups within the Shvetambara community: the Sthanakavasis and Terapanthis , who recognize a thirty-two-book canon. The other major division of Jainism, the Digambara [di-GUM-ba-ra], recognize the names of the Purva and Anga texts but assert that these texts have not survived in their original form. Topics that appear in these texts of the Shvetambara canon include monastic discipline, doctrinal issues, a discussion of non-Jaina teachings, mythology, cosmology, and biographies of those who are reborn as gods and who transcended rebirth altogether.

Practices

Jainism stresses practice rather than doctrine. It is not surprising, therefore, to find a multitude of practices for ascetics and laypersons. Both must follow five practices, known as Great Vows for ascetics, Restricted Vows for lay persons. The only distinction between the two is the degree of stringency of practice, with the demands on the ascetics much greater. The five vows are as follows:

1. abstention from violence (for ascetics, it is total; for laypersons, it is recognized that violence or injury does occur through no fault of the layperson);

2. abstention from lying;

3. abstention from taking what is not given;

4. abstention from sexual activity (for ascetics, it is complete chastity; for laypersons, any sexual activity outside of marriage); and

5. abstention from attachment. Besides these, an additional seven vows are undertaken by laypersons—three Subsidiary Vows and four Vows of Instruction.

Subsidiary Vows, which expand on the Restricted Vows, include:

1. restriction of travel;

2. restriction from certain foods (such as garlic, carrots, and ginger); and

3. restriction from certain activities that might be harmful (gambling or any activity that might promote violence).

The four Vows of Instruction include:

1. meditation (to achieve a state of equanimity);

2. further restrictions on travel;

3. fasting on certain days of the month; and

4. charity.

In addition, there are certain food restrictions (as noted in point 2 of the Subsidiary Vows above) that are almost universally practiced: not eating meat, figs, or honey nor partaking in alcohol. Vegetarianism, therefore, is strictly practiced, involving abstinence from not only meat, eggs, milk products, and fish, but also certain fruits and vegetables, such as onions, garlic, and fruit with lots of seeds. Onions and garlic are included under their notion of meat, because they are believed to possess lifeforms (perhaps due to their shape), as does the earlier-mentioned fruit.

Both ascetics and laypersons may also practice a "religious death," the practice of fasting and meditation that will gradually lead to one's demise. The practice is rare, however.

Ascetics, of which only a small proportion makes up the total Jain population, practice total renunciation. Central to all Jain practice, lay and ascetic, is nonviolence. With this in mind, any activity that might cause violence is avoided, including a number of activities that seem innocent enough: bathing, fanning oneself, walking on greenery or touching a living plant, and digging. All can be harmful to living organisms. Shvetambara Jain monks wear a mouth shield to filter out microorganisms. All ascetics undergo an initiation that symbolizes a spiritual rebirth. The male initiate then takes on the lineage name of his teacher, renounces all clothing if he is a Digambara ascetic (nuns are not allowed to go naked), takes the three robes if he is a Shvetambara ascetic, and wears a mouth shield if the male or female ascetic is a Sthanikavasi or Terapanthi. In addition to undertaking the five Great Vows, ascetics undertake certain "essential duties," which are also recommended for the laity: a form of meditation or spiritual activity known as "equanimity," praise of the twenty-four Great Teachers, homage to the ascetic's teacher, repentance, abandonment of the body (assuming a motionless position, standing or sitting), and abandonment of certain foods or activities.

Worship directed toward a Great Teacher or Tirthankara is also performed in the temple, which includes walking around the image of the Tirthankara three times, sprinkling and drying the image, offering eight substances (water, sandalwood paste, flowers, incense, a lamp, uncooked rice, sweets, fruits), reciting the names of the twenty-four Tirthankaras, and performing the waving of lamps before the image.

Certain holidays are considered very significant, such as the anniversary of Mahavira's birth (April/May) and death (or final liberation; October/November). An important event, the Paryushana Parva, takes place in August/September. For a period of eight or ten days (for Shvetambaras and Digambaras respectively), laypersons fast; worship Mahavira; listen to a recitation of his biography; and, in the concluding portion of the event, make known their sins, ask for forgiveness, and extend their own forgiveness to all. Three other holidays are shared by Jains and Hindus: Rakhi (celebration of love and friendship; August); Dusserah (celebration of good over evil; October/November); and Diwali (festival of lights; October/November).

Main Subgroups

Jains are divided into two major divisions or traditions: the *Shvetambara* and *Digambara*. The differences between the two are primarily ones of outward appearance and ascetic practice, which are regarded as an index to the proper understanding of the doctrine. One important difference is that Digambara male ascetics practice nudity; Shvetambara ascetics do not. Another is that Digambara ascetics do not use bowls for eating (only cupped hands), whereas Shvetambara ascetics do.

Besides these differences, there are important differences regarding the status of women. Women were allowed to enter mendicant (begging) orders, but Digambaras place female ascetics on a lower level than male ascetics because they are not to go naked. Shvetambaras, however, place women on a more equal level, but women ascetics are required to pay homage to even a newly initiated monk. Women cannot reach the same level of omniscience as men in the opinion of Digambaras, whereas Shvetambaras believe they can.

Another important difference is the interpretation of the Great Teachers (*jinas* or "spiritual victors"). Digambaras consider them to be omniscient, therefore devoid of sensual perception and in constant meditation. A *jina,* therefore, communicates the teachings not through the voice or by example but through means of the "divine sound." It is supposedly understood by his audience and converted to scriptural tracts by his disciples. Shvetambaras, however, believe that the *jinas* can be both omniscient and engage in human activities.

One final difference concerns the scriptures. Digambaras reject Shvetambara scriptures.

Common Misunderstandings and Stereotypes

Jainism is not well known in the United States, but pockets of Jainism are developing in major metropolitan areas. What little is known about the religion is its strict adherence to nonviolence (familiar to Americans through the Rev. Martin Luther King Jr.'s teaching and practice) and vegetarianism. A misconception that might arise is the degree of adherence to these practices. Laypersons are not expected to be as strict in these practices as ascetics.

"Total nonviolence is unrealistic."

Jains look at the outside world with its incessant violence causing death and destruction and ask how unrealistic their worldview really is.

Classroom Concerns

The Jain adherence to nonviolence and strict vegetarianism might present some problems for teachers and school administrators. Any action that is perceived as violent is ideally to be avoided by a Jain student. Dissection in biology classes presents an obvious problem. Contact sports in gym classes may also be inappropriate for the student. Discussion of violent events in history (wars, for instance) may not be viewed in the same light as that expressed in textbooks or in the classroom, especially if the war is glorified. It is recommended that teachers speak to the parents of the student should a problem arise. Vegetarian lunch choices should always be available for Jain children.

Population Data

Jainism is a small religion when compared with other traditional faiths. There are 75,000 Jains in the United States and Canada, with more than 60,000 in the United States alone. This is the figure given by the editor of the *Jain Directory* (quoted in Prothero and Tweed, p. 309). Sources such as the *World Almanac and Book of Facts 2000* (on Adherents.com) give a much lower figure: 7,000 for North America. The *Statistical Abstract of the United States, 1997: The National Data Book* (published by the U.S. Department of Commerce) places the figure at 5,000 as of 1996.[1] For a calculation on the figure 75,000-85,000, see Jain-List.[2] Adherents.com estimates the worldwide Jain population at 4.2 million.

—J.S.

Further Reading

Dundas, Paul. *The Jains.* 2nd ed. London: Routledge, 2002.

Jaini, Padmanabh S. *The Jaina Path of Purification.* Delhi: Motilal Banarsidass Publishers, 1979.

Prothero, Stephen A., and Thomas A. Tweed. *Asian Religions in America: A Documentary History.* New York: Oxford University Press, 1999.

Web Sites

http://www.beliefnet.com/story/80/story_8048_1.html

http://www.bbc.co.uk/religion/religions/jainism/index.shtml

http://philtar.ucsm.ac.uk/encyclopedia/jainism/index.html

Notes

1. Available at http://books.google.com/books?vid=ISBN0160492807&id=Nn-RQGzkcx8C& pg=PA828&ots=QvOxKXU9N1&dq=population+of+Jains+in+the+U.S. Accessed February 23, 2007.

2. Available at http://groups.yahoo.com/group/jainlist/. Accessed August 7, 2006.

The Star of David (Magen David, or *"Shield of David"* in Hebrew) *probably had no historical connection to King David. Its first use as a Jewish symbol may have been on the frieze of a synagogue in Capernaum in the second century C.E. In 1354, the Jews of Prague used it on their first state-sanctioned flag, and by the 1600s, it appeared as the official seal of the Jewish community there. In 1897, it became the seal of the First Zionist Congress, and in 1948, it was made the central emblem on the flag of the new State of Israel.*

Judaism

Origins

The Jewish people trace their origins to the biblical patriarch Abraham. Judaism as a religious system began about 1250 B.C.E. with Moses, whom God commanded to lead the Hebrew slaves out of Egypt and with whom God established a covenant or pact on Mount Sinai. Although the ancient Israelites had their own God whose sacred name was YHWH/Yahweh (see the Book of Exodus 3:14)—a name most Jews do not pronounce for fear of using it disrespectfully)—strict monotheism probably did not develop until after the Babylonian exile of the Jewish nation in 538 B.C.E.

Beliefs

Judaism centers on belief in one God (monotheism) who chose the Jews to carry on an ethical and religious lifestyle spelled out in the Torah (the first five books of the Bible and commentaries thereon). A traditional summation of Jewish belief is to imagine the Jewish people, the Torah, and the land of Israel (the promised land) as three points on a triangle with God at the center. Judaism has no elaborate creed but instead stresses the observance of the commandments in the Torah and, more generally, the living of an ethical life.

129

The essence of Jewish faith is perhaps best expressed in the words of Deuteronomy 6:4 (known in Hebrew as the Sh'ma): "Hear, O Israel, the Lord is your God, the Lord alone." It is said at every Jewish Sabbath service.

Although more traditional Jews do believe in an afterlife of rewards and punishments, Jews generally—unlike Christians and Muslims—do not emphasize the idea. In fact, more liberal Jews are quite agnostic on the point and hardly discuss it. Life is to be lived here and now for its own sake. Thus, the familiar expression *L'Haim,* "To life!"

Sacred Books/Scriptures

The Hebrew Bible (so named because it is written almost entirely in the Hebrew language) consists of three parts: the Torah (the law or recital), the Prophets (Joshua, Judges, Isaiah, Jeremiah, etc.), and the Writings (Psalms, Proverbs, the Book of Job, etc.). Its contents are the same as what Christians call the Old Testament, although arranged in a somewhat different order. Jews do not call it the "Old Testament," meaning "old covenant," because this would imply acceptance of the New Testament/covenant, which is exclusive to Christianity.

In addition to the Bible, Jewish life over the centuries has been profoundly influenced by the Talmud, an interpretation of the 613 laws found in the Torah (Genesis, Exodus, Leviticus, Numbers, and Deuteronomy). The Talmud is a vast and complex document. It explains precisely how various commandments, such as hallowing the Sabbath, are to be observed. It also presents stories about famous early rabbis, medical lore, and other material about living according to Jewish tradition.

Practices

Some Jews "keep kosher" by following a dietary code that permits only certain foods to be eaten (no pork products, shellfish, or meat-eating animals, for example). Meat must come from a kosher market (ensuring that the animal has been correctly slaughtered and all its blood removed). Also, meat and dairy products may not be eaten at the same meal. Jews who follow this system must not eat in the homes of friends who do not keep kosher or in nonkosher restaurants.

Orthodox Jewish males wear a yarmulke [YAR-mul-keh], a small head covering that signifies respect for the presence of God, and an undershirt with tassels that serves as a constant reminder of the commandments one must observe.

Jewish males are circumcised on the eighth day after birth as a sign of the covenant with God. The ritual is performed by a specially trained individual, a mohel [MOY-el]. A baby-naming ceremony for girls is now common among more liberal Jews.

The ceremony of entry into adult Jewish life is the *Bar* (son) or *Bat* (daughter) **Mitzvah** (of the commandment). Boys at age thirteen and girls at twelve or thirteen conduct a synagogue service, read part of that week's portion from the Torah in Hebrew, and address the community. A celebration follows the service, and it is customary for guests to bring a gift. Anything an ordinary teenager would like is appropriate, or religious items may be given.

The Sabbath, the most important holiday, lasts from sundown on Friday until one hour after sundown on Saturday. A festive meal ushers in this holiday. Many Jews refrain from workaday activities (including, in the case of Orthodox Jews, driving a car and using the telephone) on the Sabbath. Jews attend synagogue services, led by a rabbi, either on Friday evening or Saturday morning.

Among the other Jewish holidays—all of which are on a lunar calendar and thus movable—four have the most effect on the lives of American Jews:

> **Rosh Hashanah** [rowsh ha-SHAN-ah] (The Jewish New Year)—Although a time of rejoicing, this holiday initiates a ten-day period of reflection on how well one has lived during the year just ended. Celebrated in September/October.

> **Yom Kippur** [yohm kee-POOR] (The Day of Atonement)—This holiday is celebrated ten days after the Jewish New Year. Jews fast for twenty-four hours from all food and drink and spend time in prayer and reflection.

> **Hanukkah** [HA-nu-kah]—The Festival of Lights, celebrated in December and lasting for eight days, commemorates the Jerusalem Temple's rededication in 165 B.C.E. after a severe religious persecution. Each evening, candles are lighted in the home to commemorate the legend that the temple sanctuary light, after being rekindled, miraculously kept burning for eight days even though having enough oil for only one day. More important than the legend is that the light of Judaism, threatened with extinction, kept glowing because of the heroism of Jews who refused to forsake their faith.

> **Passover**—This March/April holiday commemorates the Hebrews' exodus or escape from Egypt and consists of an elaborate meal known as the Seder [SAY-der], in the home. No food containing yeast may be eaten during the eight days of Passover.

All Jewish holidays begin at sundown. Consequently, when a secular calendar gives a particular date as the start of a holiday, be aware that it actually begins the evening before. Most Jews will not go to work or school on the Jewish New Year, the Day of Atonement, or Passover. Orthodox and Conservative Jews will do the same on the day after the New Year, the first two and last two days of the eight-day Passover festival, and on two other holidays: Sukkot (the Feast of Tabernacles), in September/October, and Shavuot (the Feast of Weeks), in May/June.

Main Subgroups

> **Orthodox**—The most traditional Jews, the Orthodox, adhere strictly to the interpretation of Jewish life contained in the Talmud (see "Sacred Books/Scriptures," above). They comprise about 7 percent of practicing Jews in the United States. Within a notable subgroup of Orthodoxy, Hasidic Judaism, males dress in black suits and hats and wear beards.

Conservative—Although quite observant in areas such as keeping the Sabbath and the dietary laws, Conservative Jews are more willing than Orthodox to reinterpret Talmudic traditions to correspond with changed modern conditions. They will, for example, drive to the synagogue on Saturday for services. They comprise about 38 percent of practicing Jews in the United States.

Reconstructionist—A fairly recent offshoot of the Conservative movement, Reconstructionism stresses Judaism as a civilization or culture, rather than simply a religion, and rejects the notion of Jews as a chosen people. Less then 2 percent of practicing Jews are Reconstructionist, although the movement is growing.

Reform—The Reform branch is the most liberal and does not require such traditional practices as keeping kosher or strictly observing the Sabbath. Reform practice is based on the premise that the Bible is of human origin, so that each individual must decide what God wants of him or her. The movement stresses ethical conduct as the centerpiece of religion. Of practicing Jews in the United States, about 43 percent are Reform.

A note about Jews for Jesus, Messianic Jews, Hebrew Christians, and similar groups: Jews in these organizations have converted to an Evangelical form of Christianity but often continue to observe Jewish holidays and other practices. They are religiously Christian although culturally Jewish in some respects but are no longer considered part of the Jewish community in the usual sense.

Common Misunderstandings and Stereotypes

"The Jews are the 'Chosen People' who consider themselves morally superior to other people."

The Jews' status as chosen people signifies not superiority but special obligations. Jews view themselves as having a mission to live a monotheistic and ethical lifestyle, but do not view themselves as morally or socially superior to any other religious or ethnic group.

"Jews are 'Christ-Killers.'"

Although some Jewish leaders at the time of Jesus opposed him, the leader of the Roman occupation in Judea, Pontius Pilate, had Jesus crucified (the Roman form of capital punishment) for fear he would start a revolution against Roman rule.

"Jews rejected 'their Messiah.'"

Jews do not accept Jesus of Nazareth as the Messiah because (1) his followers claimed he was a divine being (contrary to Jewish belief) and (2) they do not see that his coming ushered in the expected messianic period of peace and justice, and an end to the persecution of Jews.

"Hanukkah is the 'Jewish Christmas.'"

As noted above, Hanukkah's origins are completely distinct from those of Christmas. Jews do not celebrate Christmas because they do not accept Jesus as Messiah and savior.

"Jews are greedy, as typified in the expressions, 'Jew them down,' or 'Don't be a Jew.'"

During the Middle Ages in Europe, Jews were forced into the profession of money lending because Christians considered it forbidden by the Bible. Because Jews were not allowed to own land or participate in most trades until modern times in Europe, they tended to work as small shopkeepers and pawnbrokers, and later as bankers. Jewish association with these professions led to the stereotype of Jews as greedy or obsessed with money. Shakespeare's play *The Merchant of Venice*—which features Shylock, a wealthy and stingy Jew—both reflected and perpetuated this image.

Classroom Concerns

The period surrounding the Christian holidays of Christmas and Easter can be difficult for Jewish children in public schools. It is recommended that classroom activities should not include Christmas or Easter pageants or make it appear that everyone observes these holidays. School activities scheduled on Friday evenings are also a problem because of the Jewish Sabbath. School officials should also take particular care during the fall not to schedule important school events on Rosh Hashanah or Yom Kippur. It is strongly suggested that the Nazi genocide against the Jewish people, the Holocaust, be discussed in the upper grades. It is both a unique event in history and an example of the "crimes against humanity" that have been so numerous in modern times and which humankind must strive never to repeat.[1]

Population Data

There are about 13 million Jews worldwide, with the largest concentrations in the United States (5.3 million) and Israel (5.1 million).[2] Kosmin and Keysar's survey found 2,831,000 Jewish adults (down from 3,137,000 in Kosmin and Lachman's 1990 survey).[3]

—B.H.

Further Reading

Fackenheim, Emil L. *What Is Judaism? An Interpretation for the Present Age.* New York: Summit Books, 1987.

Neusner, Jacob. *The Way of Torah: An Introduction to Judaism.* 7th ed. Belmont, CA: Wadsworth, 2003.

Solomon, Norman. *Judaism: A Very Short Introduction.* New York: Oxford, 1996.

Telushkin, Joseph. *Jewish Literacy (The Most Important Things to Know about the Jewish Religion, Its People, and Its History)*. New York: William Morrow, 1991.

Telushkin, Joseph, and Dennis Prager. *Why the Jews (The Reasons for Anti-Semitism.* 2nd rev. ed. New York: Simon & Touchstone Books, 2003.

Web Sites

http://www.aish.com (an Orthodox site)

http://www.rj.org (Reform site)

http://www.uscj.org (Conservative site)

An online encyclopedia of Judaism and the State of Israel: www.Jewishvirtuallibrary.org

Notes

1. See www.Holocaust-history.org for abundant material on this topic.

2. Tal, Rami, ed. *The Jewish People Policy Planning Institute Annual Assessment 2004–05: The Jewish People between Thriving and Decline.* Jerusalem: Gefen, 2005, pp. 152–53.

3. *Religion in a Free Market,* p. 27.

*Dream Catchers trap bad dreams that come in the
night in a web, where they remain until the morning
when they are dispersed by the sun's rays or the
evaporation of the dew. Only the good dreams know
their way through the center of the web to the sleep-
ing person.*

Native American Religions

Origins

Current theories estimate that Native Americans are descendents of people
who arrived in the New World more than 12,000 years ago.[1] By the time of Columbus (who mistakenly called them "Indians"), there were over two hundred cultural
groups, speaking different languages and following different tribal religions.

Beliefs

Traditionally, Native Americans believe that the natural world is alive
and human beings are one part of it. Because nature and humans interact in
mutually influential ways, humans should pay careful attention to nature and
show respect toward it in all its details. A major fact about nature is that it
changes: from day to night, youth to old age, seed to plant, human to animal,
material to immaterial, ignorance to wisdom, spiritual being to human being.
As one among other beings of nature, humans help to maintain the world's stability and continuity, although they have the power to interfere and disrupt as
well. Two important religious positions are (1) shamans (SHAWmuns: medicine men and women), who usually have a sacred helper (often in the form of a
spirit animal) and who cure illnesses, locate game, and retrieve lost souls; and
(2) priests, who typically don masks and dance as gods in rituals that benefit
humans and enable changes to occur. Nature is inhabited by divine beings to
whom people offer prayers or sacrifice. Other sorts of beings, both helpful and
dangerous, dwell in the forests, lakes, streams, oceans, air, and under the
ground. The aims of religious practice are to:

135

- establish and maintain good and just relationships with other human beings and with nature and all its inhabitants,

- maintain personal and communal health, and

- live a long and successful life.

Sacred Books/Scriptures

Native Americans originally had no writing. They remembered their sacred histories and myths through singing, dancing, storytelling, carving, drawing, and ritual. These histories and myths explain how everything came to be the way it is. They teach Native Americans how to live and what will happen to them after this life. By enacting their histories and myths in rituals, ceremonies, and art, Native Americans make the events of the stories tangible in their own lives.

Practices

All tribes have one or more religious leaders. Some Native Americans use amulets, charms, and songs to contact the sacred world. Others rely on visions and guardian spirits. In addition to creation myths, there are many stories of other sacred beings and events. One of the most common and widespread stories is about a shape-changing "trickster" who upsets the normal order of things but also brings about positive changes. All Native American religions incorporate dancing, singing, and drumming or rattling into their ceremonies. Two widespread practices are the Sacred Pipe and the Sweat Lodge.

- In ceremonies of the Sacred Pipe, tobacco is used to communicate with sacred beings and to heal. The pipe symbolizes the cosmos and its creation, as well as the proper relationships between humans and sacred beings. Sitting in a circle, each participant smokes the pipe and extends it in six directions—north, south, east, west, up, down—thereby summoning the attention of the natural world in all its dimensions.

- The Sweat Lodge is also symbolic, its domed shape representing the world. Participants pour water on heated stones and the steam purifies them spiritually and physically.

Characteristic practices in each of the major cultural areas include the following.

Arctic—The Inuit [IN-you-it] (Eskimo) perform hunting rituals involving taboos (especially regarding menstruating women), amulets, songs, and drums. Shamans, using drums, enter into trances to locate game or recover lost souls.

Far North—Algonquin [al-GONE-kwin] people tell stories about a cultural hero who, often by mistake, changes the landscape into the way it now appears. Shamans enter a tent and call upon the spirits, who arrive and shake the tent violently.

Great Basin—The Washo [WAH-sho] hold an annual Big Time ceremony celebrating the harvest of wild crops that includes gambling, trading, dancing, and feasting as well. A girl's puberty is celebrated in a public ritual that initiates her into womanhood.

Plateau—Boys and girls of the Flathead tribe obtain guardian spirits through visions. The guardian is "forgotten" until adulthood. When it is remembered it becomes a soul partner whose loss imperils the owner's life. A Spirit Dance is an occasion for singing about guardian spirits, dancing, and initiating youths into adulthood.

California—*Southern*: At puberty, Luiseño [lu-ee-SEN-yoh] girls are "cooked" in heated pits to initiate them into womanhood. In a youth's initiation ceremony, a tea of Jimsonweed (Datura) is drunk to obtain a vision. An annual mourning ceremony includes the burning of effigies of the dead, new clothes, or other property. *Central*: Maido [MY-do] masked dancers impersonate the creator-hero in a ceremony that indoctrinates youths into tribal ways. *Northwestern*: Hupa [HOO-paw] dancers display possessions of wealth such as white deerskins, strings of dentalium shells, and large obsidian knives in a dance of world renewal.

Northwest—The Potlatch is an occasion for Kwakiutl [KWA-kee-you-tl] families to give away large amounts of wealth, thereby earning certain rights, ranks, and privileges. Family status is represented in totem poles, which are like coats of arms. In an important initiation ritual, a boy is taken away by a cannibal monster and readmitted to society through an elaborate drama in which his savage nature is tamed.

Southwest—The Apache [uh-PATCH-ee] celebrate a girl's puberty in a public ceremony during which she becomes White Painted Woman, who brings blessings to the tribe. In the kachina [kuh-CHEE-nuh] dances of the Hopi [HOPE-ee], spirits of the dead bring rain, happiness, and health. The Navaho [NAH-vuh-ho], in their "chantways," use sand paintings for curing and maintaining the order, or beauty, of nature.

Southeast—For Cherokee [CHAIR-o-kee] people, bathing in running water is a daily ritual. Men acquire war honors through brave deeds, receive new names, and often record their achievements in tattoos on their bodies. In the Green Corn ceremony, people celebrate the harvest of corn, resolve conflicts of the past year, are purified and revitalized, and join in the renewal of the new year.

Northeast—A sick person is cured by initiation into a secret society. The patient is "shot" with a sacred shell, then the shell is extracted along with the illness. Men of the Iroquois False Face Society, wearing oddly distorted masks and dancing in high-spirited and exaggerated ways, sweep away the disease. In the Big House ceremony of the Delaware, the order of the world is recreated in the design of the ceremonial Big House itself, and the order of time is renewed through the new year's ritual of the Good White Path.

Plains—Although acquiring a guardian through visions or dreams is a widespread activity among Native Americans, the ritual of the "vision quest" seems most at home here in the plains. Lakota [luh-KOH-tuh] men elect to undergo an ordeal of isolation for several days, without food or drink. Power and healing often accompany the vision. The Sun Dance is celebrated in a specially built sacred lodge. There, men dance around the central pole, often attached to it by lines tied to skewers of wood pierced through the skin of their chests. The pole is a specially prepared tree representing the cosmos. Men pledge to undertake the dance and experience a ritual rebirth that renews not only their own lives, but the life of the tribe as well.

All Cultural Areas—Two movements arising from contact with Europeans are the following:

• The Ghost Dance, a round dance believed able to drive away all non–Native Americans, return the dead to life, and renew the world.

• The Native American Church, in which peyote, a hallucinogenic cactus eaten to induce "visions," is used as a sacrament in an all-night spiritual ceremony.

Main Subgroups

Although each tribe has its own religious traditions, some practices—such as the Ghost Dance and the Native American Church—cross tribal borders. Native Americans historically have been hunters, fishers, gatherers, and/or farmers. Because of restrictions imposed by the reservation system, few Native Americans have opportunities to follow a hunting life, but some of the ceremonies and beliefs of hunters, such as the vision quest, are still practiced. Some Native Americans—for example, the Navajo— are pastoralists; others—Hopi and Cherokee—are farmers; and still others—Kwakiutl—are seafaring fishers. Unfortunately, all too many Native Americans live in poverty or near-poverty, with limited opportunities for employment. The recent popularity of Indian gambling casinos has brought new income to many reservations, with the hope of improved conditions. As discussed in "Practices" above, tribes have been classified and divided into the following cultural areas: Arctic, Far North, Great Basin, Plateau, California, Northwest, Southwest, Southeast, Northeast, and Plains.

Common Misunderstandings and Stereotypes

With so many tribes and religious traditions, it is impossible to generalize. Nearly anything one might say about Native Americans can become a stereotype. Columbus's misnomer "Indian" is deeply ingrained in American culture. Native Americans have been called savages and demons, or innocent and gentle nobles; and they have been labeled primitive, illiterate, and uncivilized. A Native American male is called *brave, buck,* or *redskin,* and a Native American woman, *squaw.* Clichés abound: "going on the warpath," "burying the hatchet," "going to the happy hunting ground," "Indian giver," and "speaking with a forked tongue." Native Americans go to powwows, drink firewater, carry papooses, and live in teepees or wigwams. They believe in the Great Spirit, say "How," carry tomahawks, stand stoically in the way of progress, and are disappearing: "The only good Indian is a dead Indian!"

The list goes on, but Native Americans are not disappearing, and their religions are as complex and sophisticated as any of the more familiar world religions. They present a challenge to the teacher, for their traditions represent a way of life that contrasts sharply with the dominant value orientations of modern America. They are the first people of this land, the foundation of our history. Their religious values must be taken into account if we are to paint a more complete, honest picture of the history and experience of all Americans.

"White Man's Indian," the image of what Native Americans *should* be, often prevents others from seeing Native Americans as they truly are. Many speak English rather than their tribal language, live in cities such as Los Angeles and Phoenix, are married to non–Native Americans (or are themselves children of such marriages), and are active members of Christian churches or other religious organizations. At the same time, they work for tribal self-determination and are proud of their Native American heritage. Change is a central experience in tribal religions. In various ways, Native Americans are changing to meet the challenges of living in the modern United States, yet they nevertheless remain Native American.

Classroom Concerns

Students should avoid imitating Native American dance, dress, and singing. Dressing in buckskins, whooping with hand to mouth, and dancing by stomping on the ground only serve to perpetuate stereotypes that insult Native Americans. When attending religious ceremonies, visitors should avoid taking pictures, making sketches, or taking notes. Also, visitors should wear clothing appropriate to the sacredness of the occasion. Celebrations are not always solemn; many involve clowning, merrymaking, and even obscenity. However, all ceremonies are sacred.

It is not possible to teach about Native Americans in general. Rather than trying to cover all the ground, tell the sacred stories of those who live (or lived) where you now live. Teach the meanings of local Native American city, state, and geographic names—for example, Seattle ("chief of the Dwamish"), Chicago ("place of the wild onion") , and Mississippi ("big river") —and tell the stories of how these names came about. By first teaching the history of Native American religions through the stories of the native peoples who are closest at hand, you then can lead students to stories and histories from other parts of the United States. For example, if you live in Maine, first tell about how Gluscap made the Penobscot River when he cut down a yellow birch; if you live in northern California, tell about how the Yurok Jump Dance renews the balance of the world. Once local stories and histories are told, others can be compared. Be sure to teach the entire history, including what has happened to Native Americans since the Europeans arrived.

Population Data

Population estimates at the time of Columbus ranged from less than 1 million to more than 10 million. Kosmin and Keysar[2] estimate there are 1,280,000 adult Native Americans in the United States. Los Angeles has the largest city population and Oklahoma the largest state population.

Significant population reduction can be attributed to genocide and its aftermath. Because of warfare, malnutrition, disease, and massacre, there may have been no more than a quarter of a million people by the mid-1800s. Native Americans were caught up in the wars of the English, French, and Spanish; they were denied their indigenous land base for farming and hunting; they had no immunity to diseases introduced by Europeans, especially smallpox and tuberculosis; and they were slaughtered outright when they got in the way of progress.

—J.H.

Further Reading

Gill, Sam. *Native American Religions: An Introduction*. Belmont, CA: Wadsworth, 1982.

――――― . *Native American Traditions: Sources and Interpretations*. Belmont, CA: Wadsworth, 1983.

Hultkrantz, Ake. *Native Religions of North America: The Power of Visions and Fertility*. San Francisco: Harper & Row, 1987.

Martin, Joel W. *The Land Looks After Us: A History of Native American Religion*. New York: Oxford University Press, Inc., 2001.

Sullivan, Lawrence E., ed. *Native American Religions: North America*. New York: Macmillan, 1989.

―――― , ed. *Native Religions and Cultures of North America*. New York and London: Continuum, 2000.

Weaver, Jace. *Native American Religious Identity: Unforgotten Gods*. Maryknoll, New York: Orbis Books,1998.

Web Sites

Native American Sites and home of the American Indian Library Association Web Page: http://www.nativeculturelinks.com/indians.html

Ontario Consultants on Religious Tolerance: http://www.religioustolerance.org/nataspir.htm

Religious Movements Homepage Project @The University of Virginia: http://religiousmovements.lib.virginia.edu/nrms/naspirit.html

Notes

1. Smithsonian Institution, Paleoamerican Origins. Available at http://www.si.edu/resource/faq/nmnh/origin.htm. Accessed July 20, 2006.

2. *Religion in a Free Market,* p. 28.

New Age

Origins

By definition, the New Age refers to a number of loosely knit interests, orientations, practices, and beliefs. These have their origins primarily in nonmainstream and nonscientific or pseudo-scientific pursuits, including the mystical and magical. The New Age does not refer to any single and central organization, belief, creed or dogma, community, or scripture that would in any way unify this mind-set. From one standpoint, it is based on a rejection at most, a downplay at least, or perhaps even an unorthodox application of that type of knowledge produced from the scientific method. Some New Age practitioners place science and scientific knowledge on a lower rung of knowledge; some enthusiastically adapt scientific inquiry to investigate phenomena outside the purview of ordinary scientific research.

In short, the New Age advocates two seemingly contradictory pursuits: (1) It revisits those practices, philosophies, and beliefs that were dominant in pre-Enlightenment[1] times. To a large degree, therefore, it is a reformulation and, in some instances, a reinterpretation of a number of ancient practices and beliefs. (2) It applies scientific methodology to the investigation, for instance, of such practices as the paranormal.

Among the philosophies that have been incorporated from ancient times, for instance, are Neoplatonism, Gnosticism,[2] Hinduism (especially the Vedanta philosophy and practices such as *kundalini* yoga with its attendant teachings of the *cakras*[3] [CHA-kruhs], Buddhism (especially Vajrayana or Apocalyptic Buddhism), and Sufism (Islamic mysticism).

143

More recent movements or individual teachings that have contributed to the New Age Movement and that may be considered direct descendants are the teachings of Emanuel Swedenborg (1688–1772); Franz Mesmer (1734–1815); freemasonry; Rosicrucianism; transcendentalism; mesmerism; spiritualism; Theosophy (more specifically, the teachings of the modern Theosophical Movement[4] represented especially through the teachings of H. P. Blavatsky, William Q. Judge, Annie Besant, Charles W. Leadbeater, and the Theosophically inspired teachings of Alice Bailey); New Thought; the Native American religious experience and pre-Christian nature religions (paganism); and a host of other more immediate and derivative movements, such as the humanistic psychology; its offshoot, the Human Potential movement; and the various forms of transpersonal psychology. New Age, seen in this light, is an outgrowth of the esoteric and metaphysical traditions that became prominent in the nineteenth century, and of the more recent development of the Human Potential movement, and transpersonal psychology.[5]

Beliefs

There are several key beliefs in New Age spirituality:

1. A tendency to accept a form of monism, meaning that at the base of the diversity of the universe lay a fundamental unity. As an intellectual or metaphysical explanation, this echoes Hindu Vedanta philosophy in its strictest sense. As an exercise and training path, it reflects Tantric Hinduism.[6] In the West the German Idealistic tradition taught that all reality is ultimately spiritual, a teaching that replicates Neoplatonism and the theology of Emanuel Swedenborg.

2. An expression of monism is pantheism (i.e., the Divine is wholly equated with the cosmos and its components) or panentheism (only a part of the Divine comprises the cosmos and its components). The underlying assumption is that because the divine is inherently good, and because humanity is either a spark of or part of the divine, then humanity is fundamentally good. Again, variations of the basic idea reflect Swedenborg's teaching, Neoplatonism, and the cabalistic (i.e., Jewish mystical) speculation of the unfolding of the creative power of God.

3. A tendency by many (including Theosophy and Theosophically inspired groups) to accept the reality of rebirth or reincarnation, a worldwide belief that most adherents associate with the teaching of *karma*.

4. The wide acceptance of the Hindu teaching of *karma*: Good actions lead to good consequences, and bad actions to bad consequences. Should consequences not be borne out in the present life, they will be in a future life. This is also common teaching in Theosophy and Theosophically inspired groups.

5. Presence of the role of transformation, a religious experience that is not much different from the "born again" experience of evangelical Christians or the "peak experience" of psychologist Abraham Maslow (1908–70), the founder of humanistic psychology. Such a transformation is not limited to individuals but also applies to society and indeed to the whole of humanity.

6. Presence of the corollary to transformation—the role of healing, for physical and mental healing is a sign of spiritual healing or transformation.

7. A spirit of optimism: Transformation is indeed within the reach of all people, and they can achieve the ultimate goal with the right technique.

8. An emphasis on the "New," that a New World Order will come about. This was originally popularized as the "Age of Aquarius," an expression popular in the 1960s but employed extensively in the nineteenth and earlier twentieth centuries in astrological (and Theosophical) circles. It referred to the time when the Sun will be in the constellation or zodiacal sign Aquarius at the spring equinox rather than the constellation Pisces (Piscean Age). If the present Piscean Age is characterized as an age of disillusionment, the new Aquarian Age will bring, eventually, an age of peace, prosperity, and the end of discrimination—but only after a time of cataclysm and war, according to many forecasters. Similarly, the Harmonic Convergence of August 16 and 17, 1987, celebrated the next step in humanity's spiritual evolution. It is around this time (the late 1980s), coincidentally, that the expression "New Age" began to take hold in the popular imagination.

9. Psychic powers are very likely to be accepted.

10. A tendency to place more reliance on a symbolic, as opposed to a literal, interpretation of myths, art, and objects of nature, which in turn may have multiple layers of meaning. Symbolic meaning as a key to understanding the cosmos was a popular form of interpretation in the Middle Ages and the Renaissance, mainly because of individuals such as Saint Basil and Saint Ambrose, the Neoplatonism of Plotinus, and such works as the *Book of Dreams* of Artemidorus (third century C.E. philosopher) and the *Hieroglyphica* (book of Egyptian hieroglyphic signs) of Horapollo[7] (fifth-century C.E. philosopher).

Sacred Books/Scriptures

There is no common scripture for New Age practitioners. Instead, they draw on the writings of many religious traditions and philosophers (see "Beliefs" above).

Practices

The New Age includes practices based on several assumptions. First, the practices range from the maintenance of or a return to physical, mental, and spiritual health for the transformation of the individual and society. Second, many (but not all) of the practices are occult in nature. "Occult" refers to secret knowledge, that is, knowledge closed to public access and possessed only by small numbers of groups and individuals who are generally initiated into this knowledge (gnostic or liberating knowledge). Generally, this knowledge covers forces, powers, or laws that exist in the world but cannot be discerned by sensual or empirical observation. Such forces can be manipulated by certain physical, verbal, or mental practices that have come under the rubric of New Age practice.

Some of the practices are ancient, many of which are based on forms of psychic reading or divination (foretelling the future).

Akashic Records—These records may be considered Cosmic Memory, referring to the storing of every thought, emotion, and event in the *akasha* or astral light (literally, the "ether"), which can in turn be read, heard, or seen by those sensitive to these records. The Akashic Records appear in the writings and pronouncements of the American occult diagnostician of disease, Edgar Cayce (1871–1945).

Astrology—Divination based on the position of the planets and stars.

Aura reading—Divination based on the energy that is emitted from all things in nature, visible only through clairvoyance and Kirlian photography (a process that claims to record electrical discharges coming naturally from living organisms in the form of an auralike glow).

Channeling—The same as mediumship in spiritualism, in which a spirit, usually of a deceased individual who has lived hundreds or even thousands of years ago, communicates through the channeler, who is usually in a trance, giving advice or teaching.

Yijing—The ancient Chinese classic *Yijing* (*Book of Changes*)—divination based on the interpretation of sixty-four broken and solid lines arranged in hexagrams that appear in the text.

Numerology—Divination based on the notion that all things are expressed in numbers and that the cosmos is a mathematical construct.

Palmistry—Divination based on reading the lines and mounds of palms and fingers.

Pendulum movements—Divination based on dowsing, by means of which a pendulum is supposedly sensitive to energy emitted from objects and living beings; this energy can be communicated by its swinging movements.

Psychometry—Divination based on handling objects associated with persons or events.

Retrocognition—Divination about a past event through psychic power; precognition: divination about a future event.

Runes—Ancient Teutonic writing that possessed magical powers for those who were able to decipher the symbols.

Scrying—Divination based on clairvoyant visions arising from gazing on an object such as a crystal ball or mirror.

Tarot cards—Divination based on a set of playing cards showing emblematic figures that, when played in a certain way, foretell the future for the individual. The Tarot cards also have a deeper meaning, which associates them with the Tree of Life of the Cabala (Kabbala); the Cabala originally referred to Jewish mystical thought and later, during the Renaissance, to Christian Cabala. The Tree of Life reveals the relation between God, humans, and the cosmos.

New Age also emphasizes the maintenance or improvement of the body's health through a number of practices that are by no means exclusive to this movement. Such practices include:

Acupuncture—The insertion of needles into the skin at certain points of the body that help to unblock the flow of the vital force, or *qi* [chee], that circulates through the body.

Acupressure—The application of pressure using the hands and fingers on those spots where needles are ordinarily inserted in acupuncture.

Reflexology—The application of pressure from the fingers and thumb on those spots on the ball and sole of the foot that are believed to be connected to other parts and organs of the body.

Shiatsu—Japanese massage and acupressure.

Therapeutic touch—Healing by holding the hands over that area of the body that is in need of healing, or manipulating the body's energy field with hand strokes.

In general, any practice that is considered part of holistic medicine is accepted by the New Age, including alternative interpretations of the body's map. These include the acceptance of the Hindu and Buddhist yogic *cakras* (psychic centers) and the *kundalini* (psycho-divine potency) that passes through them. Various meditative techniques may also be included.

Crystals (the general term for any gem or stone that possesses a molecular pattern reflected on its surface) have been popular since the 1980s for physical and mental healing, the alleviation of stress, and the arousal of higher consciousness and creativity.

Another characteristic of New Age is its music. The general nature of New Age music is to induce relaxation and to serve as an aid in healing.

Main Subgroups

Strictly speaking, there are no subgroups because there is no mainline New Age Church. It is better to regard New Age religion in the manner considered above under Origins. The New Age, therefore, refers more to a network rather than a movement, which in turn adopts and adapts ideas and practices from the previous age and redirects and incorporates them in what is interpreted to be the New Age. Furthermore, with regard to those who participate in New Age ideas and practices, Grace Davie has argued two attitudes: "believing without belonging" and "belonging without believing."[8] Participation does not include a service or worship, but being in the milieu of the audience, that is, a group that is not bonded as a cohesive unit.

If the New Age portends a New World Order, so to speak, a legitimate question might arise regarding its relationship to a movement that closely resembles it from the preceding age, *New Thought.*

There are similarities and differences between the New Thought and New Age movements. The very names of these broad-based movements can easily cause confusion, especially when they share so much in common. Among their similarities are the following.

1. Ideas that derive from many of the same sources, including Neoplatonism, which teaches that the soul is the divine spark of God; Hindu Vedanta monistic philosophy; the Swedenborgian view that spiritual laws are both correspondent to and the cause of natural laws; the mesmeric view of a magnetic fluid (much like the Hindu *prana* and the Chinese *qi*) that permeates the universe connecting all things and humans, and Mesmer's experiments with hypnotism; and the transcendentalism of Ralph Waldo Emerson (1803–82), who wrote that "Mind is the only reality of which men and all natures are better or worse reflectors."

2. A sense of optimism.

3. An emphasis on the one power in the universe, which is considered good.

4. An emphasis on alternative medicine.

These ideas are reflected in the Declaration of Principles followed by the churches affiliated in the International New Thought Alliance. These would very likely be accepted, in whole or in part, by a majority of New Agers, whether or not they have affiliations with New Thought churches:

1. the Oneness of God and Humans;

2. freedom in matters of belief;

3. the God is supreme, eternal, and universal;

4. the Kingdom of God is within us;

5. "we" can heal the sick through prayer;

6. belief in God as the Universal Wisdom, Love, Life, Truth, Power, Peace, Plenty, Beauty, Joy;

7. the idea that a human's mental states are carried forward into manifestation and become his or her experience through the Creative Law of Cause and Effect;

8. divine Nature expresses itself through humanity and is manifested as health, wisdom, love, life, truth; and

9. a human being is an invisible spiritual dweller within a human body.

New Age and New Thought are arguably more similar than different. Yet there are differences. New Thought is older, originating in the 1880s and 1890s, about one hundred years before New Age. It is a descendent of the teachings of Phineas P. Quimby (1802–66), who emphasized "mental healing," which is based on the idea that disease was caused by delusion and error fixed within the mind. This doctrine, called by Quimby the Science of Health, attracted a number of followers, among whom was Mary Baker Eddy, the founder of the Church of Christian Science (see the chapter "Christian Science").

It was Emma Curtis Hopkins, however, who contributed more to the dissemination of New Thought ideas and institutions by training a number of students in her Christian Science Theological Seminary in Chicago. These students would later found separate organizations: Myrtle and Charles Fillmore, founders of the Unity School of Christianity; Annie Rix Militz, founder of the Homes of Truth; Melinda Cramer, founder of Divine Science; and Ernest Holmes, founder of the Church of Religious Science in 1926. Hopkins was important in helping to differentiate New Thought from Christian Science, first by breaking from Mary Baker Eddy and her church, and second by training a core of ministers (about one hundred, mostly women) to teach and practice their own variations of Christian Science, which by the end of the nineteenth century became known as New Thought. Out of this came the New Thought Alliance, later called the International New Thought Alliance, which comprises a number of independent church organizations.

A second major difference between New Thought and New Age represents more of a psychological attitude toward human conditions. New Thought was never reactionary or revolutionary in its view of the world. The teaching of Mind was the one way to deal with the problems of the individual, society, and world because they were all subject to Mind, which is inherently good.

New Age, however, perceived the situation in less optimistic terms. There was a sense that many practices and beliefs were beyond the individual's control, resulting in more pessimism with the present age. Only the replacement of the Dark Age or preceding age with a New Age—what originally was called the Aquarian Age—would change things for the better. To do so, new practices and new ideas not related to the dominant mold of the Old Age were adopted as means of making people whole. These included the occult practices (see "Practices," above) that normally would not be accepted in New Thought but certainly accepted in the New Age.

A third difference centers on who is susceptible to healing. New Thought restricts it to individuals, but New Age extends it to the entire planet.

Common Misunderstandings and Stereotypes

"The New Age movement is composed of a bunch of weirdos."

New Age practitioners are clearly out of the mainstream of American religion, but their ideas have a consistency and logic that is neither weird nor wicked. They seek the betterment of their followers and of humankind generally through the means described above. Moreover, many traditional Christian, Jewish, and other religious people have adopted one or more of the practices of New Age—especially those relating to health—without accepting the system as a whole.

Population Data

It is next to impossible to determine who is and who is not a full-time, committed member of the New Age network. However, Kosmin and Keysar (*Religion in a Free Market*, p. 27) place the number of U.S. adult adherents at 68,000 based on their 2001 survey.

—J.S.

Further Reading

Hanegraaff, Wouter J. *New Age Religion and Western culture: Esotericism in the Mirror of Secular Thought.* Albany, NY: SUNY Press, 1998.

Lewis, James R., ed. *The Encyclopedic Sourcebook of New Age Religions.* Amherst, NY: Prometheus Books, 2004.

Partridge, Christopher, ed. *New Religions: A Guide.* New York: Oxford University Press, 2004.

Pike, Sarah M. *New Age and Neopagan Religions in America.* New York: Columbia University Press, 2004.

Sutcliffe, Steven J. *Children of the New Age: A History of Alternative Spirituality.* London and New York: Routledge, 2003.

Web Sites

Ontario Consultants on Religious Tolerance: http://www.religioustolerance.org/newage.htm

http://www.newageinfo.com/index.htm

Notes

1. The Enlightenment refers to a movement in Western philosophy in the seventeenth and eighteenth centuries that was skeptical of Christian beliefs and accepted only those biblical and theological teachings that could be reconciled with reason and the methods of science.

2. Gnosticism is a religious philosophy that originated in the Near East at about the same time as Christianity. It stresses *gnosis* (esoteric or mystical knowledge) as the key to salvation.

3. *Cakras* are energy centers in the spiritual body of a person, each of which is associated with a Hindu deity.

4. Theosophy is a movement combining Western interest in the occult and mystical with Eastern religious philosophy. It strives for the unity of humankind, the study of comparative religion and philosophy, and the uncovering of the powers latent in humankind.

5. In an earlier publication, J. Gordon Melton has proposed the origins to be in "light" groups (those groups that combined Theosophical teachings and channeling), one of the most prominent of which was the spiritual community of Findhorn in northern Scotland, founded in 1962 by Peter and Eileen Caddy. More recently, Michael York has described New Age as "the self-conscious spiritualization of the human potential movement" but also notes the nineteenth century roots of the New Age. James R. Lewis and J. Gordon Melton, eds., "New Thought and the New Age," in *Perspectives on the New Age* (Albany: SUNY Press, 1992), 20; Michael York, "New Age Traditions," in *New Religions: A Guide,* ed. Christopher Partridge (New York: Oxford University Press, 2004), 309.

6. The term *Tantra* refers to a body of texts. As a general term, it refers to those practices and movements (sects or lineages) that emphasize the worship of the Female energy (*shakti*) and for adepts to gain this power in conjunction with the Unchanging Masculine Being. In cosmic terms, it is the Female energy that permeates the universe. Different techniques are employed, one of which involved *kundalini* yoga: the technique of raising the latent power *kundalini* resting at the base of the spine upward through the power centers known as *cakras*. In Tantrism, there is the fundamental assumption of an identity between absolute and phenomenal existence. In New Age metaphysics, the notions of bioenergetics, biodynamics, and synergy reflect the world in terms of energy and vibration.

7. The *Hieroglyphica* probably had the greatest influence on scholars of the Renaissance era regarding Egyptian symbols. See the *Hieroglyphics of Horapollo*, translated by George Boas with a new foreword by Anthony Grafton (Princeton, NJ: Princeton University Press, 1993 [originally copyrighted in 1950 and renewed in 1979]). On the *Book of Dreams (Oreirocriticon)*, see Claes Blum, *Studies in the Dream-Book of Artemidorus* (Uppsala, Sweden: Almqvist & Wiksell, 1936).

8. "Believing without Belonging: Is This the Future of Religion in Britain?" *Social Compass* 37 (1990): 4, quoted in *Che cos'è il New Age* by Jean Vernette. Translated from the French by Stefano Viviani (Carnago [Varese], Italy: Sugarco Edizioni, 1992), 12. This appears in Massimo Introvigne's introduction to the book.

The Lion represents Haile Selassie I of Ethiopia as the Conquering Lion of Judah and the King of Kings. The dreadlocks worn by Rastafaris simulate the spirited mane of the lion.

Rastafarianism

Origins

Rastafarianism originated in Jamaica in the 1930s as a repatriation movement among descendants of African slaves. In their longing for a better life, they turned to Marcus Garvey's[1] Back-to-Africa movement, which promised the decolonization of Africa and the return of freedom and dignity to those who were enslaved by white society. When Ras (Duke) Tafari Makonnen was crowned emperor of Ethiopia (November 2, 1930), he took the name Haile Selassie I ("Might of the Trinity") and the titles "King of Kings," "Elect of God," and "Conquering Lion of the Tribe of Judah" (Book of Revelation 19:16). He claimed to be the descendent of Menelik I, founder of the kingdom of Ethiopia in the tenth century B.C.E. and the first son of King Solomon and the Queen of Sheba. Selassie thus represented an original, pure, biblically grounded (many Rastafaris claim to be the original Israelites)—and black—heritage, free from the evils of colonialism. Rastafaris call him "Jah,"[2] and look to him as the Messiah who will lead them to the "Promised Land of Moses"—meaning Africa.

Two important events followed the emergence of the Rastafari religion:

1. Haile Selassie visited Jamaica on April 21, 1966, and told the Rastas they should not immigrate to Ethiopia until they had found freedom in Jamaica. They called this "liberation before repatriation." They understood it to mean they should keep themselves free from the pollution and corruption of the dominant culture while awaiting the summons to restoration.

153

2. Haile Selassie died August 27, 1975. Many believed, though, that because he was Jah, he did not really die. They were convinced he would return someday to lead the righteous to the Promised Land of Africa, where they would live in peace and harmony. Other Rastas put more emphasis on social reform in Jamaica, or wherever they found themselves. Worldwide recognition of the Rastafari religion can be attributed to migration and, remarkably, the popularity of the reggae music of Bob Marley and others.

Beliefs

The Rastafari movement has been called a "way of life" and not a mere intellectual "belief." In addition, Rastas rely on individual interpretation of doctrine and have no single authoritative source. Nevertheless, two beliefs are common:

- **Babylon:** White culture and white Christianity have created the slavery, poverty, illiteracy, and inequality of Africans, who are held captive, just as the Jews were held in Babylon. Jamaica is the land of exile, but by following Jah Rastafari, one will find one's true identity and freedom, which is to be African in Africa. This millennial hope is for an "everliving" life of peace and harmony, not an afterlife in heaven or hell.

- **Jah:** Haile Selassie I is Jah, although it is up to each Rasta to interpret just how he is Jah: as God, Messiah, King, Savior, or several together. Following Jah means establishing and maintaining a bond of identity between God and all humankind. This is expressed by the phrase "I and I," meaning God is within us and we are therefore all one person, beyond personal, cultural, social, or racial differences. It should be obvious that this view implies nonviolence, because any violence would be toward oneself as well as toward Jah.

Sacred Books/Scriptures

The Bible, especially the New Testament Book of Revelation: Rastas accept the Bible in part but believe it has been distorted by "Babylon" and must be interpreted critically.

The Holy Piby: An Afrocentric "Bible" was written by Robert Athlyi Rogers in 1928 and later adopted by Rastafaris.

Kebra Negast: This national epic traces the history of the Kings of Ethiopia.

Practices

Language: Many words and phrases contrast the worldview of Rastas and the colonial language of Jamaica. For example:

1. "I and I," instead of you and I, expresses the equality of all people, who are bound together by one God.

2. "Everliving," instead of everlasting, to emphasize bodily immortality.[3]

3. "Overstanding," instead of understanding, because knowledge is by participation in the life of Jah, who "comes over I and I."

4. "Downpression," instead of oppression, to show that victims are pressed down upon from a higher position of power.

5. Rastafari pronounced as Rasta-FAR-"I," with the *I* sound of the letter I. The same for the title of Haile Selassie "I," which is understood as the ordinal *first*. The "I" in both cases expresses an original and personal relationship with God.

6. "Zion" describes heaven, specifically Ethiopia, which is symbolic of all of Africa.

7. Rastas avoid using "-*isms*" such as capital*ism*, commun*ism*, and especially Rastafarian*ism*, because these are colonialist ways of classifying people. One can "trod" the path without -*isms*.

8. "Ital" (I-tal) means vital and refers to Rastafaris' diet, the "I" pointing to the unity of nature.

9. Rastafari use the term "Livication," instead of *ded*-ication, because of the sound of death.

Ganja: Marijuana (cannabis), called the "wisdom weed," is used as an herb in spiritual life, a sacrament in ritual settings, an aid in meditation, and medicine. It is not advocated for recreational use. As might be expected, Rastafaris have faced legal and social opposition to this practice.

Dreadlocks: Many, but not all, Rastafaris grow their hair long and "locked"[4] as an expression of naturalness and as a representation of the symbolic "Lion of Judah." Dreadlocks are said to provide spiritual energy. To form locks, the hair is allowed to grow naturally and is washed with pure water, but no razor, scissors, or comb is used, as these are considered instruments of Babylon. The word "dread" is explained in one or more ways:

- They look "dreadful" to "baldheads."

- Dread means fear of the Lord.

- Mau Mau freedom fighters in Kenya with locked hair were 'dreaded' by the colonial British.

- They express rebellion against the establishment and its norms.

- They are a symbol of ethnic and racial identity.

- They signify devotion to Jah.

- Locks may have been inspired by the Biblical injunction against cutting hair.[5]

As might be expected, Rastas who wear dreadlocks have had to face legal, social, and economic discrimination.

> **Diet:** Rastas advocate I-tal food, natural and free of chemicals. Many are vegetarian, although fish—particularly small fish—is often eaten. They avoid liquor, milk, coffee, soft drinks, and "artificial" foods, including canned or dried food.

> **Music and Art:** Music is an integral part of Rastafari life and worship. Much of the reggae music of Bob Marley and others expresses suffering in slavery, devotion to Ras Tafari, and longing for return to Africa.

The colors of the Ethiopian flag—red, gold, and green—are symbolic of the Rastafari movement. One interpretation is that red stands for the blood of martyrs, gold for the wealth of Africa, and green for the beauty and vegetation of Africa. Black is another important color, representing Africans and their descendants.

The Lion represents Haile Selassie I as the Conquering Lion of Judah and the King of Kings. Rastas' dreadlocks simulate the spirited mane of the male Lion.

> **Ceremonies:** Rastas say "I am the temple." There are no centers of worship and no official practices. Each person chooses the appropriate degree and type of worship. In general, though, there are weekly and monthly meetings, and there are special meetings called Nyahbinghi. Weekly meetings are "reasonings" where ethical, social, and religious issues are discussed. Monthly meetings include music, prayers, inspirational talks, and dancing, and these may last all night. Nyahbinghi meetings last from one or two days up to a week and involve exhortations, feasting, socializing, and—as in the other gatherings—smoking of ganja. In the early days, ceremonies were for men only. Later, they were opened to both men and women.

Important dates:

- January 7, Ethiopian Christmas

- February 6, Bob Marley's birthday

- April 21, *Grounation Day*, the anniversary of Haile Selassie's visit to Jamaica

- July 23, Birthday of Emperor Haile Selassie I

- August 17, Marcus Garvey's birthday

- November 2, Coronation of Emperor Haile Selassie I

Main Subgroups

The Rastafari religion consists of autonomous groups and individuals who hold some beliefs and practices in common. Groups are referred to as *Houses* or *Mansions*. Some groups are more highly organized than others. Because there is no head leadership over all Rastafaris, groups may coalesce, change, or dissolve. Three of the major groups are the following:

- **Nyahbinghi**—Nyahbinghi believe in Haile Selassie as Messiah, the incarnation of the Supreme Deity.

- **Bobo Ashanti**—Bobos believe in Haile Selassie as King or God.

- **Twelve Tribes of Israel**—Twelve Tribes believe Haile Selassie is a divinely anointed king representing the line of David.

Common Misunderstandings and Stereotypes

"Rastafaris, with their dreadlocks, are violent social dissidents."

This notoriety is due more to imitators than to true Rastas. Although Rastas may hold the millennial hope that blacks will rule the world, they are also convinced that it will be achieved by peaceful means. In the meantime, tolerance is enjoined toward all races and religions. Dreadlocks may appear to "baldheads" as unkempt, but they are an expression of personal spirituality that Rastas say puts them in touch with nature and God.

"Rastafaris are potheads who smoke marijuana in violation of the law."

Although imitators may use the cover of the Rastafari movement to smoke ganja recreationally, it is not a practice sanctioned by the religion. Marijuana is to be used solely for sacramental or spiritual purposes. Accommodations have been made for the religious use of controlled substances in the United States, and the 1993 Religious Freedom Restoration Act has been cited in efforts to protect the use of ganja.[6]

Classroom Concerns

Rastafaris appear set apart from mainstream U.S. culture and religion because they wear dreadlocks, smoke ganja, worship Haile Selassie I as Jah, and use an edited version of the Bible. But Rastas affirm their humanity through these beliefs and practices, however different they may be from more familiar ones. Perhaps Rastafari can be better understood as a religion nurtured by the intercultural and interracial milieu of Caribbean life, which includes other religious movements such as Santería, Shongo, Candomblé, Macumba, Vodou, and Obeah.

Santería can be cited for comparison because it is perhaps the best known of these Caribbean religions because of publicity surrounding the ritual sacrifice of animals. Santería is a syncretistic religion which venerates the *Orisha,* divine guardians of Bantu and Yoruba people. When forced into slavery in the Caribbean, African people were baptized in the Roman Catholic Church, but many kept their native religion alive by disguising the Orisha as Catholic saints. Orishas need food, so they are fed ritually killed animals, mainly chickens. This practice brings good luck, purifies, and forgives sins. There is sufficient precedent to ensure Santería the religious freedom in the United States to continue sacrificing chickens in their ceremonies.[7]

The variety of religious movements in just one area of the world, the Caribbean, should draw attention to the multiplicity of American religions generally and to their legal right to worship in their own way, regardless of size or difference.

Population Data

Although Rastafaris in the past have been predominately male and of African ancestry, more recently women and people from around the world have become Rastas. Kosmin and Keysar[8] estimate that there are 11,000 adult Rastafaris in the United States.

Further Reading

Barrett, Leonard E., Sr. *The Rastafarians*. Boston: Beacon Press, 1997.

Nettleford, Rex M. *Mirror, Mirror: Identity, Race and Protest in Jamaica*. Kingston: William Collins & Sangster, 1970.

Web Sites

First Amendment Center: http://www.firstamendmentcenter.org

Harvard Pluralism Project: http://www.pluralism.org

Ontario Consultants on Religious Tolerance: http://www.religioustolerance.org

Ras Adam's Haile Selassie/Rastafari Links: http://web.syr.edu/~affellem/raslinx.html

University of Virginia Religious Movements Project: http://religiousmovements.lib. virginia.edu/nrms/rast.html

Notes

1. Marcus Mosiah Garvey (1887–1940), founder of the Universal Negro Improvement Association and the African Communities League, advocated the unification in Africa of all people of African ancestry, where they would rule themselves.

2. Rastas cite Psalm 68.4 (in the King James Version) as authority for this term: "Sing unto God, sing praises to his name: extol him that rideth upon the heavens by his name JAH, and rejoice before him."

3. It is said that Bob Marley refused to write a will because that would mean he was subject to death rather than *everliving* life.

4. If allowed to grow naturally, the hair will form itself into matted ropes or "locks."

5. Leviticus 21:5; Numbers 6:5.

6. Tony Mauro, "Religious Liberty Gets Boost in Hallucinogenic-tea Case." Available at http://www.firstamendmentcenter.org//analysis.aspx?id=16524&SearchString=marijuana. Accessed July 3, 2006.

7. *Church of the Lukumi Babalu Aye, Inc., et al. v. City of Hialeah* (Supreme Court, 1993).

8. *Religion in a Free Market*, p. 28.

Secular Humanism/ Atheism

Origins

Secular Humanism, which considers humanity as a substitute for God, is partly rooted in the Enlightenment movement of the eighteenth century within Western philosophy. The Enlightenment philosophers, although not denying God's existence, were critical of the nonrational elements of religion, such as belief in miracles. One offshoot of the Enlightenment was Deism, the notion that God created the world but then left it up to humanity to work out its destiny with no divine intervention. Deism significantly influenced the founding fathers of the United States, including Benjamin Franklin, George Washington, Thomas Jefferson, James Madison, and John Adams. This is particularly true of the framing of the First Amendment's provisions for no official, state-sponsored church and for the free exercise of any religion by U.S. citizens. The framers' awareness of the history of religious persecution in Europe also influenced the Amendment's contents.

Along with the Enlightenment, the other principal sources of Humanism were the ideas of French philosopher August Comte (1798–1857), who organized a Church of Humanity in Paris; and the American Humanistic Association (AHA), begun in the 1920s. In 1933, the AHA, which included prominent American philosopher John Dewey, issued a Humanist Manifesto, which rejected supernatural explanations for the origins of the universe and regarded humanity as part of nature. Several Unitarian ministers were also prominent in the movement (see the chapter "Unitarian Universalism"). In 1973, the AHA issued a second manifesto stressing the importance of technology in preserving the environment, alleviating poverty, reducing disease, prolonging life, and discovering new ways to make human existence more meaningful. AHA published a third manifesto in 2003, the platform of which is summarized under "Beliefs," below.

159

Beliefs

Secular Humanists reject belief in a supernatural being or beings and are, in effect, atheists. They believe in humanity and its ability to solve human problems without divine assistance. Philosophical or so-called existential atheists, such as French philosopher Jean-Paul Sartre, argue that to be authentically free in the universe, it is necessary that God(s) not exist, because their existence would limit human freedom. The 2003 manifesto stresses six points: (1) Knowledge of the world derives from observation, experimentation, and rational analysis. (2) Humans are an integral part of nature resulting from "unguided evolutionary change." (3) Ethical values stem from human needs and the inherent worth and dignity of each person. (4) Life's fulfillment comes from an appreciation and cultivation of the joys and beauties of human existence while realizing the inevitability and finality of death. (5) Social by nature, humans must work cooperatively and nonviolently to enrich the lives of all people. (6) Working to benefit society produces individual happiness. Humanists are concerned for the well-being of everyone, to diversity of viewpoints and to civil liberties. They view participation in the democratic process and the protection of nature as everyone's responsibility. In sum, humanity has the ability to make progress towards its highest ideals and is solely responsible for producing the kind of world we live in.[1]

Sacred Books/Scriptures

There is no single writing that Secular Humanists accept as normative for their movement. Documents such as *Humanist Manifestos I, II,* and *III* are certainly important, but so are the writings of August Comte, British philosopher Bertrand Russell, and many others.

Practices

In place of clergy, the AHA licenses counselors to conduct weddings and funerals for Humanists. Not surprisingly, there are no rituals within the Humanist movement. However, some self-described Humanists belong to the Unitarian Universalist Association and participate in the nontheistic services of this group (see the chapter "Unitarian Universalism"). There are also small Humanist groups such as the Ethical Culture Society and the Society for Humanistic Judaism, whose tenets are similar to those of the AHA and Unitarian Universalists. The Society for Humanistic Judaism does conduct services, but they are nontheistic.

Main Subgroups

It is important to realize that many Secular Humanists/atheists are not affiliated with any official group but simply hold a philosophical position that parallels that of "card-carrying" Humanists. There are several Humanistic organizations in the United

States, such as the AHA and Ethical Culture Society; the Council for Democratic and Secular Humanism, which publishes a magazine *Free Inquiry*; and the Alliance of Secular Humanist Societies, with local affiliates around the country. Finally, there is a global alliance of Humanists, the International Humanist Ethical Union.

Common Misunderstandings and Stereotypes

"Secular Humanists hate religion and seek to suppress it."

Although Humanists do not accept the religious teachings of Christianity or any other faith, they respect religious people insofar as they work for the betterment of humanity. Humanists in no way seek to keep religious people from practicing their faiths.

"Secular Humanists are godless and immoral."

The term *secular* is sometimes used by conservative religionists to cast Humanists in a bad light. Although Humanists reject belief in God(s), it does not follow that they lack morals. In fact, they tend to be very ethical individuals with a deep dedication to improving living conditions for people everywhere.

Classroom Concerns

Teachers should try to be sensitive to the unique situation of a child whose parents are Humanists or atheists. Teachers will very often be unaware of the nonreligious background of such children. It is important for teachers not to denigrate Humanism/atheism in their classrooms, even though it might not agree with their worldviews.

Humanist students may be reluctant to salute the flag because of the words "under God" in the Pledge of Allegiance. They should be informed that they may either stand silently while other students do so or be excused from class during the recitation.

Population Data

Kosmin and Keysar found that more than 14 percent of the adult population in the United States describe themselves as having no religious affiliation (29.5 million vs. 14.3 million in the comparable 1990 Kosmin and Lachman survey).[2] Of these 29.5 million, 27.5 million responded in the 2001 Kosmin and Keysar survey that they had "no religion"; 902,000 described themselves as; "Atheist," 991, 000 as; "Agnostic," 49,000 as "Humanist," and 53,000 as; "Secular." It is not clear how many of the "no religion" respondents would be comfortable with the philosophy of Humanism, but some certainly would. Moreover, there are 629,000 adult Unitarians according to Kosmin and Keysar, most of whom hold a Humanist worldview (see chapter "Unitarian Universalism").

—B.H.

Further Reading

Herrick, Jim. *Humanism: An Introduction*. Amherst, NY: Prometheus Books, 2005.

Jacoby, Susan. *Freethinkers: A History of American Secularism*. New York: Henry Holt, 2004.

Kurtz, Paul. *The Humanist Alternative: Some Definitions of Humanism*. Buffalo, NY: Prometheus Press, 1973.

Web Sites

http://www.AmericanHumanist.org

http://www.infidels.org/news/atheism

Notes

1.   Available at http://www.AmericanHumanist.org. Accessed June 20, 2006.

2.   Kosmin and Keysar, *Religion in a Free Market*, pp. 24, 27.

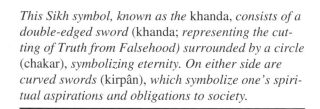

This Sikh symbol, known as the khanda, *consists of a double-edged sword* (khanda; *representing the cutting of Truth from Falsehood) surrounded by a circle* (chakar), *symbolizing eternity. On either side are curved swords* (kirpân), *which symbolize one's spiritual aspirations and obligations to society.*

Sikhism

Origins

The founder of the Sikh [SEEK] religion was Guru Nanak (1469–1539). Raised Hindu in the Panjab region of northern India, his religious background reflects the devotional (*bhakti*) traditions within Hinduism, most especially the *Sant* (Saint) tradition. The designation *sant* applies to those poet-saints in the Panjab belonging to a loose collection of devotional groups who taught that the Supreme God was beyond all comprehension. According to biographical accounts, Nanak opposed both Muslim fanaticism and Hindu ritual and caste by teaching his followers to meditate on God's Name. As a religious teacher or spiritual guide who came face to face with God to receive his mandate, he became a Guru: one who is a spiritual guide, or according to the popular etymology, the Light (i.e., the Divine Light) that dispels darkness. To Sikhs, Guru Nanak—and all Sikh leaders who were given the title Guru—was the vehicle through which God transmitted His teaching. The Guru is therefore primarily a teacher; he is neither God nor a Messiah. A follower of the Guru is known as a Sikh (disciple), hence the religion's name. By definition, a Sikh may be defined as one who is a disciple of the ten human Gurus, from Guru Nanak to Guru Gobind (Guruship: 1675–1708, b. 1666–1708) and the sacred book that replaced the human Guru, the Guru Granth Sahib [GOO-roo grunth sa-HEEB] or Adi [AH-dee] Granth.

Beliefs

The fundamental belief is found in the opening lines of the sacred book of the Sikhs, the Guru Granth Sahib. These lines declare that God is One, Absolute, Creator, Without Fear or Hatred, Timeless, Unborn, Self-Existent, Omnipresent, and the Supreme Truth. Hindu traditional beliefs were accepted by Nanak, such as *karma* (actions and their consequences; according to Sikhs, the rewards and punishments for actions are determined by God) and the cycle of existence or rebirth. The purpose of human life is to dispel ignorance, egoism, and suffering and to achieve purity and illumination of mind by God's Grace and by constant repetition of the name of God. This practice produces a God-Conscious and Godlike person. In other words, a human cannot become God but, according to Guru Arjan (Guruship: 1581–1606, b. 1563–1606), there is ultimately no difference between God and a God-Conscious soul.

Sacred Books/Scriptures

The Guru Granth Sahib/Adi Granth is considered the living Guru of the Sikhs. This status was conferred upon it with the death of the tenth and last human Guru, Gobind, who declared shortly before his death that the Guru Granth Sahib be his successor. Although the Guru Granth Sahib underwent development from the time of Guru Nanak, it received its distinctive form under the fifth Guru, Arjan. It was later expanded by the last Guru, Gobind, who added hymns of his father, the ninth Guru, Tegh Bahadur Ji (Guruship 1664–75, b. 1621–75). The Guru Granth Sahib now consists of a standardized 1,430 pages, written in Gurmukhi (lit., "from the mouth of the Guru") pertaining to the Gurmukhs or Sikhs) script. What is unique is that Hindu and Muslim poet-saints are also included in the collection. The total number of hymns is 5,894, with the largest contribution by Guru Arjan (2,218). The Adi Granth is made up of three main sections consisting of thirty-three divisions: (1) the first section made up of the prayers for sunrise, sunset, and the end of the day; (2) the hymns making up thirty-one subsections comprising the melodic modes or *rag-s;* and (3) the final section consisting of miscellaneous verses.

Practices

Practices include dress, life-cycle rituals, festivals, and worship in the temple (Gurdwara). Since the time of Guru Gobind (the founder of the Khalsa—the Community of warrior-Sikhs or the initiated Sikh Brotherhood—) on Vaisakhi (Baisakhi) Day (April 13), initiated or baptized Sikhs began to share certain practices and forms of dress. Initiated as a Khalsa ("pure") by means of the baptism ritual (Amrit), the Sikh must now follow a strict regimen of abstaining from destructive practices such as the taking of intoxicants and tobacco, not committing adultery and infanticide, not eating the meat of animals killed in any religious ceremony, and exhibiting the physical signs of the Khalsa—the Five Ks. These are (1) to leave the hair (kesh) uncut (over which a turban is worn), (2) to keep a comb (kangha) within the hair, (3) to carry a steel dagger (kirpan), (4) to wear a steel bracelet (kara), and (5) to wear a specific knee-length undergarment (kacch). All Sikh males take the name Singh (lion), and all women take the additional name Kaur (princess). These designations replaced the traditional name that indicated one's caste, an institution that was rejected by Sikhs.

Life-cycle rites include the name giving (Nam Karan), baptism (Pahul), marriage (Anand Karaj), and funeral rites. Sikhs participate in many festivals, but of those that are celebrated, five are universally observed:

> **Birthday of Guru Nanak**—October/November.
>
> **Birthday of Guru Gobind**—December 22.
>
> **Installation of the Guru Granth Sahib as Guru** commemorates the date in 1604 when the sacred book was installed at the Golden Temple in Amritsar; celebrated September/October.
>
> **Vaisakhi** (the New Year) (Baisakhi) is celebrated on April 13, a day that is especially important because this was the day that the Khalsa order was founded by Guru Gobind in 1699. Also during Guru Amar Das' Guruship (1552–74, b. 1479), the first annual gathering of Sikhs was initiated at the center of pilgrimage, Goindwal.
>
> **Diwali**—A festival of light similar to the Hindu and Jain festivals of the same name but marking the return of the sixth Guru, Har Gobind (Guruship: 1606–44, b. 1595–1644), to the holy city of Amritsar after his release from prison (October/November).

All the festivals, open to men and women, include hymnal singing, lectures, and consecrated and free food provided by the communal kitchen. One feature of the Gurpurb (or Gurupurab: a specific type of celebration reserved for the anniversaries of the birth, ascendancy to guruship, martyrdom, and death of the ten Gurus, the installation of the Guru Granth Sahib as the successor to the human Gurus, and the deaths of the sons of Guru Gobind) is the continuous reading of the Guru Granth Sahib, which takes about forty-eight hours. The dates of the Gurpurb follow a lunar calendar, so the days will vary from year to year.

Sikh temples serve a number of purposes. Services consist of singing passages from the Guru Granth Sahib, exposition of a passage by a *granthi* (one who is versed in the text), the concluding prayer, and the meal that is taken by the congregation.

A note about the Golden Temple and Sikh temples in general: By the eighteenth century, the city of Amritsar, the Sikh holy city wherein the Golden Temple is located, served as the gathering spot for Sikhs especially after the death of the last Guru. The Golden Temple was built during Guru Arjan's time, the foundation stone laid in 1588. It is in the midst of an artificial lake, Amritsar (the Pool of Nectar), in the city of the same name, and is the center of Sikh religious power. The Temple was attacked in June 1984 by the Indian army to flush out Sikh fundamentalists. Many hundreds or thousands of pilgrims lost their lives, leading to an animosity toward the Indian government that has not healed. A direct outcome of this attack was the assassination of the Indian prime minister, Indira Gandhi.

Main Subgroups

Sikhs in the United States generally are of Indian, and more specifically, Panjabi origin. Subgroups do exist based on the issues of Guru succession, ritual, and customs. For instance, Khalsa Sikhs of Guru Gobind (the Singhs) only accept the ten Gurus ending with Gobind; two reform movements, the *Namdharis* (founded by Baba Balak Singh, 1797–1862) and *Nirankaris* (founded by Baba Dayal Das, 1783–1855), worship living Gurus. The first movement believed that the last Guru (Gobind Singh, b. 1675) did not die in 1708 but continued to live until the age of 137 (c. 1812), late enough to confer the Guruship on Balak Singh, who in turn passed the Guruship on to Ram Singh (1816–85), the twelfth Guru, upon his death in 1862. This continued line of personal Gurus defines them as unorthodox among most Sikhs. Some of their practices include vegetarianism, cow worship, the fire ceremony at which time some performers would achieve ecstasy and "shriek," a term by which they are identified: "Kukas" (from *kuk*, "shriek"). Namdharis take their name from their practice—namely, repeating the name of God. They are identified by the clothing they wear (made of white cloth) and their method of tying the turban, among other features.

The second movement, the Nirankaris, opposed the assimilation of the Sikhs into Hinduism. The name of the group refers to the renewed emphasis on the Absolute as *nirankar* or "Formless" Being, rather than the idolatry practiced by the Sikhs and Hindus with the exception of Guru Nanak and the Guru Granth Sahib.

Another movement is the Udasi sect, founded by Guru Nanak's son, Shri Chand (1494–1629). By its very name Udasis (*udas/udasin:* "one who is indifferent to" or "one who renounces" the world) are more ascetically inclined than other groups.

A twofold division may be considered to separate the Sikh community: the Kesadharis ("keeping one's hair uncut") and the Sahajdharis (the Easy Goers or Slow Adopters), who do not follow this practice. The first refers to a Sikh who does not cut his hair, an article of faith for Khalsa Sikhs who practice the five Ks.

One group, however, that is predominantly Western is the 3HO, or the Healthy, Happy, and Holy Organization, founded by Sardar Harbhajan Singh Puri (Yogi Bhajan, 1929–2004) in 1969. The members of this organization are recognizable by the wearing of white, Indian-style clothing and turbans by men and women. Both traditional Sikhs and 3HO adherents share in the basic beliefs and practices, with members visiting the temples of either community.

Common Misunderstandings and Stereotypes

"Why do they wear those turbans?"

The main area of concern is unfamiliarity with the dress codes of the Sikh community. Before a boy is initiated, his hair is allowed to grow with a cloth covering it. This might cause comment among other students to the discomfort of the Sikh student. If sufficiently mature, the student might be willing to explain these customs in class or in a paper.

"Should Sikh students be allowed to carry a weapon to school?"

Once initiated into practice, the Five Ks, especially leaving the hair uncut, over which a turban is worn, and carrying a steel dagger (the "dagger" is actually only a few inches long and is concealed) are clearly a concern for school officials because of the "zero tolerance" weapons policy of most schools nationwide. This is a time-honored practice among Panjabi Sikhs and so must be handled with discretion by teachers and administrators alike. Consultation with the Sikh parents is recommended. The Ninth Circuit Court of Appeals ruled in 1995 (*Cheemah v. Thompson*) that Sikh students could carry the dagger to school as long as it was sewn into its sheath.

Sikh holidays and festivals are not generally recognized in U.S. schools, but it must be remembered that certain obligations have to be carried out by the Sikh community that might require the student to miss school. It is advisable that the teacher and administrator discuss with the parents ahead of time which days might require the student to be away from class.

Population Data

According to the 2001 Indian census, there are 19,215,730 Sikhs residing in India, almost 2 percent of the population. Most reside in the Panjab (14,592,387), comprising almost 60 percent of the population. Globally, there are about 23 million Sikhs. Sikhs have emigrated to all parts of the world, including Great Britain, Canada, the United States, Africa, and other parts of Asia. The emigration was accelerated after the partition of India in 1947. The Sikhs who entered the United States and Canada were mainly professionals (doctors, teachers, and engineers), although many who came to California prior to this time worked as farm laborers. Many eventually bought farmland and now own sizable orchards and farms in California. A liberalization of the immigration laws after 1965 allowed many more Sikhs to enter. Kosmin and Keysar[1] report 57,000 adult Sikhs in the United States. The estimated number of Sikh adherents to the 3HO is fairly small, ranging from 5,000 to 10,000 members.

—*J.S.*

Further Reading

Cole, W. Owen. *Understanding Sikhism.* Edinburgh: Dunedin Academic, 2004.

Hawley, John Stratton, and Gurunder Singh Mann, eds. *Studying the Sikhs: Issues for North America.* Albany, NY: SUNY Press, 1993.

Mann, Gurunder Singh. *Sikhism.* Upper Saddle River, NJ: Prentice Hall, 2004.

_____. *The Making of Sikh Scripture.* New York: Oxford University Press, 2001.

McLeod, W. H. *Sikhs and Sikhism.* New Delhi and Oxford: Oxford University Press, 2004.

Singh, Pashaura. *The Guru Granth Sahib: Canon, Meaning and Authority.* New Delhi: Oxford University Press, 2000.

Web Sites

http://www.sikhs.org

http://www.bbc.co.uk/religion/religions/sikhism/

http://www.allaboutsikhs.com/introduction/introduction-to-sikhism.html

http://www.adherents.com

Notes

1. *Religion in a Free Market,* p. 27.

Unitarian Universalism

Origins

Unitarians trace their roots to such" "free thinkers" of the Reformation era as Michael Servetus (1511–53) and to liberal movements in Poland, Transylvania (part of present-day Romania), and England from the sixteenth to eighteenth centuries. Joseph Priestly, a refugee from England because of his beliefs, formed one of the first Unitarian churches in the United States in about 1794. During the early 1800s, a number of New England Congregationalist (United Church of Christ) churches embraced Unitarianism. Universalism, begun by John Murray, was a distinct but similar movement until its merger with the Unitarians in 1961. Unitarians formed their first congregation in 1779 in Gloucester, Massachusetts.

Beliefs

Unitarian Universalists (UUs), as the name implies, reject the trinitarian nature of God and thus the divinity of Jesus. In fact, belief in God is not required for membership. They also believe that salvation is universal, open to everyone in the world. UUs rely on their own reason and the teachings of the great religious and philosophical thinkers of all cultures for guidance. Although UUs revere the ethical teachings of Jesus, he is not their final religious authority. Hence, UUs are not considered Christian. UUs stress the inherent worth and dignity of each person; justice, equality, and compassion in human relations; the goal of world community with peace, liberty, and justice for all; and respect for the interdependent nature of all existence. They draw wisdom from the great religious traditions, but also from humanist teachings which prize reason, and earth-centered traditions which counsel living in harmony with nature.[1]

169

Sacred Books/Scriptures

There are no official scriptures; instead, UUs draw on the sacred writings of many religious traditions for inspiration and read from them and the works of poets and philosophers in their weekly services.

Practices

UUs have no sacraments as such but have rituals dedicating their children to the service of humanity, recognizing their coming of age, celebrating marriage, and remembering the dead.

UUs have Sunday services that consist of readings from various religious traditions, poets, and philosophers; a sermon; the singing of hymns; sharing of thoughts from the congregation; and a social hour afterward. UUs are very committed to social outreach—various activities to help people in need and to gain the passage of legislation that will better conditions for such people.

Main Subgroups

Given the tolerant and nondogmatic characteristics of the church, there are no subgroups, although individual churches are fully independent and thus free to emphasize different styles of worship, different social service agendas, and so on.

Common Misunderstandings and Stereotypes

"Unitarian Universalists are anti-Christian."

Although UUs accept neither belief in the Trinity nor Jesus' divinity, they bear no resentment towards Christianity. In fact, they applied in the past for membership in the National Council of Churches of Christ but were denied admittance. They do, however, work cooperatively with the Council and other religious groups on common concerns.

"Unitarian Universalists promote atheism."

Although UUs leave the decision about whether to believe in a higher power or God in the hands of individual members, they make no attempt whatsoever to convince people to become atheists. In fact, UUs do not actively seek converts, though they will gladly explain their teachings to anyone interested.

Classroom Concerns

It is recommended that Unitarian Universalist students not be lumped under the headings of Protestant or atheist. UUs are Humanists, or noncreedal free thinkers, who may personally hold a variety of beliefs but are united by their dedication to the principles of freedom, reason, and tolerance. (See the chapter "Secular Humanism/Atheism.") Like other non-Christian students, UUs do not celebrate Christian holidays, and teachers should be mindful of this.

It is recommended that teachers mention to their students the number of prominent Americans who either practiced Unitarian Universalism or were sympathetic to its philosophy: Thomas Jefferson, John Adams, John Quincy Adams, Benjamin Franklin, Thomas Paine, James Madison, Ralph Waldo Emerson, Theodore Parker, Nathaniel Hawthorne, Henry Wadsworth Longfellow, Herman Melville, Amy Lowell, Louisa May Alcott, Susan B. Anthony, and Clara Barton, among others.

Population Data

Kosmin and Keysar's survey found 629,000 adult Unitarian Universalists in the United States.[2] Adherents.com estimates the worldwide UU population at 800,000.[3]

—*B.H.*

Further Reading

Almstrom, Sydney E., and Jonathan S. Carey, eds. *An American Reformation: A Documentary History of Unitarian Christianity.* Lanham, MD: International Scholars Publications, 1997.

Buehrens, John A. *A Chosen Faith: An Introduction to Unitarian Universalism.* Boston: Beacon Press, 1988.

Mendelsohn, Jack. *Being Liberal in an Illiberal Age: Why I Am a Unitarian-Universalist.* Boston: Beacon Press, 1985.

Robinson, David. *The Unitarians and Universalists.* Westport, CT: Greenwood Press, 1985.

Web Sites

Ontario Consultants on Religious Tolerance: http://www.religioustolerance.org/u-u.htm

Official UU Web site: http://www.uua.org

Notes

1. "Unitarian Universalist Association Principles and Purposes." Available at http://www.uua.org. Accessed August 5, 2006.

2. *Religion in a Free Market*, p. 27.

3. http://www.adherents.com. Accessed on June 27, 2006.

The Pentacle is a five-pointed star within a circle, having a single point at the top and two points at the base; it is commonly worn as a protective amulet. Some Wiccans believe that four points of the star represent air, fire, water, and earth, and the fifth at the top is the quintessential element, or spirit.

Wicca

Origins

Wicca is the Old English word for *witch*. Witches (usually women, but also men) were people who used charms, spells, and herbs in rituals of healing, and as aids in childbirth, matchmaking, and spiritual guidance. Such practices have been the traditional province of religious specialists throughout the world who have been known as shaman, doctors, medicine men and women, magicians, healers . . . and witches. The belief underlying these practices is that health is established and maintained by living in harmony with nature. Witches apply their skills in witchcraft to the prevention or removal of harmful or evil influences that could cause illness and death or interfere with the flow of natural life. At the same time, because they deal with evil forces, witches have been accused of consorting with the devil, casting spells, and causing harm. It was fear of witches' dark powers (real or imagined) that caused Christian Europe to bring to trial, torture, and execute so many during the "burning times" (fifteenth–eighteenth centuries).

The Wiccan religion is part of contemporary Paganism (or Neo-Paganism).[1] It is based on non-Christian traditions—mainly Celtic and pre-Celtic—found, constructed, or imagined from archaeological and historical European sources. Although Wicca as a religion has been known since the early twentieth century, it is only with the repeal of laws against witchcraft in England[2] in 1951 that it has become more generally recognized and accepted. A major source of this recognition is Gerald Gardner (1884–1964), who published several influential books on the subject beginning in 1954. Since then, Wicca has taken on many forms. It is not a single organization but consists of diverse, decentralized groups (some of which are "covens")[3] and "eclectic" or "solitary practitioners," each having distinct traditions, beliefs, and practices.

Some Wiccans and Wiccan groups follow certain pre-Christian practices, which they believe to be original and authentic, often calling them the Old Religion. Others are more syncretistic, combining elements from several religions, ancient and modern. Still others believe that personal experience is sufficient for the construction of new rituals, beliefs and practices.

People become Wiccans for various reasons. For some, Wicca is a vital alternative to stale, out-dated religious practices; others discover that Wicca's practices and beliefs are similar to what they have felt and known already but for which they had no name for; for still others, Wicca is a modern form of traditional ethnic and cultural practices, sometimes handed down through family lines, sometimes constructed from fragments of myths, archaeological artifacts, literature, and history.

Wicca has grown rapidly in the United States, in part because it coincided with the countercultural revolution of the 1960s and 1970s and partly because it encouraged the participation of women. It is a recognized religion receiving the same protections under the Constitution as other religions.[4] Wiccans are found as advocates of environmental protection, opponents of discrimination against witches and witchcraft, and supporters of freedom of religion throughout the world.

Beliefs

Because Wiccans emphasize experience more than belief, there are those who say it doesn't matter what you believe, it is the inner experience that counts. However, most Wiccans agree with the following beliefs:

Nature: The universe is alive and human beings are one part of it. Wiccans communicate with, and influence, this interconnected web of nature through magic but never in a negative way.

The Rede: *"An (i.e., If) it harm none, do what thou wilt."* Wiccans are free to do whatever they wish, as long as it harms nobody, including themselves.

The Threefold Law: Many believe the harm one does will return three times over; so, too, will the good. In more general terms, whatever one does has repercussions, because everything is interconnected and affects everything else.

Reincarnation: Wiccans do not believe in hell. Many believe in rebirth in the present world and in reincarnation as a way of gaining enlightenment. Some believe that after death one goes to a netherworld (called Summerland) before being reborn.

Gods and Goddesses: Wiccans hold a range of belief: Some believe there is a single creative force in the universe; some believe in one God or Goddess; some are polytheistic (more than one Deity); some pantheistic (Deity is everywhere, or everything is Deity); and some panentheistic (Deity is everywhere, but also transcendent). Some Wiccans are agnostic, some atheistic. Many Wiccans are dualistic, believing in both a Goddess and a God. The Goddess is associated with the earth and the moon. She is seen as Maiden, Mother, and Crone, who stands for the creative cycle of the seasons and represents sensuality, fertility, and wisdom. The God is often pictured with horns. He is seen as Hunter and Lover, bringer of fertility but also death. Harmony and balance derive from the balance between God and Goddess.

Wicca is an earth-centered religion. It stresses living in harmony with nature, puts emphasis on feminine deities, and holds celebrations according to the "Wheel of the Year."

Sacred Books/Scriptures

Wicca has no holy text, although some Wiccans keep a workbook called the *Book of Shadows,* which contains rituals, spells, poetry, herbal lore, and commentary. Some of these books have been published, others are private journals.

Practices

Wheel of the Year: Festivals take place during the solar equinoxes and solstices, and the cross-quarter days between them. The Wheel begins with Samhain (SOW-en or SOW-ain), the Wiccan New Year. Other festivals are according to the phases of the moon. In addition, rituals may happen whenever needed, such as for initiation, birth, death, the union between couples (called handfasting), divorce, healing, or other life-cycle passages. Many Wiccans create their own rituals and ceremonies.

Some festivals are said to predate Christianity and have influenced Christian festivals. The most important festivals are:

Samhain (October 31, Halloween)

Beltane (May 1, spring festival, May Day)

Other festivals include:

Yule (December 21, Winter solstice, Christmas)

Imbolc (February 1, Candlemas, Groundhog Day)

Ostara (March 21, spring equinox, Easter)

Litha (June 21, summer solstice, Midsummer Night's Eve)

Lughnasadh (LOO-nah-sah, August 1, First Harvest)

Mabon (September 21, autumn equinox, Michaelmas).

Ritual: Wiccan groups meet in natural settings or private homes. A circle is drawn on the ground and consecrated by rituals that bring into focus the various dimensions of reality, symbolized by the elements (earth, air, fire, water, some add spirit); directions (north, east, south, west); colors (green, yellow, red, blue); human characteristics (stability, wisdom, will, regeneration); symbols (salt, incense, candle, chalice); spirit beings;

and others. The correspondence among these dimensions enables access to the interconnectedness of human beings, nature, and the world of the spirit. Rituals usually include:

- Consecration of the sacred circle.

- Invocation of Deity.

- Ritual actions: spells, magic, dancing, singing, teaching, healing, discussion, readings, and other nature-based, life-affirming activities. A communal meal usually follows the rituals.

- Banishing the circle and restoration of ordinary space.

Objects used in rituals include many everyday implements—salt, candles, a bell, a broom—as well as some less common ones, such as:

- A ritual knife—Athamé (ATH-ah-may)—although never used to injure.

- An altar

- Incense

- Pentacle, a five-pointed star (pentagram) within a circle

- A chalice or goblet

- A cauldron for mixing herbs

The work of healing and spiritual development is called Magic and may take place privately or in gatherings. Magic includes casting spells; preparing and administering potions; using talismans, chants, and charms; and meditation. In light of the Rede's ethics, one must use Magic only for good, never to harm.

Main Subgroups

Most Wiccans consider Wicca a subgroup of Paganism or Neo-Paganism.[5] The Wiccan religion is a series of independent, self-governing groups and individuals with no overarching authority. Wiccans usually belong to particular traditions or paths based on family heritage, historical tradition, mythic construction, or self-authenticating personal experience. Some of the traditions are known as Hereditary, Shamanic, Gardnerian, Alexandrian, Celtic, Traditionalist, Dianic, Faerie, and Eclectic. Solitary Wiccans may follow their own paths or one of the established traditions.

Common Misunderstandings and Stereotypes

"Wiccans are Satanists who worship the Devil."

Although many people think Wicca is a form of Satanism, Wiccans reject this association. The Wiccan Rede contradicts the practice of witchcraft for harmful purposes. Wiccans trace their religion to non-Christian and pre-Christian sources, whereas Satan is more often found among biblically-based religions. Numerous satanic cults have appeared in modern times and often are confused with Wicca. Although there are a few similarities such as meeting in a circle, practicing magic, and using a five-pointed star, Wiccans do not worship the Devil.

> *"Wicca is anti-Christian. If it is not stamped out, it will destroy Christian civilization."*

There are many popular folktales and legends about witchcraft, some of which may arouse feelings of terror and loathing. Stories of witches fascinate and repel, especially as portrayed in motion pictures and children's literature. Many common assumptions about witches, such as changing into animals, flying through the air, and causing storms, can be traced to the 1487 publication, *Malleus Maleficarum* (*The Witches' Hammer*[6]), which was instrumental in identifying witches during the "burning times." Unfortunately, Wicca has inherited this stigma of evil. Wicca may seem unusual, strange, or different, but there is no reason to fear it. Wiccans are devoted to doing good, not evil; to healing and reconciliation with nature, not its exploitation; and to reconciliation among religions, not the destruction of Christianity. Wicca teaches that there is much to be learned about the strange and wonderful world we live in. Through Wiccans' efforts to bring about peaceful resolutions to religious and racial differences, they show that unusual or strange religions may have good qualities even though they are "not like my religion." Wicca may not be Christian, but it should be taken as seriously as any other religion.

Classroom Concerns

Because witches are part of the popular mythology of Halloween, the season of Halloween presents an opportunity to explore the history and meaning of witches and witchcraft. For example, students might study how and why witches suffered persecution during the "burning times." Also, Halloween is one of several days of the year celebrated by Wiccans. Discussing the "wheel of the year" and the history of solar and lunar festivals could help children understand some of the relationships between nature and culture. In addition, comparing witchcraft with similar traditions worldwide, such as shamanism, may show how ideas of healing and health differ because of different worldviews. The Wiccan religion might be studied as an example of a non-biblically-based religion that is earth-friendly and teaches the equality of all religions.

If there are parents who are opposed to teaching about Halloween, teachers should make an effort to inform them that the study of witches and witchcraft is taught historically and objectively. In addition, Wicca is neither anti-Christian nor Satanic, as some parents might think.

Because Wicca often brings out stereotypes and prejudices, studying witches and witchcraft may be a good occasion for looking at how perceptions of reality get distorted. Wiccans are frequently available to help teach about stereotypes.

Occasionally, school policies prohibit students from wearing a pentacle or other signs of witchcraft. Once again, Wiccans are usually willing to help resolve discriminatory policies.

The following two Web sites may be of help in locating Wiccans willing to be of assistance:

- Larry Cornett, "Directory of Public Earth Religion Rights Contacts": http://members.aol.com/lcorncalen/directory.htm

- Larry Cornett, "Topic-Specific Links for Help and Guidance Concerning Religious Discrimination and Associated Legal Problems": http://members.aol.com/lcorncalen/helplink.htm

Population Data

Kosmin and Keysar estimate there has been a seventeen-fold increase in self-identified adult Wiccans between 1990 and 2001, from 8,000 to 134,000, making Wicca one of the fastest-growing religions in the United States.[7]

Wiccans tend to be "white, college-educated and middle class."[8] The largest groups are students, computer analysts, writers, and housewives; one-third are men, two-thirds are women.

—J.H.

Further Reading

Adler, Margot. *Drawing Down the Moon: Witches, Druids, Goddess-Worshippers, and Other Pagans in America Today.* New York: Penguin Books, 1986.

Cunningham, Scott. *Wicca: A Guide for the Solitary Practitioner.* St. Paul: Llewellyn, 1988.

Gardner, Gerald. *Witchcraft Today.* New York: The Citadel Press, 1954.

Lewis, James R., ed. *Magical Religion and Modern Witchcraft.* Albany: SUNYPress, 1996.

Starhawk. *The Spiral Dance: A Rebirth of the Ancient Religion of the Goddess.* Rev. ed. San Francisco: Harper and Row, 1989.

Web Sites

American Religion Data Archive: http://www.thearda.com/

Circle Sanctuary: http://www.circlesanctuary.org/aboutpagan/guide.htm

Law Enforcement Guide to Witchcraft, Wicca and Other Earth Religions: http://www.tylwytheg.com/lawguide/lawguide1.html

Ontario Consultants on Religious Tolerance: http://www.religioustolerance.org/mist_404.htm

Pluralism Project: http://www.pluralism.org/news/search.php

Religious Movements Homepage Project @The University of Virginia: http://religiousmovements.lib.virginia.edu/nrms/wicca.html

Witches Voice: http://www.witchvox.com/

Notes

1. The differences between Pagans and Neo-Pagans are too controversial and complex to include in this essay. See Ontario Consultants on Religious Tolerance Web page *Neopagan-Pagan Religious Traditions* Available at http:religioustolerance.org/neo_paga.htm. Accessed March 16, 2007.

2. Laws against witches and witchcraft had existed in England since 1401.

3. Groups of people, usually no more than thirteen in number, who meet periodically to participate in Wiccan rituals.

4. In *Dettmer v. Landon* (1985), the District Court of Virginia ruled that Wicca is a legally recognized religion and is afforded all the benefits accorded to it by law. Available at http://en.wikipedia.org/wiki/Wicca. Accessed February 21, 2006.

5. See note 1 above.

6. Jacob Sprenger and Heinrich Kramer, *Malleus Maleficarum.* University of Cologne, 1487. http://en.wikipedia.org/wiki/Malleus_Maleficarum. Accessed February 21, 2006.

7. *Religion in a Free Market*, p. 28.

8. *The Washington Post*, October 31, 2003, quoted in the Pluralism Project, http://www.pluralism.org/news/search.php. Accessed April 14, 2006.

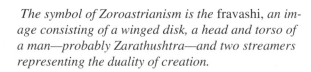

The symbol of Zoroastrianism is the fravashi, *an image consisting of a winged disk, a head and torso of a man—probably Zarathushtra—and two streamers representing the duality of creation.*

Zoroastrianism

Origins

The Iranian reformer responsible for establishing the Zoroastrian religion is known either by his Iranian name, Zarathushtra, or his Greco-Latin name Zoroaster. Although very little is known about him, he is one of the very few traditional founders of a major religious tradition who left a written record. Known as an astrologer and the founder of magic in Western esoteric texts, Zarathushtra also was considered the arch-representative of the Magi (a priestly tribe of the Medes, according to Herodotus) by many Greek and Roman writers. Because the Magi were associated with oneiromancy (divination through dreams), astrology, and magic, Zarathushtra was considered a great practitioner of magic as well as being a great sage and prophet. As sage and prophet, he represented Persian wisdom. It is little wonder that the three Wise Men mentioned in Matthew 2:1 13 were also representatives of Eastern (Persian) wisdom and astrology.

Zarathushtra's dates are uncertain. Some scholars suggest an earlier date between 1000–700 B.C.E., and others propose 660–583 B.C.E. or 630–553 B.C.E. The life of the prophet may be divided between what few facts can be discerned from early sources to the legendary accounts that developed from the Younger Avesta and later Pahlavi or Middle Persian works. He was born in Iran, perhaps western Iran, into the Median Spitaman family. His parents, Pourushaspa and Dughdhova, named him Zarathushtra, "he who can manage camels," thus giving him the full name of Spitama Zarathushtra. He chose, or his parents chose for him, his profession as a priest (*zaotar*), beginning formal training at the age of seven. According to tradition, he was initiated as a *zaotar* at age fifteen, left the home of his parents at age twenty, and retired from the world in search for truth. At age thirty, he experienced his first vision when Vohu Manah, "Good Intention," an aspect of the Supreme God (Ahura

181

Mazda) appeared to him and arranged a conference with Ahura Mazda. The upshot of this revelation was the call to the service of God. In the following seven or eight years, six additional revelations or visions are said to have occurred, each emphasizing the cardinal virtues of the teaching.

Following the first vision, Zarathushtra undertook the spread of the new teaching, but only his cousin, Maidhyoi-maonha, was converted, and he not until the tenth year of the religion. Because of his failure to attract followers, he left his native land and traveled to the court of Vishtaspa, where he first attracted the attention of the queen, Hutaosa, and later the king. This apparently took place when he was forty-two and gained him a place of honor in the kingdom. He married three times, had three daughters and a son with his first wife, and two sons with his second wife. His religion grew because of the numerous battles undertaken by Vishtaspa, now a devout follower.

The religion spread throughout Iran and beyond its borders to Turkistan. Later, it became the dominant religion of the Archaemenian Empire (549–331 B.C.E.), the Parthian Arcasid Empire (141 B.C.E.–224 C.E.), and the Sassanian Empire (224–642 C.E.). After the Arab conquest of Iran and the Sassanians, Zoroastrianism lost much of its influence except for pockets of influence in parts of Iran and beyond. From the seventh century on, Zoroastrians, under Muslim control, were considered People of the Book (*dhimmis*). As early as the eighth century C.E., some Zoroastrians traveled to Gujurat (India) and adjacent areas to escape Muslim persecution. They are known there as Parsis (meaning "Persians" in Gujarati) and were allowed to settle. Thus, the Zoroastrian community is divided to this day between the Iranis and Parsis.

Beliefs

The teaching of Zarathushtra did not arise in a vacuum. His was a reaction to the traditional Iranian religion and to the social, economic, and political realities of his time. The traditional religion shared many features with the Vedic or pre-Hindu religion described in the Vedas (see chapter on Hinduism). When compared to those sections in the Avesta (the Zoroastrian scripture) that retain elements of the traditional religion, we can surmise that it accepted many gods and that a hierarchy may have existed including the *ahuras,* a class of divinity that was associated with creation and the cosmic order. The *ahuras* were therefore associated with "good" or "orderly" gods. In the Iranian traditional religion *ahuras* were high deities, as they were also in the earliest portion of the Indian Vedas, the *Rigveda.* Zarathushtra, curiously, ignored the *ahuras* as a class of divinity but it is obvious that his Supreme God was an *ahura,* perhaps *the* Ahura or Wise (Mazda) Ahura who was considered by his tribal group to be the special god of the Aryans or highest social class.

Zarathushtra's unique insight was to proclaim Ahura Mazda, the "Wise Lord"—to whom Zarathushtra was introduced during his first Revelation—as the Supreme God for all of society. This God was described in a manner similar to what the Hebrews (Jews) understood their God to be: One; the Creator of heaven and earth and of the spiritual and material world; the Source of both light and darkness; the Lawgiver and Judge who created laws that would guide humans to truth; the One who is omniscient, omnipresent, and omnipotent and exercises absolute sovereignty—in brief, God Almighty.

The Question of Dualism

Among the teachings about Ahura Mazda is that concerning the Holy or Beneficent Spirit (Spanta Mainyu). The problem with Spanta Mainyu is whether he is identical with Ahura Mazda, or a principle or aspect of God. Understanding the true relationship between the two explains the nature of the religion. Is Zoroastrianism a monotheistic religion or dualistic? The ultimate question that a monotheistic religion faces is the origin of evil. If God is All-Good, then whence comes evil? This is the issue that confronted Zarathushtra and his later followers. Whether both Goodness and Evil originate from God cannot be answered, although the expectation and wish is that only Goodness can come from the Supreme Being. The fact that both exist is incontestable and of paramount importance in the conduct of the Zoroastrian's life. The issue arises in the Gathas ("hymns" or "songs" composed by Zarathushtra included in the Avesta or scripture, specifically Yasna 30), which posits two spirits—twins—one wicked (Angra Mainyu), the other good (Spanta Mainyu), both of whom in the beginning revealed themselves in thought, word, and deed. These two made choices at the beginning of creation: the wicked twin chose to do wicked deeds, known as the Lie (Druj), whereas the good twin chose justice and Truth (Asha). Thus a paradigm or model is created that emphasizes the choice between Good and Evil. The dualism of Zoroastrianism, therefore, is most definitely an ethical dualism based on free will; whether it is a monotheistic religion in which there is one creator, or a cosmic dualism wherein a creator of good and a creator of evil were posited, was open to debate and controversy in the religion. (See the section on "Main Subgroups.") What is important, however, is that Zoroastrians side with the good and the Creator of good, and their whole purpose on earth is to choose the good and to live the good life. This, after all, reflects the action of Ahura Mazda Himself, who chose "holy and good right-mindedness" (Yasna 32.2). As God chooses Truth, so, too, must his followers. The same Yasna (32.3–5), also states that Ahura rejects the false gods and their followers, an indication that Zarathushtra's reform places humanity on the right track in conformity with God's choice.

Free choice does not have consequences only in this world. Zarathushtra certainly expected to reform the world (Gatha 34.6), but it would come as a result of the continuous struggle against evil by those who chose the Truth (Asha). Conformity to God's Will, which involves choosing the Good or Truth and rejecting the Lie (Druj) is manifested as three forms of action: good words, good thoughts, good deeds. This is the ethical foundation of Zoroastrianism.

Besides the transformation of this world, a second existence is mentioned in Gatha 45.1, which obviously refers to the spiritual realm. When death occurs, the soul (*urvan*) survives and, on the third day after death, departs the earth and is met by a female figure, the *daena*, a figure perhaps representing the soul's conscience, who accompanies the soul to the place of judgment at the Bridge of the Separator where they are met by the Judge, Ahura Mazda Himself. If good actions outweigh bad actions, the soul is allowed in Heaven with the *daena*; if bad actions outweigh good, the soul falls into Hell; if the actions are balanced, then the soul goes to a "Place of the Mixed," an abode without joy and sorrow.

Salvation also includes a Final and General Judgment. In later Zoroastrianism, this teaching is given through an explanation of choice between Truth or Good and Lie or Evil. In addition, a grand dualism is described involving the battle between Ohrmazd or the God of all that is Good, and Ahriman, the demonic Evil one. The battle would last twelve thousand years. Their influence would abide in the two states of existence: the incorporeal or spiritual (Pahlavi *menog*) and corporeal or material (*getig*). The corporeal creation is open to corruption and the assault of Ahriman. Within limited, historical time, as opposed to eternity, two periods are established: (1) the creation by Ohrmazd of both *menog* and *getig* which took place when the two (Ohrmazd and Ahriman) made their choices and (2) the subsequent assault by Ahriman of the *getig* sphere. This second period is the contention of good and evil, which is followed by the Frashokarati "Making Wonderful," "Rehabilitation," when eternity now manifests itself and history ends. Evil is destroyed and a "Separation" (*Wizarishn*) of good from evil occurs, resulting in all humans—along with Ohrmazd and the *yazatas* (lesser divinities worthy of worship)—living in harmony, peace, and goodness.

This battle between the forces of good and evil will result in the triumph of Truth over the Lie, which is purged from this world when all creation, including humanity, will undergo an ordeal of submerging everything in a river of molten metal, with the righteous being blessed and the wicked destroyed. This was Zarathushtra's interpretation of the Last Period, a time when the utter destruction of evil and the annihilation of sinners would take place. What happens with those in the "Place of the Mixed" is not clear.

In later Zoroastrianism, a substantial change occurs with respect to the Last Time. The damnation of the wicked is no longer considered permanent. The ordeal, rather than destroying the wicked souls, will purge them of sin with molten metal, so that the suffering souls are now repentant after realizing God's (Ohrmazd's) goodness. This account also introduces the Messianic figure Saoshyant (or three Saoshyants, depending on the version), who is responsible for the Rehabilitation and final victory over evil. Born of the seed of Zarathushtra, a human and warrior-hero-priest, the Saoshyant or Savior is also responsible for resurrecting the bodies of the dead and uniting them with their souls now restored to a pure state.

Where the three Saoshyants are mentioned, the number conforms to the division of the "world-year," that period of twelve thousand years from the time of the beginning of the conflict between Ohrmazd and Ahriman to the Frashokarati or beginning of eternity. The "world-year" is divided into four periods of three-thousandyears each. In the last three-thousand-year period a Saoshyant is born every thousand years, each contributing to the Rehabilitation. The final Saoshyant participates in the last battle, the Resurrection, and the Frashokarati.[1]

Sacred Books/Scriptures

The sacred writings of the Zoroastrians is known as the Avesta, a term only occurring in Pahlavi or Middle Persian as *avistak,* from the Sassanian Period (third to seventh centuries C.E.). Only a fragment of the original set of works comprising the Avesta still exists. Tradition states that it once contained twenty-one books (*Nasks*), of which the only complete work, *Nask* 19, titled the *Videvdad*, survives. Fragments of two other *Nasks* also exist. The present Avesta is divided into the following parts:

1. The *Yasna* "sacrifice, worship, offering." It consists of seventy-two chapters and, as the name suggests, is primarily concerned with worship. Chapters 1–27 contain the invocation to the Supreme God, Ahura Mazda, and to other divinities. The following chapters—28–34, 43–51, and 53—comprised the Gathas, or the songs composed by Zarathushtra (excepting 53). Written slightly later are chapters 35–42, known as the "Seven Chapters." The remaining chapters (52, 54–72), known as the Later Yasna, contain praises and thanksgiving offerings to various divinities.

2. The *Visperad* ("All the Lords") consists of invocations to the lords mentioned therein.

3. The *Yashts* are the "songs of praise." Consisting of twenty-one altogether, they are directed to the divinities or angels.

4. The *Videvdad* is a priestly code somewhat similar to the biblical Book of Leviticus. The story of the progenitor of the human race, Yima, is narrated along with a version of the Flood.

5. The *Khordah Avesta* or "Little Avesta." A number of minor texts including special "Prayers."

6. Fragments of numerous other scriptures also survive.

Practices

1. **Calendar**—Zoroastrians observe a number of festivals and holidays. When they occur is confusing because of the different calendars. Three are current: Fasli ("seasonal"), Shahanshahi (Shenshai), and the Qadimi ("ancient") calendars. The first follows the Gregorian calendar and fixes New Year's Day on March 21. The Shahanshahi calendar is followed by the Parsis and is "theoretically synchronized with the seasons by inserting a month every 120 years." New Year's was observed on August 23, 1995 *(The Qadimi* calendar supposedly represents the ancient tradition and "is one month ahead of the Shahanshahi)."[2]

2. **Initiation Rite**—The Navjote or initiation rite occurs between the ages of seven and fifteen years for both boys and girls at a time when the child is capable of offering the Zoroastrian prayers and observing its rituals and customs. Two garments are given to the child: the shirt and thread or cord. The cord is tied around the shirt three times signifying good thoughts, good words, and good deeds.

3. **Prayer**—Prayer ideally occurs five times a day (dawn, sunrise, noon, afternoon, and night) requiring ablutions for all those above age seven who pray. Ritual cleanliness is important and a sacred cord is tied around the waist for each prayer.

4. **Funeral rites**—These rites are fairly well known because of the method of disposal of the body. The body is exposed to the elements as the only means of disposing of the corpse. In Mumbai (Bombay), "towers of silence" exist specifically for this purpose. The body is exposed until picked clean by vultures or from the elements, and the bones are bleached by the sun. This practice is becoming more difficult, however, because of the scarcity of vultures in Mumbai. Solar panels are now being suggested to aid in the disposal of bodies.

5. **Holidays**—Six seasonal festivals are celebrated to honor the sky, waters, earth, plants, cattle, and humanity. These represent the six stages of Creation. Other festivals include the birthday of Zarathushtra in August or September, the death of Zarathushtra, and the birth of the fire. New Year's Day (No Roz, Naw Ruz, or Norouz) is celebrated on the first day of spring or around the time of the vernal equinox when prayers are offered at the Fire Temple before the fire. This is the most important day of the year. The feast of "All Souls" is celebrated a few days before the New Year. The festival of Fire is celebrated about fifty days before the New Year as a midwinter celebration.

Main Subgroups

Many subgroups, both sectarian and heretical, have been recorded throughout Zoroastrian history. One of the earlier movements, Zurvanism, was an attempt to interpret one of the most perplexing teachings in Zoroastrianism: the twin spirits mentioned by Zarathushtra himself (see "Beliefs," above). In the *Monotheistic view* Spanta Mainyu, the Holy or Bounteous Spirit, is an aspect or function of Ahura Mazda, as may have been the case in Zarathushtra's teaching. If so, then Ahura Mazda is only associated with Spanta Mainyu (the good spirit), not Angra Mainyu (the wicked). So the religion must be considered monotheistic. Yet the position of Angra Mainyu is open to misinterpretation if Zarathushtra's teaching reflects an absolute monotheism. What if Spanta Mainyu is a literal twin of Angra Mainyu, and therefore identical to Ahura Mazda? If this is so, then Spanta Mainyu was the creator of good, while his twin brother, Angra Mainyu, the creator of evil. This was more the view during Sassanian times (third–seventh centuries C.E.) and is today considered the orthodox position within Zoroastrianism.

Zurvanism or the dualistic view, on the other hand, which developed as early as the Achaemenid Dynasty (549–331 B.C.E.), posited a totally new entity who is parent to both Spirits: Zurvan "Supreme Time." Then, neither Spanta Mainyu-Ahura Mazda (Ohrmazd) nor Angra Mainyu (Ahriman) was transcendent. Both were limited but derived from Infinite Time (Zurvan). This "heretical" sect (at least in the eyes of the orthodox Zoroastrians) lasted to the seventh century C.E.

It is difficult to determine whether differences of opinion comprise different subcommunities within the Zoroastrian community. A Web site operated by the Zarathushtrian Assembly considers those who use different calendars (the Shahanshahis, Faslis and Qadimis) to be "denominations."[3] The Philosophy, Theology, and Religion Website belonging to St. Martin's College[4] includes more recent movements, such as Ilm-i Kshnoom,[5] an occult movement established by Behramshah Shroff (1857–1927), whose philosophy is explained in *A Manual of Khshnoom: The Zoroastrian Occult Knowledge* by Phiroz Nasarvanji Tavaria.

Of the other possible divisions within Zoroastrianism, perhaps only the Mazdaznan Movement is a genuine offshoot of Zoroastrianism. Founded by the Rev. Dr. Otoman Zar-Adhusht Hanish (d. 1936), monotheism centered on Ahura Mazda, who is described in Trinitarian terms: the Father, Mother, and Child. Breath control, chanting, and rhythmic praying are means of perfecting the body. Vegetarianism is also practiced. The Movement is currently headquartered in Encinitas, California.[6]

Common Misunderstandings and Stereotypes

Zoroastrianism is not known well enough to generate many misunderstandings. Any that do exist come from an unlikely source. Writers—reporters or even textbook writers—often misconstrue the purpose of the fire in the Zoroastrian temple, which they misidentify as Ahura Mazda or as the *fravashi* (see below).

"Zoroastrians worship fire."

Zoroastrians are not fire-worshippers; rather, they regard fire as associated with Truth (Asha), purification, the sun, and ultimately the light or sun of Ahura Mazda. It is also thought of as the representative of the religion. As such, fire dispels darkness or the Evil Spirit (Angra Mainyu or Ahriman). Rituals are usually performed before the fire housed in the fire temples known as Atash Kadeh or Dar-e Mihr.

The *fravashi* is representative of the soul. Because other terms are used for soul (*urvan, daena*), it is problematic what this term, never used by Zarathushta, meant. One scholar (H. W. Bailey) suggests it is the spirit of the hero. In its earliest mention (Yasna 37.3), *fravashis* are associated with the departed souls of the just. Most probably, it is a term referring to the departed righteous, in some passages the preexistent souls of the just, and often a protector of humans or guardian spirit. The image of the *fravashi,* and symbol of the religion itself, is shown at the beginning of the chapter.

Classroom/Community Concerns

The concerns of the Zoroastrian community resemble those of the Jewish community. Stated in traditionalist terms, how do Zoroastrians maintain their uniqueness? How do they prevent assimilation into the larger community—Indian, American, or European? What is the proper attitude toward marriage, that is, may Zoroastrians marry outside the faith or must they marry Zoroastrian women or men? The declining birthrate and the emphasis on marrying in endogamy by the traditionalists may lead to oblivion, yet marriage outside the community may lead to the loss of identity. Another issue relating to marrying out is the fate of children. In India, entrée into the religion by means of the Initiation Ceremony (Navjote) is through Zoroastrian men, so those children who are born of a Zoroastrian woman and non-Zoroastrian man are not allowed entry into the religion. In the United States, however, the community is more accepting. This does not detract from the common opinion within the Zoroastrian community at large that the religion is ethnic and that membership is determined by birth. In other words, ethnic identity is no different from religious identity.

Although some conversions have taken place, the accepted teaching within the Irani and Parsi communities is that conversions are not allowed. The result of this exclusivism is a sharp decline in the Parsi population. Special mention is given in the Population Analysis of the Indian Census of 2001 of the decline of population of the Parsi community in India from 79,382 in the 1991 census of India to 69,601 in the 2001 census. The final portion of the report states: "This is a clear, visible but extremely unfortunate decline of a rich civilization of Zoroastrians and its people. It is apparent from 2001 census results that urgent and drastic interventions are required by all concerned including possibly by the government and definitely the Parsi community leaders to ensure survival of Parsi population in India."[7]

Another issue is the strict adherence to ritual and ancient symbols. Should rituals be retained in their pristine purity or should there be reform? Reformers wish to discard excessive ceremonialism and certain beliefs. An outcome of the reformist movement is the abandonment of ancient dress, such as the sacred shirt and cord. The fire temples are seldom visited. There is a blending with other religions, such as Hinduism, Theosophy, and Christianity. The time-honored ceremony of exposure of the dead body is now being replaced by burial or cremation.

Population Data

Zoroastrians number under 200,000 worldwide. It is very likely that the number is closer to 150,000, with the largest number in India (about 60,000), 30,000 in Iran, and about 25,000 in North America. It is a religion in decline, largely because of the tradition of not allowing conversions. A falling birthrate is especially evident in India because many Parsi women marry late. (Figures are provided by www.Adherents.com.) The decline in population is also the subject of a *Boston Globe* article (September 5, 2004) by Jehangir Pocha.[8]

—*J.S.*

Further Reading

Boyce, Mary. *A History of Zoroastrianism.* 3 vols. Leiden: E. J. Brill, 1989. (Vol. I: *The Early Period.* Second impression with corrections; originally published 1975; Vol. II: *Under the Achaemenians,* 1982; Vol. III: *Under Macedonian and Roman Rule,* 1992).

_____, ed. and trans. *Textual Sources for the Study of Zoroastrianism.* Totowa, NJ: Barnes & Noble Books, 1984.

_____. *Zoroastrianism: A Shadowy but Powerful Presence in the Judeo-Christian World.* London: Dr. William's Trust, 1987.

_____. *Zoroastrianism: Its Antiquity and Constant Vigour.* Costa Mesa, CA: Mazda, 1992.

Gnoli, Gherardo. *Zoroaster in History.* New York: Bibliotheca Persica Press, 2000.

Gray, Louis H. *The Foundations of the Iranian Religions.* Bombay: D. B. Taraporevala Sons, 1930.

Modi, Jivanji Jamshedji. *Religious Ceremonies and Customs of the Parsees.* 2nd ed. Bombay: Jehangir B. Karani's Sons, 1937.

Moulton, James Hope. *Early Zoroastrianism.* London: Williams and Norgate, 1913; reprint: New York: AMS Press, 1980.

Zaehner, R. C. *The Dawn and Twilight of Zoroastrianism.* New York: Putnam, 1961.

Web Sites

http://www.avesta.org/

http://www.sacred-texts.com/zor/

http://www.bbc.co.uk/religion/religions/zoroastrian

http://www.vohuman.org

http://www.zoroastrian.org

Notes

1. Mary Boyce, *A History of Zoroastrianism,* Vol. I. Leiden: Brill, 1989, pp. 286-87.

2. Available at http://www.avesta.org/zcal.html. Accessed August 22, 2006.

3. Available at http://www.zoroastrian.org/other/faq.htm. Accessed August 24, 2006.

4. Available at http://www.philtar.ucsm.ac.uk/encyclopedia/zorast. Accessed August 24, 2006.

5. Available at http://www.tenets.zoroastrianiam.com/AManualofKshnoon.pdf. Accessed August 28, 2006.

6. Available at http://www.philtar.ucsm.ac.uk/encyclopedia/zoroast/mazdaz.html. Accessed September 1, 2006.

7. Available at http://www.censusindia.net/results/religion_main.html. Accessed September 6, 2006.

8. Available at http://www.boston.com/news/world/articles/2004/09/05/shrinking_population_threatens_an_ancient_faith. Accessed September 6, 2006.

General Bibliography

Note: For books on specific religions, see the "Further Reading" lists at the end of each chapter.

Encyclopedias/Dictionaries

Bell, Daniel A., and Hahm Chaibong, eds. *Confucianism for the Modern World.* Cambridge, England: Cambridge University Press, 2003.

Coulter, Charles R., and Patricia Turner. *The Encyclopedia of Ancient Deities.* London: McFarland, 2000.

de Bary, William Theodore, and Irend Bloom, eds. *Sources of Chinese Tradition.* 2nd ed. New York: Columbia University Press, 1999–2000.

Eliade, Mircea, ed. *The Encyclopedia of Religion.* 16 vols. New York: Macmillan, 1987.
     The most detailed and comprehensive reference work in English on the world's religions; includes extensive bibliographies.

Freedman, David Noel, ed. *The Anchor Bible Dictionary.* 6 vols. New York: Doubleday, 1992.

Glasse, Cyril. *The Concise Encyclopedia of Islam.* New York: Harper & Row, 1989.

Guastad, Edwin. *Religious History of America.* New York: Harper & Row, 1974.
     A collection of documents from the religious history of the United States, with commentary by the author.

Haboush, Jahyun Kim, Dorothy Ko, and Joan R. Piggott, eds. *Women and Confucian Cultures in Premodern China, Korea and Japan.* Berkeley: University of California Press, 2003.

Hejtmanek, Milan, Alan Wachman, and Tu Weiming, eds. *The Confucian World Observed: A Contemporary Discussion of Confucian Humanism in East Asia.* Honolulu: East-West Center, 1992.

Hillcrbrand, Hans, ed. *The Encyclopedia of Protestantism.* 4 vols. New York: Routledge, 2004.

Keck, Leander, ed. *The New Interpreter's Bible.* 13 vols. Nashville, TN: Abingdon, 1994.

Kohn, Livia. *Daoism and Chinese Culture.* Cambridge, MA: Three Pines Press, 2001.

Laozi. *A Translation of Lao Tzu's* Tao Te Ching *and* Wang Pi's Commentary. Ann Arbor: Center for Chinese Studies, University of Michigan, 1977.

Livingstone, E.A. *The Oxford Dictionary of the Christian Church,* 3rd ed. Oxford: Oxford University Press, 1997.

Lopez, Donald W., ed. *Religions of China in Practice.* Princeton: Princeton University Press, 1996.

Marthaler, Berard, ed. *The New Catholic Encyclopedia,* 2nd ed. 19 vols. Washington, DC: Catholic University Press and Thomson-Gale, 2003.

191

Martin, Richard C., ed. *The Encyclopedia of the Muslim World.* 2 vols. New York: Thomson-Gale, 2004.

McBrien, Richard P., ed. *The HarperCollins Encyclopedia of Catholicism.* New York: HarperCollins, 1995.

Melton, J. Gordon. *Encyclopedic Handbook of Cults in America.* New York: Garland, 1992.

Melton, J. Gordon, and Martin Baumann, eds. *Religions of the World (A Comprehensive Encyclopedia of Beliefs and Practices).* 4 vols., illustrated. Santa Barbara, CA: ABC-CLIO Press, 2002.

Neusner, Jacob, Alan J. Avery-Peck, and Wm. Scott Green, eds. *The Encyclopedia of Judaism.* 3 vols. New York, Continuum, 1999.

Roth, Cecil, and Geoffrey Widgoder, eds. *Encyclopedia Judaica.* 16 vols. Jerusalem: Keter, 1972.

Slote, Walter H., and George A. De Vos, eds. *Confucianism and the Family.* Albany, NY: SUNY Press, 1998.

Smith, Jonathan Z., and William Scott Green, eds. *The HarperCollins Dictionary of Religion.* San Francisco: Harper, 1995.

Stein, Gordon, ed. *The Encyclopedia of Unbelief.* 2 vols. Buffalo, NY: Prometheus Books, 1985.

Wigoder, Geoffrey, ed. *The New Encyclopedia of Judaism.* New York: NYU Press, 2002.

Zhuangzi. *Basic Writings/Chuang Tzu.* Burton Watson, trans. New York: Columbia University Press, 1996.

Religion and Public Education (annotated)

Council on Islamic Education. *Teaching about Islam in the Public School Classroom: A Handbook for Educators.* 3rd ed. Fountain Valley, CA: Council on Islamic Education, 1995.

    A balanced, rich resource for teaching about Islam.

Gaddy, Barbara, T. William Hall, and Robert Marzano. *School Wars: Resolving Our Conflicts over Religion and Values.* San Francisco: Jossey-Bass, 1996.

    A balanced look at the controversies surrounding religion and education. A useful guide to help parents, teachers, and community leaders understand the background of these disputes.

Greenawalt, Kent. *Does God Belong in Public Schools?* Princeton, NJ: Princeton University Press, 2005.

    Covers some of the same ground about the legitimate place of religion in public schools as the books by Charles Haynes (below) but more from the standpoint of a legal scholar.

Haynes, Charles, et al. *The First Amendment in Schools.* Nashville, TN: First Amendment Center and Association for Supervision and Curriculum Development, 2003.

A concise guide to the five freedoms enunciated in the First Amendment (religion, speech, press, assembly, and petition) with a summary of judicial decisions that interpret these freedoms as they relate to public schools.

_____, ed. *Finding Common Ground: A First Amendment Guide to Religion and Public Education.* Nashville, TN: First Amendment Center, 1994.

A comprehensive and useful teacher's resource manual for First Amendment issues. Includes materials for teaching about religion.

———. *Religion in American History: What to Teach and How.* Alexandria, VA: Association for Supervision and Curriculum Development, 1990.

_____ and Warren A. Nord. *Taking Religion Seriously across the Curriculum.* Nashville: First Amendment Center, 1998.

Discusses the importance of integrating factual information about world religions, religion in American history and character education into the curriculum at appropriate levels, and explains how to do so.

Nord, Warren A. *Religion and American Education: Rethinking a National Dilemma.* Chapel Hill: University of North Carolina Press, 1995.

A pivotal book in the dialogue on religion's place in the public school classroom. Thorough, lengthy, and controversial, but basic for educational policy making.

Web Sites (annotated)

Note: For Web sites on specific religions, see the sites listed at the end of each chapter.

http://www.beliefnet.org

A very valuable site that combines breaking religion news with a stable of some eighty columnists and essays on virtually every one of the world's principal religions.

http://www.religioustolerance.org

Similar in some respects to Beliefnet but with greater stress on inter-religious understanding. Excellent essays both on specific religions and controversial issues (e.g., biblical inerrancy).

Appendix A
Ramona Unified School District Policy Instruction

Recognition of Religious Beliefs and Customs

The Governing Board recognizes that students' education would be incomplete without an understanding of the role of religion in history and current society. It is both proper and important for teachers to objectively discuss the influences of various religions, using religious works and symbols to illustrate their relationship with society, literature or the arts. The Board expects that such instruction will identify differences and principles common to all religions and foster respect for the multiple creeds practiced by the peoples of the world.

In order to respect each student's individual right to freedom of religious practice, religious indoctrination is clearly forbidden in the public schools. Instruction about religion must not favor, promote or demean the beliefs or customs of any particular religion or sect. Staff shall be highly sensitive to its obligation not to interfere with the religious development of any student in whatever tradition the student embraces.

Statement of Purpose

The Board endorses teaching about religion where the curriculum guides indicate it is appropriate and when the classroom atmosphere encourages both teachers and students to be responsible and to respect the rights of each person.

Such teaching must foster knowledge *about* religion, not indoctrination into religion; it should be academic, not devotional or testimonial; it should promote awareness of religion, not sponsor its practice, nor be hostile towards it; it should inform students about the diversity of religious views rather than impose one particular view; and it should promote understanding of different religious views as well as respect for the rights of persons who hold such views.

Staff shall not endorse, encourage or solicit religious or anti-religious expression or activities among students. They shall not lead students in prayer or participate in student-initiated prayer. However, staff shall not prohibit or discourage any student from praying or otherwise expressing his/her religious belief as long as this does not disrupt the classroom.

Students may express their beliefs about religion in their homework, artwork and other written and oral reports if the expression is germane to the assignment. Such work shall be judged by ordinary academic standards, free of discrimination based on religious content.

Rights and Responsibility of Students/Staff

Students have the right to pray individually or in groups or to discuss their religious views with their peers so long as they are not disruptive. Because the Establishment Clause does not apply to purely private speech, students enjoy the right to read religious literature, pray before meals, and before tests, and discuss religion with other student listeners as long as the listener(s) are not coerced or harassed. However, the right to engage in voluntary prayer does not include, for example, the right to have a captive audience listen or to compel other students to participate.

Teachers and school administrators, when acting in those capacities, are representatives of the state, and, in those capacities, are themselves prohibited from encouraging or soliciting student religious or anti-religious activity. Similarly, when acting in their official capacities, teachers may not engage in religious activities with their students. However, teachers may engage in private religious activity during duty free and non-contractual hours.

As a general rule, students may express their religious viewpoints in the form of reports, both oral and written, homework and artwork. Teachers may not reject or correct such submissions simply because they include a religious symbol, address religious themes or include references from sacred writings. Likewise, teachers may not require students to modify, include or excise religious views in their assignments, if germane. These assignments should be judged by ordinary academic standards of substance, relevance, appearance and grammar. As noted, however, teachers should not allow students to use a captive, classroom audience to proselytize or conduct religious activities.

Students have the right to distribute religious literature to their schoolmates, subject to those reasonable time, place, and manner or other constitutionally-acceptable restrictions imposed on the distribution of all non-school literature. Thus, a school may confine distribution of all literature to a particular table at particular times. It may not single out religious literature for burdensome regulation.

Student participation in before- or after-school religious events on campus is permissible. School officials, acting in an official capacity, may neither discourage nor encourage participation in such an event.

Students have the right to speak to, and attempt to persuade, their peers about religious topics just as they do with regard to political topics. But school officials should intercede to stop student religious speech if it turns into religious harassment aimed at a student or a small group of students.

Student religious clubs in secondary schools are permitted to meet and to have equal access to campus media to announce their meetings. Teachers may not actively participate in these club activities and "non-school persons" may not control or regularly attend club meetings.

Religious Holidays

Seasonal class parties are appropriate insofar as they are consistent with the approved curriculum. In keeping with district goals, such parties must not unduly interfere with regular academic activities.

Whereas teaching about religious holidays is a permissible part of the educational program, school-sponsored programs shall not be, nor have the effect of being, religiously oriented, a religious ceremony, or an overt celebration of a particular holiday.

School and classroom decorations may express seasonal themes that are secular or have attained a secular status in our society. Additionally, the use of religious symbols that are a part of religious holidays are permitted as teaching aids or as resources, provided such symbols are used as examples and are inclusive of a broad cultural understanding of, and respect for, the religious heritage of celebration and are limited to a brief or temporary period of instruction.

Upon written request of the parent/guardian, a student shall be excused from any part of health, family life or sex education which conflicts with the religious training, beliefs, or personal moral convictions of the parent/guardian or student. (Education Code 51240)

Alternate activities shall be provided for students who are so excused.

Staff shall make every effort to avoid scheduling examinations, school-sponsored trips, special laboratories, picture-taking days and class parties on established religious holidays.

Religion in Curriculum and Instruction

Students may be taught about religion, but public schools may not teach religion. As the U.S. Supreme Court has repeatedly said, "[I]t might well be said that one's education is not complete without a study of comparative religion, or the history of religion and its relationship to the advancement of civilization." It would be difficult to teach art, music, literature and most social studies without considering religious influences.The history of religion, comparative religion, the Bible or other religious texts as literature (either as a separate course or within some other existing course) are all permissible public school subjects. It is both permissible and desirable to teach objectively about the role of religion in the history of the United States and other countries. As a part of the curriculum, religious literature, music, drama and the arts may be included, provided each is intrinsic to the learning experience in the various fields of study and is presented objectively.

Also, as part of the curriculum, students may be asked to read selections from sacred writings for their literary and historical qualities, but not for devotional purposes. The approach to religion shall be one of instruction, not one of indoctrination. The purpose is to educate, not convert. The focus shall be on the study of what all people believe and must not be on teaching a student what to believe. At all levels, the study of religious music as part of a musical appreciation course, as a musical experience, as part of a study of various lands and cultures is to be encouraged. Seasonally appropriate religious music may be studied during the season when interest is highest. In all public school programs and study, care must be taken to avoid presentation of the music as an endorsement of a particular religion or religious holiday, to ensure that there is no bias shown for or against any religion or non religion and that there is balance in the curriculum. Schools may teach civic virtues, including honesty, good citizenship, sportsmanship, courage, respect for the rights and freedoms of others, respect for persons and their property, civility, the virtues of moral conviction, tolerance and hard work. Although schools may teach about the role religion may play in character and values formation, schools may not invoke religious authority.

Religious Symbolism

Religious messages on T-shirts and the like may not be singled out for suppression. Students may wear religious attire, such as yarmulkes and head scarves, and they may not be forced to wear gym clothes that they regard, on religious grounds, as immodest.

UNIFIED SCHOOL DISTRICT, Ramona California Policy adopted: May 25, 2006

Programs and Exhibits

When school programs and exhibits are in any way related to instruction about religion or religious holidays, the following guidelines shall be observed:

1. The principal or designee shall ensure that school-sponsored programs are not, or do not have the effect of being, religiously oriented or a religious celebration.

2. The principal or designee shall participate in planning the program or exhibit and shall be kept informed of its development.

3. Program or exhibit planners shall take into consideration the diverse religious faiths represented in the community, student body and staff.

4. Students and staff whose beliefs prohibit their participation in a program shall be excused without penalty, and an alternate activity shall be provided for any such students.

Legal References

CALIFORNIA EDUCATION CODE

233.5(a) Character Education

51240 Excuse from health instruction and family life and sex education due to religious belief

51511 Religious matters properly included in courses of study

UNITED STATES CODE, TITLE 20

> 6061 School prayer

COURT DECISIONS

> *Walleye v. Gaffer (1985) 472 U.S. 38*
> *Lemon v. Kurtzman (1971) 403 U.S. 602*
> *School Dist. of Abington v. Schempp (1963) 374 U.S. 203*

Management Resources

U.S. DEPARTMENT OF EDUCATION

> "Religion in the Public Schools: A Joint Statement of Current Law,"
> April 1995
> "Religious Expression in Public Schools," United States Department of
> Education, August 1995

RAMONA UNIFIED SCHOOL DISTRICT, Ramona, California

> Regulation approved: October 12, 2004
> Contact: Dr. Robert W. Graeff, Ed. D.
> Assistant Superintendent, Education Services
> Ramona Unified School District
> 720 North Ninth St.
> Ramona, CA 92065
> (760) 787-2012
> Bgraeff@Ramonausd.net

Appendix B

Interfaith Calendar:
2007–2008

Note: Holy days marked with an asterisk (*) begin at sundown the day before this date. For descriptions of these holidays, see the chapter for the religion in question. **The authors are indebted to Professor Emeritus James K. Uphoff of Wright State University for assistance in preparing this appendix**.

For the years following 2008, consult the Interfaith Calendar provided by the National Conference for Community and Justice: www.nccjsocal.org.

2007

JANUARY 2007
12/31/06–1/2/07 'Id Al Adha—Muslim
1 Feast of St. Basil—Orthodox Christian
5 Birth of Guru Gobind Singh—Sikh
6 Epiphany—All Christians
7 Christmas—Orthodox Christian
20 Al Hijra—Islamic New Year[1]
29 Ashura—Islam

FEBRUARY 2007
4 Four Chaplains Sunday—Interfaith[2]
8 Nirvana Day—Buddhism[3]
18 Chinese and Vietnamese New Year
21 Ash Wednesday—Catholic, Protestant

MARCH 2007
4 Purim*—Jewish
3 Holi—Hindu
21 No Roz/Naw Ruz (New Years)—Baha'i and Zoroastrian

APRIL 2007

1 Palm Sunday—Christian

3*–10 Pesach (Passover)—Jewish

6 Good Friday—Christian

8 Easter—Catholic, Protestant Easter/Pascha—Orthodox Christian

14 Vaisakhi—Sikh

15 Yom HaShoah* (Holocaust Remembrance Day)—Jewish

21 First Day of Ridvan—Baha'i

30 St. James the Great Day—Orthodox Christian

MAY 2007

2 Buddha Day—Buddhist[4]

17 Ascension of Christ—Christian

23–24 Shavuot*—Jewish

27 Pentecost—Orthodox Christian

JUNE 2007

9 Pentecost—Catholic, Protestant

JULY 2007

9 Martydom of the Bab—Baha'i

11 St. Benedict Day—Catholic Christian

24 Pioneer Day—Mormon Christian

AUGUST 2007

15 Assumption of Blessed Virgin Mary—Catholic

SEPTEMBER 2007

13 Rosh HaShanah*—Jewish

13 Ramadan begins—Islam

22 Yom Kippur*—Jewish

27–28 Sukkot*—Jewish

OCTOBER 2007

4 St. Francis Day—Catholic

5 Simchat Torah*—Jewish

13 'Id al Fitr (Ramadan ends)—Islam

20 Birth of the B'ab—Baha'i

27 Reformation Day—Protestant Christian Dassehra, Hindu

31 All Hallows Eve—Christian

NOVEMBER 2007

1 All Saints Day—Christian

12 Birth of Baha'u'llah—Baha'i

22 Thanksgiving—Interfaith

DECEMBER 2007

2 First Sunday of Advent—Christian

5–12 Hanukkah*—Jewish

8 Immaculate Conception—Catholic

12 Feast Day of Our Lady of Guadalupe—Catholic

25 Christmas—Catholic, Protestant

2008

JANUARY 2008

1 Feast of St. Basil—Orthodox Christian Birth of Guru Gobind Singh—Sikh

6 Epiphany—All Christians

7 Christmas—Orthodox Christian

10 Al Hijra—Islamic New Year

19 Ashura—Islam

FEBRUARY 2008

3 Four Chaplains Sunday—Interfaith

6 Ash Wednesday—Catholic, Protestant

7 Chinese and Vietnamese New Year

8 Nirvana Day—Buddhism

MARCH 2008

16 Palm Sunday—Christian

21 Good Friday—Christian Purim*—Jewish Holi—Hindu No Roz/Naw
      Ruz—Baha'i and Zoroastrian

23 Easter—Catholic, Protestant

APRIL 2008

13 Vaisakhi—Sikh

20–27 Pesach (Passover)—Jewish

27 Easter/Pascha—Orthodox Christian

30 St. James the Great Day—Orthodox Christian

MAY 2008
1 Ascension Day—Catholic, Protestant
2 Yom HaSho'ah* (Holocaust Remembrance Day)—Jewish
20 Buddha Day—Buddhist
25 Pentecost—Catholic, Protestant

JUNE 2008
4 Pentecost—Orthodox Christian
9–10 Shavuot*—Jewish

JULY 2008
9 Martydom of the Bab—Baha'i
24 Pioneer Day—Mormon Christian
25 St. James the Great Day—Orthodox Christian

AUGUST 2008
15 Assumption of Blessed Virgin Mary—Catholic

SEPTEMBER 2008
2 Ramadan begins—Islam
10 Hijra—New Year—Islam
29–30 Rosh HaShanah*—Jewish

OCTOBER 2008
2 'Id al Fitr—Islam
4   St. Francis Day—Catholic
9 Yom Kippur*—Jewish Dussehra—Hindu
14–15 Sukkot*—Jewish
20 Birth of the B'ab—Baha'i
22 Simchat Torah*—Jewish
27 Reformation Day—Protestant Christian
31 All Hallows Eve—Christian

NOVEMBER 2008
1 All Saints Day—Christian
2 All Souls' Day—Catholic Christian
12 Birth of Baha'u'llah—Baha'i
26 Day of Covenant—Baha'i
27 Thanksgiving—Interfaith
30 First Sunday of Advent—Christian

DECEMBER 2008
8 Immaculate Conception—Catholic
12 Feast Day of Our Lady of Guadalupe—Catholic
21–24 'Id al Adha—Islam
22–29 Hanukkah *—Jewish
25 Christmas—Catholic, Protestant

Notes

1. Commemorates the migration of Prophet Muhammad from Mecca to Medina and marks the year 0 of the Muslim calendar.

2. Commemorates the event in World War II when four Jewish, Catholic, and Protestant chaplains gave their life jackets to GIs as a troop ship was sinking in the Atlantic Ocean.

3. In northern/Mahayana Buddhist nations (China, Korea, Japan), this day marks the Buddha's passing.

4. The birthday of Siddhartha Gautama, the Buddha.

Index

207

About the Authors

BENJAMIN J. HUBBARD (PhD, University of Iowa) is professor emeritus of comparative religion at California State University, Fullerton, where he was department chair for fifteen years. He has been a frequent contributor on religion-related issues to the *Los Angeles Times*/Orange County and the *Orange County Register*. His specialties include Judaic studies, the interfaith movement, and religion and media studies.

JOHN T. HATFIELD (PhD, Claremont Graduate University) is professor emeritus of Ethnic and Women's Studies at California State Polytechnic University, Pomona. He is a past president of the American Academy of Religion's Western Region and of the Far Western Philosophy of Religion Society. His special interests include Native American religion, and religion and public education.

JAMES A. SANTUCCI (PhD, Australian National University) is professor and chair of the Department of Comparative Religion, California State University, Fullerton. For nearly twenty years, he has edited the journal *Theosophical History*. He is an expert on theosophy and other nontraditional religious movements, as well as the religions of South Asia (Hinduism, Buddhism and Jainism).